CHINA–AFGHANISTAN RELATIONS

Hope, Hype and More

CHINA–AFGHANISTAN RELATIONS

Hope, Hype and More

Vishal Chandra

MANOHAR PARRIKAR
idsa
MANOHAR PARRIKAR INSTITUTE FOR DEFENCE STUDIES AND ANALYSES
मनोहर पर्रिकर रक्षा अध्ययन एवं विश्लेषण संस्थान

PENTAGON PRESS LLP

First published in 2025 by

PENTAGON PRESS LLP
206, Peacock Lane, Shahpur Jat
New Delhi-110049, India
Contact: 011-26490600

Typeset in AGaramond, 11.5 Point
Printed by Aegean Offset Printers, Greater Noida

ISBN 978-81-991162-4-5

www.pentagonpress.in

To

Buddhas of Mes Aynak

Contents

Acknowledgements

I am grateful to Amb Sujan R. Chinoy, Director General MP-IDSA; Gp Capt (Dr) Ajey Lele, Retd, Deputy Director General MP-IDSA; and my colleague Dr Ashok Behuria, Senior Fellow and Centre Coordinator South Asia, for their valuable support and guidance. I also owe gratitude to my senior colleague Dr Uttam Sinha for his warm encouragement during the finalisation of the book.

I also thank the Pentagon Press for publishing this book in an efficient manner.

I am most indebted to my wife and to my daughters Varenya and Aradhya for their tremendous patience and support, without which it would not have been possible to finalise the book for publication.

Vishal Chandra

List of Abbreviations

ANDS	Afghanistan National Development Strategy
ANDSF	Afghan National Defence and Security Forces
APEC	Asia-Pacific Economic Cooperation
AQ	al-Qaeda
BRI	Belt and Road Initiative
BSA	Bilateral Security Agreement
CARs	Central Asian Republics
CCTV	China Central Television
CNPC	China National Petroleum Corporation
CPC	Communist Party of China
CPEC	China-Pakistan Economic Corridor
CRI	China Radio International
ETIM	East Turkistan Islamic Movement
EU	European Union
FDI	Foreign Direct Investment
IMU	Islamic Movement of Uzbekistan
ISIS	Islamic State of Iraq and Syria
IS-K	Islamic State Khorasan
MCC	Metallurgical Corporation of China Limited (China Metallurgical Group Corporation)
MCIT	Ministry of Communications and Information Technology
MoU	Memorandum of Understanding
NATO	North Atlantic Treaty Organisation

NUG	National Unity Government
PDPA	People's Democratic Party of Afghanistan
PLA	People's Liberation Army
PRC	People's Republic of China
QCG	Quadrilateral Coordination Group
ROC	Republic of China
SAARC	South Asian Association for Regional Cooperation
SCO	Shanghai Cooperation Organisation
UN	United Nations
US	United States (of America)
USAID	United States Agency for International Development
ZTE	Zhong Xing Telecommunication Equipment Co. Ltd.

Maps, Tables, and Images

Maps

Tables

Images

Map I: Afghanistan–China Border

Source: GIS Section, MP-IDSA, Map not to scale.

Introduction

At the time of finalising the introduction to the book, there were reports about the Taliban prime minister's office annulling the long-term contract with a Chinese company to extract oil from the Amu Darya basin in northern Afghanistan. The spokesperson of the Afghan ministry of mines and petroleum was said to have stated that "The contract was annulled due to repeated violations by the contracting company of its commitments."[1] In case of the Aynak copper mine project, which was awarded to a Chinese consortium way back in 2007 and is yet to be fully implemented, the acting Taliban minister of mines and petroleum had last year urged the contracting Chinese company to fulfil its commitments and carry out full copper processing within the country.[2] A lot goes into the making, unmaking, and remaking of such deals. It is the hype and hope built around these huge foreign investment projects that overshadow the various challenges to executing such projects to the satisfaction of all sides and stakeholders concerned.

China has been a part of the Afghan maze, but landlocked Afghanistan seemed to have factored either marginally or episodically in its geopolitical quests in the past seven decades. While the role of certain regional actors in Afghanistan has been far widely debated and analysed, China's role, particularly the nature and scope of its bilateral interactions and engagements with various Afghan regimes in Kabul, from Zahir Shah to the Taliban, has remained comparatively understudied. This book is a modest effort in that direction. An attempt has been made to keep the focus limited to the nature and scope of bilateral interactions between the two countries, joined by perhaps the shortest border both share with any of their other respective neighbours, as part of the author's broader ongoing academic endeavour to examine geopolitics around the Hindukush–Pamir region in both historical and contemporary contexts. The book also builds and where required copiously draws upon the author's earlier shorter publications examining the trajectory of China–Afghanistan bilateral relations in the contemporary context.[3]

While the significance of China for Kabul has been widely known, perhaps what still begs scrutiny is what Kabul has meant for Beijing over the past seven decades. In more recent years, it was not until Beijing began to directly re-engage the Taliban 2014–2015 onwards that it caught the regional and international attention. The pace at which Beijing has since attempted to position itself on the centre stage of the competing politics of peace mediation in Afghanistan was bound to attract attention and scrutiny. China is no longer seen as a distant and reluctant player in the Afghan theatre.

In retrospect, China may not have directly or explicitly backed or sided with any particular 'mujahideen' faction in the 1980s and the 1990s, but it had played a key role in resourcing the so-called anti-Soviet 'jihad' in Afghanistan that left the country militarised and radicalised. Right from backing Zia-ul-Haq's Pakistan to engaging the first Taliban regime in the late 1990s; from being a member of the 'six-plus-two' regional platform to supporting the United States' (US) Operation Enduring Freedom launched against the Taliban regime post the 9/11 terrorist attacks; and thereafter, from emerging as the largest foreign direct investor in the Afghan mining industry in 2007–2008 to concluding a Strategic and Cooperative Partnership with Afghanistan in June 2012 to undertaking several diplomatic initiatives to bring Kabul and Rawalpindi closer, China all along and through had been involved and engaged in and on Afghanistan. Post-2008, China had the strongest ever economic presence inside Afghanistan since the establishment of full diplomatic ties between the two countries in 1955. After the overthrow of the 'Islamic Republic' in August 2021, China emerged as one the most active diplomatic supporters of the second Taliban regime in Kabul.

Post-2021, China has also renewed its invitation to the Taliban government to join the BRI, particularly its flagship CPEC project. Interestingly, like the previous government in Kabul, the Taliban government has sought to open direct trade with China via the Wakhan Corridor, bypassing Pakistan. Beijing has thus far avoided making any commitment on the issue of opening of direct land trade with Afghanistan. Interestingly, the Wakhan Corridor that both separates and joins China and Afghanistan has been in the news for various reasons for quite some time now, but much of what has been reported thus far remains largely speculative, and has not been covered in detail to retain the focus on the defining theme of the book.

The book is divided into three broad chapters, covering a long period spanning seven decades, with the first chapter, 'Making and Unmaking of Bilateral Relations', focused on the first five decades of bilateral interaction between the two countries, which saw the slow and modest building of bilateral ties in the 1950s and the 1960s before it came to a near halt with the 1978 coup in Kabul and following the Soviet invasion in 1979. In the next decade, one finds China and the US-bloc on the same side against the Soviet Union, and thereafter in the 1990s, following the Soviet withdrawal from Afghanistan and the collapse of the Soviet Union, shutting down its embassy in Kabul as the civil war raged in the country, and returning later at the end of the decade to explore the prospects of engaging the Pakistan-backed Islamist Taliban ruling from Kandahar and Kabul.

The second chapter, 'China and the Islamic Republic of Afghanistan', which covers the two decade period during which Afghanistan turned into an 'Islamic Republic,' saw the rebuilding of state-to-state ties between Kabul and Beijing, defined by high level visits mostly from Kabul and the issuance of series of joint statements and also the signing of the Strategic and Cooperative Partnership. It was followed by Beijing's active trilateral diplomacy to draw Kabul and Islamabad closer while supporting the latter's effort to project and position itself as the facilitator of 'peace' in Afghanistan, and in a way also between the US and the Taliban, and to boost prospects of integrating Afghanistan into its regional connectivity ventures, particularly the CPEC, post the Western military withdrawal.

The third chapter, 'China and the Second Taliban "Emirate"', which covers the shortest but crucial four year period since the Taliban returned to power, is focused on Beijing's proactive trilateral diplomatic efforts to facilitate the dialogue between Islamabad and the Taliban-ruled Kabul. It is the Taliban's evolving or changed role from a full-blown jihadi insurgent group to an Islamist ruling authority in Afghanistan that sets a new context and scope for Beijing's bilateral interaction with Kabul.

The book ends with concluding observations anchored in the contemporary context to add further value to the book. A broad sweep of the nature of past levels of bilateral interaction and engagement should help in understanding China's ongoing proactive engagement with the second Taliban regime.

This book should be of reference value to those interested in Afghanistan, and take the discourse on the theme forward.

NOTES

1 "Taliban Cancels Landmark Oil Deal With Chinese Company Over Contract Violations", *Afghanistan International*, 17 June 2025, at https://www.afintl.com/en/202506175674; Liluma Qadiry, "Termination of 25-Year Contract with Chinese Company Sparks Reactions", *Tolo News*, 20 June 2025, at https://tolonews.com/business-194722.

2 "Acting Mines Minister Emphasizes 100% Copper Processing Inside the Country", *Bakhtar News Agency*, 3 April 2024, at https://www.bakhtarnews.af/en/acting-mines-minister-emphasizes-100-copper-processing-inside-the-country/.

3 Vishal Chandra, "Beijing: Kabul's 'Reliable' Strategic Partner", in Jagannath P. Panda (ed.), *IDSA China Year Book 2015—China's Transition under Xi Jinping*, Pentagon Press, New Delhi, 2016, pp. 314–336; Vishal Chandra, *The Unfinished War in Afghanistan: 2001–2014*, IDSA, Pentagon Press, 2015, pp. 230–257; and Vishal Chandra and Ashok K. Behuria, "Afghanistan Beyond 2014: The China Factor", in S.D. Muni and Vivek Chadha (eds.), *IDSA Asian Strategic Review*, Pentagon Press, 2013, pp. 31–49.

"Afghanistan exports an extremely small variety of commodities, [and] they are moreover not what our country needs. Afghanistan has a need for complete sets of light industrial equipment; we plan to signal our readiness to supply them and to consider payment in installments or providing credit (temporarily set limits at one million British pounds), and to provide technical assistance." *

—Draft Report, Chinese Ministry of Foreign Trade, March 1955.

* * *

*"...Chinese interest in Afghanistan was simply one aspect of a broader regional policy, reflecting the ebb and flow of relations with the Soviet Union and Pakistan. In that sense the Beijing government has always considered Kabul a second-rank partner."***

—Encyclopaedia Iranica.

---

* "Report from the Chinese Ministry of Foreign Trade, 'Scheme for Our Participation in the Trade Activities of the Asian-African Conference (Revised Draft) (Preliminary Paper)'", 12 March 1955, Wilson Center Digital Archive, PRC FMA 207-00070-03, 86-94, at https://digitalarchive.wilsoncenter.org/document/report-chinese-ministry-foreign-trade-scheme-our-participation-trade-activities-asian.

** Daniel Balland, "Chinese–Iranian Relations. vi. Relations with Afghanistan in the Modern Period", *Encyclopaedia Iranica*, Vol. 5, Fascicle 4, 15 December 1991, Online Edition. Last Updated 14 October 2011, pp. 441–443, at https://www.iranicaonline.org/articles/chinese-iranian-vi.

1

Making and Unmaking of Bilateral Relations The First Five Decades

Afghanistan was among the first countries to recognise the establishment of the Central People's Government by the Communist Party of China (CPC) in Peking (now romanised as Beijing) on 1 October 1949. Afghanistan formally notified the People's Government of its decision to establish the diplomatic relations with the 'People's Republic of China' (PRC) on 12 January 1950, thus cutting off ties with the Kuomintang or the Chinese Nationalist Party's 'Republic of China' (ROC). Afghanistan thereafter consistently supported the PRC in its long-drawn struggle to replace the ROC as the legitimate representative of China at the United Nations (UN) and also as a permanent member of the Security Council.[1]

Interestingly, the ROC and Afghanistan had signed a Treaty of Amity in Ankara on 2 March 1944 and exchanged ratifications six months later in Ankara on 30 September. The treaty was signed by Chinese Minister to Turkey (now Türkiye) Tsou Shang-yu and Afghan Ambassador in Ankara Faiz Mohammed Khan. Shortly thereafter, Tsou was transferred as the Chinese Minister to Afghanistan.[2] According to the archived diplomatic correspondence of the British Government in India, Tsou presented his credentials to Afghan King Mohammad Zahir Shah on 23 September 1945.[3] Afghanistan subsequently appointed its former deputy minister of foreign affairs and former envoy to Japan, Habibullah Khan Tarzi, as its envoy to China in 1946. However, within a few months, Tarzi was appointed as the first official Afghan Ambassador to the United States (US) where he served until 1953.

Interestingly, the British correspondence while commenting on China's efforts in the early 1940s to establish diplomatic relations with Afghanistan noted that given Kabul's reluctance, the Chinese Government had sought the assistance of the British Government in India to persuade the Afghans. The Chinese Government was said to be wary of the Japanese activities in Afghanistan and possible attempts by Axis Powers to establish lines of communication through Afghanistan.[4]

Slow and Modest Beginnings: 1950–1979

Despite Afghanistan severing ties with the ROK and making early diplomatic overtures to the PRC in January 1950, it took five years before the two countries restored diplomatic relations on 20 January 1955. By 1 October 1953, the Central People's Government, within four years of its formation, claimed to have established diplomatic relations with 19 countries: the Union of Soviet Socialist Republics, Bulgaria, Romania, Hungary, Korea, Czechoslovakia (now the Czech Republic and the Slovak Republic), Poland, Mongolia, Germany, Albania, Burma (now Myanmar), India, Vietnam, Denmark, Sweden, Switzerland, Indonesia, Pakistan, and Finland. Meanwhile, another seven countries—Afghanistan, Britain, Ceylon (Sri Lanka), Norway, Israel, and the Netherlands—were said to have notified Peking (now Beijing) of their willingness to establish diplomatic relations.[5]

Ting Kuo-yu (now romanised as Ding Guoyu) was appointed as the PRC's first ambassador to Afghanistan in March 1955. In April, Chinese Premier and Minister of Foreign Affairs Chou En-lai (now romanised as Zhou Enlai) and Vice Premier Chen I (now romanised as Chen Yi) met Afghan Deputy Prime Minister and Minister of Foreign Affairs Sardar Mohammad Naim Khan at the Asian-African Conference held at Bandung in Indonesia from 18 to 24 April 1955. Next month, in May, Ding presented his credentials to King Zahir Shah and served in Afghanistan until July 1958. He thereafter had a long stint as China's ambassador to Pakistan from December 1959 to July 1966, during which the so-called China–Pakistan 'boundary agreement'[6] of 2 March 1963 was negotiated and signed.[7] Kabul reciprocated by appointing

Abdul Samad as its first ambassador to the PRC. Samad presented his credentials to Chairman Mao Tse-tung (now romanised as Mao Zedong) on 22 January 1956.[8]

Afghanistan was among the last of the bordering states with which the PRC established diplomatic relations, the other exceptions being Nepal and Laos. It is important to note that the PRC had established diplomatic relations with Pakistan in May 1951, almost four years before establishing diplomatic ties with Afghanistan in 1955. Pakistan despite joining the US-led bloc came to hold certain strategic value for the PRC in the late 1950s and the early 1960s, particularly in relation to the PRC's deteriorating ties with India over border disputes followed by a border conflict in 1962. Meanwhile, Pakistan signed a Mutual Defense Assistance Agreement with the US in May 1954 and was a founder member of the anti-Communist/Soviet collective defence pacts, such as the Southeast Asia Treaty Organisation (SEATO) formed in September 1954 in Manila and the Baghdad Pact of February 1955, renamed as the Central Treaty Organization (CENTO) in August 1959.

Pakistan at that time was wary of the security threat from Chinese expansionism and Red Imperialism. Perturbed by Chinese incursions in Hunza and military action in Tibet, Pakistan's military leader General (Gen) Mohammad Ayub Khan had proposed a 'joint defence' of the Subcontinent to India in April 1959 but with "the solution of big problems like Kashmir and the canal waters" as the prerequisite, which India rejected.[9] Pakistan had earlier rejected the 'no-war declaration' proposed by Prime Minister Jawaharlal Nehru in late 1949. Meanwhile, China in view of its deteriorating political and economic ties with the Soviet Union late 1950s onwards had begun to increasingly engage with the non-communist countries, or the so-called Free World. China being landlocked from three sides also began to prioritise ties with Pakistan, which unlike landlocked Afghanistan had direct maritime access to the Arabian Sea in the Indian Ocean.

Shen-Yu Dai in his article published in *The China Quarterly* in 1966, citing reports by *Survey of China Mainland Press* and *New China News Agency*, attributed the delay in Beijing's response to Kabul's diplomatic overtures to its initial apprehensions over American construction projects in Afghanistan, basically alluding to the construction of the high-speed road system in southern

Afghanistan from 1947 onwards, and Afghanistan's initiative to modernise its educational system on the American model.[10] He, however, added:

> In 1953-54, with Afghanistan increasingly oriented towards neutralism and friendship with (in response to aid from) the Soviet Union, Peking gradually became amenable to establishing formal diplomatic relations with Kabul. This took place in January, 1955, four years after Afghanistan had taken the initiative. From this point onwards, aided by continued common irritation with Pakistan, Sino-Afghan relations took a decisive turn for the better, with Peking watching for Kabul's interests vis-a-vis Washington.[11]

Later, Yaacov Vertzberger in his article published in the *Problems of Communism* in 1982 stated:

> It [PRC] perceived hardly any promise for a Marxist party or movement of any significance in Afghanistan. It likewise saw only the slightest prospect for success–if indeed any at all–in penetrating Afghanistan's society and economy, characterised by tribalism and Islamic religious fanaticism, all particularly marked in the agrarian sector, which, according to the Maoist scheme, should have been the first target.[12]

Afghanistan's close links with the Soviet Union, with which the PRC had a major ideological split by the end of the 1950s, was seen as a limiting factor in the China–Afghanistan relations, although Afghanistan given its policy of 'active neutrality' tried to balance its ties with both the Soviet Union and the PRC. If Afghanistan refused to take sides in the Sino-Soviet rift despite the Chinese pressure, it also disapproved of the Soviet Union's collective security schemes, which in Beijing's perception were directed against it.[13]

Perhaps, what brought the two countries together was their common disapproval of bloc politics and collective security mechanisms, and the need for a balance of power in the region to preserve their sovereignty and independence. Kabul's policy of neutrality or *betarafi* towards bloc politics and Beijing's growing geopolitical rift with Moscow also provided Beijing with an opportunity to shore up its diplomatic engagement with Kabul. Perhaps, Beijing was also trying to balance its ties with both pro-West Pakistan and supposedly neutral Afghanistan.

The China–Afghanistan relations in the late 1950s and the 1960s were marked by exchange of high-level visits and modest economic cooperation. By the summer of 1956, China was exporting tea to Afghanistan via the land route and the Chinese Red Crescent Society had provided aid for the Afghan flood victims, followed by exchange of cultural delegations between the two countries. By October 1956, Kabul's Mayor had paid a goodwill visit to Beijing and a Chinese haj mission had called on King Zahir Shah in Kabul on its way back from Mecca.[14]

However, the most important moment in the nascent bilateral relations came when Chinese Premier and Minister of Foreign Affairs Zhou Enlai, along with Vice-Premier Ho Lung (later romanised as He Long), visited Kabul on his way back from Moscow in January 1957. Zhou arrived in Kabul on 19 January and left for New Delhi on 24 January 1957. During his visit, Zhou met King Zahir Shah and held meetings with Prime Minister Sardar Mohammad Daoud Khan, Deputy Prime Minister Ali Mohammad and Deputy Prime Minister and Minister of Foreign Affairs Sardar Mohammad Naim Khan. Zhou was said to have emphasised the "common border", "contacts since time immemorial", "suffering under colonialism", and the "common struggle for independence" in his interactions in Kabul. He stated how "the victory attained by the Afghan people in their struggle for national independence inspired the Chinese people in fighting for their own national independence". Zhou was said to have noted "with utmost satisfaction" the "healthy development" of relations between the two countries "on the basis of mutual respect."[15]

Afghan Prime Minister Daoud Khan defended Afghanistan's neutralism stating that "those who criticise neutrality are, in fact, trying to find an excuse for their own blocs. It is evident that the present system of blocs has been the cause of discord and has especially created differences among the peoples of Asia and Africa." Kabul's Mayor focusing on bilateral ties stated that "more efforts would be exerted to extend the exchange in economic, cultural and technical fields as well as in personal contact."[16]

Within days of Premier Zhou's visit to Kabul in January 1957, the first Afghan trade delegation visited Beijing at the end of the same month and the first trade agreement was inked between the two countries the very next month in mid-February. Five months later, on 28 July 1957, the Agreement for the Exchange of Goods and Payments was signed in Kabul. It was said to be the first trade agreement between the two countries since the establishment of diplomatic ties in 1955.[17] In the following months, Afghan sports team visited China in November 1957; Chinese water conservancy delegation visited Afghanistan in December 1957; Chinese dance troupe visited Afghanistan in August and September 1958;[18] Afghan football team toured China in October 1958;[19] Afghan cultural delegation led by renowned Afghan historian and archaeologist Ahmad Ali Kohzad[20] visited China in November 1958;[21] and Chinese cultural delegates and acrobats visited Afghanistan in June and August of 1959. By September 1958, *Peking Radio* had started playing Afghan folk music.[22] A 17-member Afghan cultural troupe, led by noted Afghan composer and painter Abdul Ghafur Breshna, visited China in August 1960. Chinese Premier Zhou Enlai and Vice Premier Chen Yi attended the premiere of the Afghan troupe in Beijing.[23]

Following Chinese Premier's first visit to Kabul in January 1957, Afghan Prime Minister Daoud Khan visited Beijing in late October 1957, during which he met Chairman Mao and interacted with Vice Chairman Marshal Chu Teh (later romanised as Zhu De) and Chairman Liu Shao-chi (later romanised as Liu Shaoqi) of the Standing Committee of the National People's Congress. Two years later, Afghan Deputy Prime Minister and Minister of Foreign Affairs Naim Khan visited China at the invitation of Premier Zhou Enlai from 5 September to 14 September 1959. He was received at the Beijing Airport by Premier Zhou.[24] Naim Khan was accompanied by Minister of Commerce Sardar Ghulam Mohammad Sherzad and other senior officials. He met Chairman of the PRC Liu Shaoqi and held meetings with Premier Zhou and Vice Premier of the State Council and Minister of Foreign Affairs Marshal Chen Yi. Zhou in his public speeches "praised Afghanistan's consistent implementation of the policy of peace and neutrality."[25]

In the Joint Communiqué issued by Naim Khan and Chen Yi in Beijing on 9 September 1959, the two leaders agreed to develop and strengthen the economic and cultural ties and expand the scope of technical cooperation between the two countries. It is noteworthy that both the sides also welcomed the forthcoming exchange of visits between the Soviet and American leaders.[26]

During his five-day stay in capital Beijing, Naim Khan visited the construction site of the Tiananmen Square, the Miyun Reservoir Project, and the Central Institute of Nationalities. He thereafter visited Chengchow (later romanised as Zhengzhou), capital of the central Henan Province; Shanghai; Hangchow (later romanised as Hangzhou), capital of the eastern Zhejiang Province; Wuhan, capital of the central Hubei Province; and Canton or Kwangchow (later romanised as Guangzhou), capital of the southern Guangdong Province.[27]

About a year later, the bilateral relations were further cemented when Chinese Vice-Premier and Minister of Foreign Affairs Marshal Chen Yi paid a state visit to Kabul from 21 August to 27 August 1960. Chen was accompanied by Kung Yuan, Deputy Director of the Office of the State Council in Charge of Foreign Affairs; Keng Piao, Vice Minister of Foreign Affairs; Hsiung Hsiang-hui, Division Head of the Office of the State Council in Charge of Foreign Affairs, and other senior officials. Vice-Premier Chen was received at the Kabul Airport by Afghan Prime Minister Daoud Khan and Deputy Prime Minister and Minister of Foreign Affairs Naim Khan. During his week-long visit to Kabul, Chen Yi met King Zahir Shah, attended the 42nd Afghan Independence Day celebrations and conducted talks with Prime Minister Daoud Khan and Deputy Prime Ministers Ali Mohammad and Naim Khan.[28]

On 26 August 1960, Chen Yi and Naim Khan signed the Treaty of Friendship and Mutual Non-Aggression and renewed the Agreement for the Exchange of Goods and Payments signed earlier in July 1957, and issued a Joint Communiqué. By then the PRC had already signed the Treaty of Friendship with Yemen in January 1958, Treaty of Friendship and Mutual Non-Aggression with Burma (now Myanmar) in January 1960, and the Treaty of Peace and Friendship with Nepal in April 1960. In his banquet speech, Chen referred to statements made by Naim Khan during the latter's visit to China in September 1959 and said that the China–Afghanistan relations "are a living example of peaceful cooperation between two nations with different political, economic and social systems."[29]

In his farewell statement, Chen characterised the friendship and non-aggression treaty with Kabul as the "crystallization of the profound friendship" between the two countries and "an embodiment and development of the Five

Principles of Peaceful Coexistence and the Bandung spirit."[30] The official newspaper of the CPC Central Committee, *Renmin Ribao* or the 'People's Daily', in its editorial described the treaty as "a fresh victory of the Five Principles of Peaceful Coexistence and of the Bandung spirit" and "of great significance in promoting Asian-African solidarity and of preserving peace in Asia and the world."[31] Chen appreciated Afghanistan's foreign policy of "peace and neutrality" and described it as "brilliant and correct".[32] On behalf of Chairman of the State Council Liu Shaoqi, he extended an invitation to King Zahir Shah to visit China, which the latter obliged four years later in 1964.

The next significant step in the China–Afghanistan relations was the settlement of the boundary between the two countries along the Wakhan region. China had already signed boundary agreements/treaties and border protocols with Burma (now Myanmar) in October 1960, Nepal in October 1961, Mongolia in December 1962, and the so-called 'Boundary Agreement' with Pakistan in March 1963. The China–Afghanistan Boundary Treaty was signed by Chinese Vice-Premier and Minister of Foreign Affairs Chen Yi and Afghan Minister of Interior Abdul Kayeum on 22 November 1963 in Beijing (see Appendix I). The Boundary Protocol between the two countries was signed during Vice-Premier Chen Yi's second visit to Kabul in March 1965.

Meanwhile, King Zahir Shah and Queen Homaira paid a state visit to China from 30 October to 13 November 1964; just two weeks after China conducted its first nuclear test at Lop Nur site in Sinkiang (later romanised as Xinjiang) bordering Afghanistan. The king and the queen were received at the airport by Chairman of the PRC Liu Shaoqi, Vice-Chairman Tung Pi-wu (later romanised as Dong Biwu), Chairman Marshal Zhu De of the Standing Committee of the National People's Congress, and Premier of the State Council Zhou Enlai. Both Liu and Zhao were accompanied by their wives on the occasion. Zahir Shah during his stay in Beijing met Chairman Mao and held talks with Chairman Liu, Premier Zhou and Vice-Premier He Long. The royal couple left Beijing on 3 November for a tour to Wuhan, Canton (now Guangzhou), Nanking (now Nanjing), Shanghai, and Hangchow (now Hangzhou).

Liu in his remarks praised the "anti-imperialist tradition of the Afghan people" and the "non-alignment policy of peace and neutrality" and "independent foreign policy" of Afghanistan. Interestingly, while speaking at the state banquet hosted in honour of Afghan King and Queen, he referred to the nuclear test that China had conducted just two weeks before and reiterated the Chinese proposal for "complete prohibition and thorough destruction of nuclear weapons" by all the nuclear powers.[33] Zahir Shah in his address referred to the Treaty of Friendship and Non-Aggression signed between the two countries in August 1960 and described the close ties the two countries share as an example of good relations between neighbouring countries with different social and political systems.[34] During the welcome rally organised at the Great Hall of the People, Zahir Shah stated how "reciprocal friendly sentiments" enabled the two countries to amicably settle matters pertaining formal demarcation of the joint boundary and setting up of frontier pillars. He described it as the "strengthening influence" in the friendly relations between the two countries.[35]

In the Joint Communiqué issued on 12 November in Beijing by Chairman Liu Shaoqi and King Zahir Shah, the two countries reaffirmed their commitment to the April 1955 Bandung Declaration and endorsed the outcomes of the first two summits of the non-aligned countries (the September 1961 Belgrade and October 1964 Cairo summits of the Non-Aligned Movement). The two sides also agreed to further develop their economic and technical and cultural cooperation.[36] In the farewell banquet hosted by King Zahir Shah and Queen Homaira in the Great Hall of the People on 12 November, Chairman Liu stated that the relations between the two countries will be "further strengthened and developed on the basis of the Five Principles of Peaceful Coexistence and the Ten Principles of the Bandung Conference."[37]

Four months after Zahir Shah's visit to China, Vice-Premier and Minister of Foreign Affairs Chen Yi visited Kabul from 22 March to 24 March 1965. He was on a three nation tour that included Afghanistan, Pakistan, and Nepal. During his three-day visit, Chen and Afghan Deputy Prime Minister Abdul Zahir signed the Boundary Protocol on 24 March 1965. According to the Afghanistan–China Boundary Protocol, the length of the border line between the two countries is 92.45 kms.[38] However, according to the official website of the Afghan Ministry of Borders and Tribal Affairs, the two countries share a 96 km joint border (see Image I).

Image I: Afghanistan–China Border
Website of Afghan Ministry of Borders and Tribal Affairs

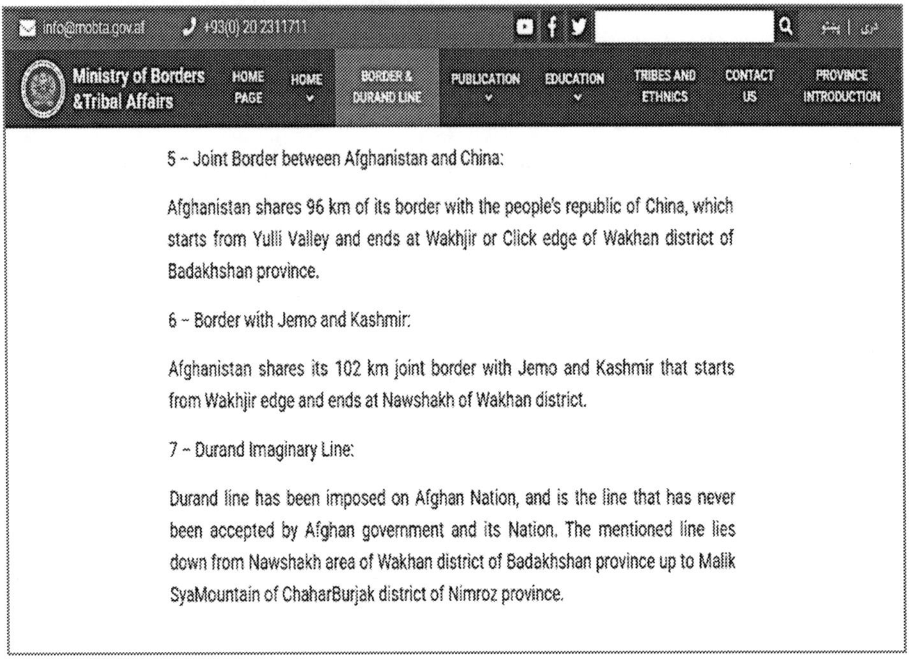

info@mobta.gov.af +93(0) 20 2311711

Ministry of Borders &Tribal Affairs | HOME PAGE | HOME | BORDER & DURAND LINE | PUBLICATION | EDUCATION | TRIBES AND ETHNICS | CONTACT US | PROVINCE INTRODUCTION

5 – Joint Border between Afghanistan and China:

Afghanistan shares 96 km of its border with the people's republic of China, which starts from Yulli Valley and ends at Wakhjir or Click edge of Wakhan district of Badakhshan province.

6 – Border with Jemo and Kashmir:

Afghanistan shares its 102 km joint border with Jemo and Kashmir that starts from Wakhjir edge and ends at Nawshakh of Wakhan district.

7 – Durand Imaginary Line:

Durand line has been imposed on Afghan Nation, and is the line that has never been accepted by Afghan government and its Nation. The mentioned line lies down from Nawshakh area of Wakhan district of Badakhshan province up to Malik SyaMountain of ChaharBurjak district of Nimroz province.

Source: Border and Durand Line section, Afghan Ministry of Border and Tribal Affairs, Kabul, at https://mobta.gov.af/en/borders-durand-line (Accessed 15 January 2025).

Besides the Border Protocol, Vice-Premier Chen signed an Agreement on Cultural Cooperation with Afghan Education Minister Mohammad Anas and an Agreement on Economic and Technical Cooperation with Afghan Finance Minister Qasim Rishtiya. Chen also met King Zahir Shah and held talks with newly-appointed Afghan Prime Minister and Minister of Foreign Affairs Mohammad Yusouf and Deputy Prime Minister Zahir. Under the Agreement on Cultural Cooperation, the two countries decided to promote exchanges in the field of culture, education, science, literature, art, religion, medicine and hygiene, physical culture, film, and journalism and broadcasting.[39]

Under the Agreement on Economic and Technical Cooperation, China agreed to grant a long-term non-interest loan equivalent to 10-million-pounds sterling (approximately US$ 28 million) to Afghanistan within a period of five years from 1 July 1965 to 30 June 1970. It coincided with Afghanistan's second five-year plan (1962–1967) and the third plan (1967–1971). The grant was to be given in installments and in the form of complete set equipment, single equipments, and consumer goods. The technical assistance was to be extended in the field of agriculture and industry. Afghanistan was to repay the abovementioned loan within a period of 10 years from 1 July 1975 to 30 June 1985, with one-tenth of the loan to be repaid per annum in the form of Afghan export goods. The agreement also stated that China would send experts and technicians and that the Central Bank of Afghanistan, or *Da* Afghanistan Bank, and the People's Bank of China would conclude a technical arrangement for accounting procedures related to the implementation of the agreement.[40] With this agreement, China for the first time made its presence felt in Afghanistan and which in due course proved to be short-lived.

Chen thereafter left for Rawalpindi on 25 March. The very next day, on 26 March 1965, Vice-Premier Chen and then Pakistani Foreign Minister Zulfiqar Ali Bhutto signed the China–Pakistan Border Protocol. Chen also visited Karachi and Dhaka (the administrative capital of what was then East Pakistan and later Independent Bangladesh since 1971) before leaving for Nepal on 30 March. Chen again visited Kabul later that year as part of his multi-nation tour and met Afghan Prime Minister and Foreign Minister Yusouf in September 1965.

The next and also the last significant visit from the Chinese side to Afghanistan until the turn of the century was that of Chairman Liu Shaoqi and Vice Premier Chen Yi, both of whom were accompanied by their wives, from 4 April to 8 April 1966. It is important to note here that no Chinese Head of State has since paid visit to Afghanistan. Their visit to Afghanistan was followed by a visit to Pakistan, including East Pakistan. Chinese leaders visiting Pakistan in the 1960s would have a visit to Dhaka (the administrative capital of what was then East Pakistan and later Independent Bangladesh since 1971) in their itinerary. Liu's visit came in the backdrop of the 1965 India–Pakistan War; Beijing's rising tension with the Soviet Union, Japan, Indonesia, and the US, including on the latter's continued support to the ROC (Taiwan); and growing conflict among or within countries in Southeast Asia, particularly between Thailand and Cambodia and the war in Vietnam. The statements made by Liu in Afghanistan and Pakistan were repetitive and mostly rhetorical, aimed at presenting the PRC as the leader of the Afro-Asian world, champion of non-alignment and promoter of global peace and stability, and a lead voice against perceived Soviet revisionism, American-led imperialism, and colonialism and neo-colonialism.

The next high level visit from the Afghan side to China was that of Foreign Minister Mohammad Musa Shafiq on 17 April 1972. Musa met Chinese Foreign Minister Chi Peng-fei and Vice-Foreign Minister Han Nien-lung. Vice-Chairman Kuo Mo-jo of the Standing Committee of the National People's Congress interacted with the Afghan delegation. The Afghan delegation also visited the southern parts of China. Three months after Shafiq's visit, the two countries signed a civil air transportation agreement on 26 July 1972 in Kabul. Afghan Prime Minister Abdul Zahir and Foreign Minister Shafiq met the visiting Chinese civil aviation officials.[41] Three months later, an Afghan delegation led by Sardar Sultan Mahmoud Ghazi, President of the Afghanistan–China Friendship Association and President of the Afghan Civil Aviation and Tourism Authority, visited Beijing and met Premier Zhou on 19 October 1972 and held discussions with Chinese government officials.[42]

The perceived sense of isolation and encirclement that gripped the Chinese leadership at that time was explicitly reflected in the *Renmin Ribao*'s editorial of 21 April 1966. The editorial stated under the subhead '"Cordon" Around China—A Paper Wall' that:

> For well over 10 years, U.S. imperialism has been building a "crescent cordon" around China. Actually, this "cordon" is no more than a paper wall. Politically, it *cannot contain the tremendous influence of China's foreign policy of peace*, nor can it play any significant role militarily. This "cordon" is, in fact, a noose that U.S. imperialism has put around its own neck. The grand and warm welcome which Chairman Liu Shao-chi received in Pakistan, Afghanistan and Burma is another testimony to China's foreign policy of peace. It *proves that China's foreign policy is fully correct.* The adverse anti-China current which the imperialists, modern revisionists and reactionaries of all countries recently have gone all out to stir up has not hurt China a whit. The fact remains that *China has friends all over the world.* The friendship between the Chinese people and the Afro-Asian and all other peoples of the world will be consolidated and developed further. The Chinese people will, as they did in the past, unite with the Afro-Asian and all other peoples of the world, and resolutely carry through

> to the end the struggle against the U.S. imperialist policies of aggression and war and for peace in Asia and Africa and the whole world (emphasis added).[43]

Fearing Soviet and American encirclement, the Chinese leadership and particularly the Chinese state-run media often played up conspiracy theories and made unprofessional remarks about countries and their leadership with which Beijing failed to resolve disputes or those which resisted its territorial aggression and expansionist policies. One also sees growing contradictions in the PRC's regional conduct even as it routinely swore by the Five Principles of Peaceful Coexistence and the Bandung Spirit in its interactions with post-colonial Asian and African states. The so-called 'Boundary Agreement' and 'Border Protocol' that China signed with Pakistan was clearly in contradiction to its stated stance that Kashmir was an issue to be resolved between India and Pakistan. It was an opportunistic and divisive move aimed at complicating the Kashmir issue and sowing seeds of future conflict in the Subcontinent. In the coming decades, one finds Pakistan playing second fiddle to both US and China, seeking to benefit from both, and in the process adding to its vulnerability to the big power politics and dependence on external military and economic aid, which remains the case to this day. China in return found a politically and militarily pliant and economically cheap ally in Pakistan Army. Unpopular autocratic leaders and regimes in neighbouring countries often played to the Chinese agenda to strengthen their claim to power and secure political legitimacy. *Renmin Ribao* editorials often went overboard in eulogising the popularity of its leaders among the neighbouring countries, particularly Pakistan, Afghanistan and Myanmar, even as Beijing failed to resolve disputes with several of its neighbours.

One finds that the impetus for China's improved relations with Afghanistan and other South Asian countries came from its strained ties with the Soviet Union and India. Vertzberger, with regard to China's boundary agreements/treaties with Afghanistan and other southern neighbours, observed that, "In so doing, it [China] hoped to gain an additional means of isolating India and to win a propaganda advantage in the Third World: China could contrast India's 'rigid attitude' with its own readiness to act 'fairly' and 'moderately' in settling border disputes."[44]

China's deteriorating relationship with India at the time was seen by scholars like Vertzberger as one of the core determinants of its relations with the other South Asian countries, particularly Afghanistan, Pakistan, Nepal, Bhutan, and Myanmar. Another significant determinant of China's policy towards its immediate neighbourhood was its ideological split with the Soviet Union, whose growing proximity with Afghanistan and the West Asian (or the Middle East) countries was perceived by China as yet another instance of the Soviet attempt to encircle China. Fearing that the Soviet Union may use Afghanistan as a springboard to make inroads into South Asia to fulfill its long-held desire for access to the warm waters of the Indian Ocean, China began to expand its diplomatic engagement with Afghanistan and Pakistan given their strategic location at the crossroads of South Asia and West Asia.

Vertzberger seemed to suggest that China, by settling its borders with its South Asian neighbours and concluding treaties of friendship and mutual non-aggression with them, was trying to project itself, especially among its smaller southern and southeastern neighbours, as a stabilising factor in the region, a dependable entity worth partnering, a reliable partner amenable to adjustments and compromises in the common interest and progress of the region. Perhaps, the PRC was trying to project itself as more deserving a partner than India to play a lead role in the region and in strengthening the Afro-Asian solidarity against bloc politics.

In the 1950s and the 1960s, the nascent PRC leadership must have had lot of insecurities and apprehensions with regard to the prevailing regional environment as it adjusted and formulated its foreign policy. It needed to have a stable and peaceful periphery to consolidate its domestic hold and to execute crucial political and economic reforms. This led China, especially given its strained relations with two of its large neighbours—the Soviet Union and India, and also in view of its tenuous hold over its largely unstable bordering regions of Tibet, Xinjiang and Inner Mongolia, to secure its periphery by settling borders (often renouncing its earlier territorial claims and positions as was the case in its border settlement with Afghanistan in 1963–64) through instruments of boundary treaties, which invariably contained the provisions of 'mutual non-aggression'.

The emphasis on the provision of 'mutual non-aggression' was probably to project the image of PRC as a benign and peaceful neighbour with no expansionist motives, for it was understood that countries like Afghanistan, Pakistan, Nepal and Burma (now Myanmar) were unlikely to have conducted any military aggression against the PRC. It was likely intended to send a message to the neighbouring countries with which it had adversarial ties, including India where a large number of Tibetans had taken refuge after the ruthless suppression of the Tibetan Uprising in March 1959.

Economic Relations

The China–Afghanistan relations thus rose and ebbed depending upon China's perception of its regional environment. After the signing of the boundary agreement with Afghanistan in November 1963, China further cemented its ties with Afghanistan. Soon China–Afghanistan Friendship Association was formed in Beijing, and an air link agreement was signed in December 1963. In October 1964, China, having conducted its first atomic test in Xinjiang, proposed an international summit to ban nuclear weapons, to which Afghan Prime Minister Daoud Khan extended his country's full support. In March 1965, when Chinese Foreign Minister Chen Yi visited Kabul to sign the boundary protocol, the two countries also signed a cultural agreement and a technical and economic cooperation agreement.

It is interesting to note that as the Sino-Soviet rivalry increased in the early 1960s, China sought to balance the Soviet influence in Afghanistan by increasing its aid and accelerating its economic investment in Afghanistan. The Sino-Afghan relations in the early 1960s, it may be said, were coming out of the initial hitches and apprehensions that had marked their relations through the 1950s. Though Chinese assistance was no match to the huge aid and investments being made by the US and the Soviet Union in restructuring the Afghan economy since the mid-1950s, still, by 1973, China had reportedly committed aid amounting to nearly $76.5 million to Afghanistan, which was said to be less than three per cent of the total foreign aid Afghanistan received.

Some of the major projects undertaken by China in Afghanistan during the period were: construction of Bagrami textile, printing & dyeing combined mill near Kabul; Darunta Experimental Fish-Breeding Centre in the eastern Nangarhar Province; development of the Parwan Irrigation Project, including the construction of a hydro-electric power station on the Charikar Canal in the north east and also a water storage dam; extension of aid in developing the Farah Rud River Project; and an experimental tea growing farm in the eastern Kunar Province.[45] In August 1971, the Chinese Red Cross Society also donated RMB 5 million Yuan to the Afghan Red Crescent Society as contribution for the purchase of 15,000 tonnes of wheat, 3,000 tonnes of maize and 5,000 blankets for Afghan flood and drought victims.[46]

Despite China's aid and increased economic assistance, Afghanistan all through remained heavily dependent on both the American and the Soviet economic and military aid. According to a World Bank report published in March 1978, between 1950 and 1970, foreign aid to Afghanistan averaged about $65 million per year, with about 50 per cent coming from the Soviet Union and 30 per cent from the US.[47] In fact, much of the developmental work, be it the agricultural, industrial or the infrastructure sector, was dependent on the flow of foreign aid and investment. The China–Afghanistan trade from 1966 to 1972 also remained insignificant (See Table I below). It was said to be less than one per cent of Afghanistan's total foreign trade at the time.

Table I: China–Afghanistan Trade: 1966–72

Year	*Afghan Imports ($ '000)*	*Afghan Exports ($ '000)*
1966	3,055	1,027
1969	10,362	500
1970	410	not available
1971	638	"
1972	866	"

Source: Sreedhar, "Sino-Afghan Economic Relations", *China Report*, Vol. 12, Issue 5–6, 1976, p. 9.

The steady China–Afghanistan relations suffered a brief jolt when former Afghan Prime Minster Daoud Khan, who was regarded by China as the architect of the special relationship between Afghanistan and the Soviet Union, staged a coup against King Zahir Shah and took over as the first president of the 'Republic of Afghanistan' on 16 July 1973, calling it a "national and progressive revolution".[48] Initially, China perceived the coup as part of a 'Soviet plot' and 'another move in the Soviet drive southward to the Indian Ocean' as well as an attempt to 'encircle China'.[49] Though China recognised the Daoud regime on 28 July 1973, it remained apprehensive of the new government as the pro-Soviet Parcham Party was a partner in the coup.

In order to allay China's apprehensions, President Daoud sent his brother and the former deputy prime minister and minister of foreign affairs, Naim Khan, as his special envoy to China. Naim accompanied by Afghan Deputy Foreign Minister Sayed Waheed Abdullah reached Beijing on 6 December 1974. He met the ailing Chinese Premier Zhou Enlai and held talks with Vice-Premier Li Hsien-nien (now romanised as Li Xiannian) and Foreign Minister Chiao Kuan-hua (now romanised as Qiao Guanhua). A fresh Agreement on Economic and Technical Cooperation was signed in the presence of Special Envoy Naim Khan and Vice-Premier Li on 8 December 1974.[50] Under the agreement, China extended economic assistance and announced another long-term and interest free loan to Afghanistan.

Backing the Anti-Soviet 'Jihad': 1979–1989

The *Saur* or 'April Revolution' in 1978, which led to the overthrow of the Daoud regime by the pro-Soviet People's Democratic Party of Afghanistan (PDPA), took China by surprise. However, a more surprising aspect of the China–Afghanistan relations in the 1970s was China's lack of initiative in extending recognition to the regimes of both President Daoud Khan and President Nur Mohammad Taraki until approached by Kabul. Despite Taraki's stated commitment to the values of non-alignment and active and positive neutrality, China remained apprehensive of the PDPA leaders. At the request of the Taraki Government, the PRC extended recognition to the new regime on 7 May 1978. Soon Kabul received Chinese Foreign Minister Huang Hua on 16 May 1978. However, the signing of the Treaty of Peace and Friendship by Kabul and Moscow in December 1978 and their growing military ties exacerbated China's anxiety over the developments in the region.

The role of the Soviet Union in the power struggle that followed between the two key constituents of the PDPA—Parcham and Khalq factions—added to China's fears about Afghanistan being taken over by the Soviet Union. The Soviet invasion of Afghanistan in December 1979 and the signing of the Soviet–

Afghan Treaty on Border Demarcation pertaining to the Wakhan Corridor bordering China in June 1981 further fuelled China's concerns. These developments, including the Soviet Union's peace and friendship treaties with Afghanistan, Mongolia, Vietnam, and India, basically countries bordering China, reinforced the Chinese narrative about the Soviet encirclement of China. On 3 April 1980, China decided not to extend the 30-year February 1950 Treaty of Friendship, Alliance and Mutual Assistance with the Soviet Union beyond the expiration date. China also saw a connection between the Soviet invasion of Afghanistan and the Moscow-backed Vietnamese intervention in Cambodia, which it believed was part of the larger Soviet game plan to expand its influence from the Strait of Hormuz in the Persian Gulf to the Malacca Straits in Southeast Asia.

After the Soviet invasion of Afghanistan, China decided to support the anti-Soviet Afghan resistance, which it perceived as the "people's war" and a "national liberation struggle," against both the pro-Soviet PDPA Government in Kabul and what it regarded as the Soviet imperialism and hegemonism in Afghanistan. The PDPA regime in Kabul had apparently become redundant for China. In the above context, it was remarked by Gargi Dutt:

> For Beijing the die had been cast. The conclusion of the (friendship) treaty and Kabul's support for a (Soviet-led collective) security system in Asia precluded any further attempt on the part of Beijing at keeping up good relations with the Kabul regime. Kabul had passed under the Soviet orbit. The time for opposing it and struggling against it had arrived. It indicated the arrival of a new stage in the approach towards developments in this area. Increasingly Beijing turned its attention towards the struggle in Afghanistan, towards the rebel movement and its potentiality, and towards the opportunities afforded by that situation.[51]

Soon China was part of the anti-Soviet front in Afghanistan, which was mainly supported by the US-led Western bloc, Saudi Arabia, Egypt, Arab Gulf states, and Pakistan and Iran. Deng Xiaoping declared that "the task of opposing the Soviet hegemonism will be on our daily agenda."[52] China reportedly supplied anti-Soviet Afghan fighters with "recoilless rifles, Soviet designed rifles and light machine guns, and mines." China was also said to have "provided training to a limited number of Afghans."[53] The Soviet media accused China of using Karakoram Highway for sending arms, ammunition and propaganda material for subversive activities in Afghanistan. Soviet sources talked of a Sino-Pakistan conspiracy to support the Afghan insurgency in close cooperation with the US.[54]

In fact, there were detailed reports of Chinese instructors training Afghan resistance fighters not only in training camps located within Pakistan, but also in its Xinjiang Region to train 'counter-revolutionary bands'. In the early years of the anti-Soviet resistance in Afghanistan, China had reportedly supplied nearly 2,000 heavy machine guns, 1,000 antitank rockets, Chinese version of AK-47, and nearly half a million rounds of ammunition.[55] In the meantime, apprehensive over a possible Soviet invasion of Pakistan, China began to further consolidate its friendly ties with Pakistan by enhancing its defence cooperation. During his visit to Islamabad in March 1980, China's Vice Minister of Defence Xio Ke made it clear that:

> Our friends can rest assured the Chinese people and army will firmly stand forever by the side of the Pakistan people and armed forces in their just struggle against hegemonic aggression and intervention to safeguard national independence and state sovereignty.[56]

It was interesting to note that China gradually adopted an extremely rigid attitude towards the Soviet military presence in Afghanistan. Fearing that Soviets may retain bases in Afghanistan, China consistently demanded a complete and an unconditional withdrawal of the Soviet forces from Afghanistan. Any idea of a partial or conditional Soviet withdrawal was not acceptable to China, although China knew it had little influence over the eventual outcome of the Afghan war. China had also proposed a possible Sino–US–Japan or Sino–US–Pakistan front to check 'Soviet hegemonism' and 'advancing imperialism' in Asia, and consistently warned the West against any détente with the 'polar bear'. In fact, the Soviet invasion of Afghanistan further afforded an opportunity for the ongoing rapprochement between China and the US, as Vice Premier Deng Xiapong made a visit to the US in late January 1979. In return, US Secretary of Defence Harold Brown visited China in January 1980 to begin the process of a 'joint strategic response' to the Soviet military presence in Afghanistan. Perhaps, a parallel can be seen in the Sino-US counter-terrorism cooperation attempted in the immediate aftermath of the 9/11 attacks.

However, with the ascendance of Mikhail Gorbachev in 1985, the foreign policy of the Soviet Union underwent drastic changes. As a result of the Soviet realisation of the futility of their Afghan venture, the Geneva peace process began in 1987. Though China was not part of the peace process, it showed keen interest in it. At another level, China was assisting its ally Pakistan in finalising the process of the Soviet withdrawal from Afghanistan. When the Geneva Accords finally came through in April 1988, China welcomed it as a 'positive development,' and regarded it as the 'new thinking' in the Soviet foreign policy. Within days of the signing of the Geneva Accords, *The New York Times* published a report in which it referred to US operations in Afghanistan as "one of the biggest ever mounted by the Central Intelligence Agency," based on interviews with officials representing different sections of the American establishment. The report stated upfront that "With help from China and many Moslem nations, the United States led a huge international operation over the last eight years to arm the Afghan guerrillas with the weapons they needed to drive the Soviet Army from their country." The report quoted a US military officer who served at the American Embassy in Beijing as having stated that China "worked hand in glove with the United States" in supplying arms such as rocket launchers to the anti-Soviet resistance fighters in Afghanistan. The report mentioned that as the US budget for covert operations in Afghanistan more than doubled, from $122 million in 1984 to $280 million in 1985, the Afghan resistance fighters "got their first effective surface-to-surface weapons, 107-millimeter multiple rocket launchers made in China."[57] However, it was noteworthy that when the Geneva negotiations were on, China came forward as a guarantor of the Accords but the Chinese proposal was rejected by then UN Secretary General Diego Cordoves.

Thereafter, as the US withdrew from Afghanistan and as the Soviet Union disintegrated, China had a new set of domestic and foreign policy priorities. At the domestic level, there were challenges in the form of the pro-democracy movement leading to the Tiananmen Square episode in Beijing in 1989, and also the ongoing economic reforms. At the external level, the absence of the Soviet threat and the emergence of resource-rich five Central Asian Republics (CARs) close to its borders afforded an entirely new gamut of opportunities and challenges to its foreign policy. China was no more interested in the faction-ridden domestic politics of the post-Soviet Afghanistan, especially as capital

Kabul turned into a battleground of factional rivalries, leading to the closure of its embassy in February 1993.

Like the West, China forgot Afghanistan until its western frontiers were threatened by the emergence of a more radical militant Islamist force, the Taliban. China had taken note of the rising power of the Taliban since the mid-1990s, and was later part of the "six-plus-two" Group, a UN sponsored initiative comprising Afghanistan's six neighbouring countries plus Russia and the US, which was formed to explore peaceful ways to resolve the Afghan conflict.

Direct Engagement with the Taliban: 1999–2001

In the early days of February 1999, China began to directly engage the Taliban. A Chinese delegation of five senior diplomats arrived in Kabul and for the first time met the Taliban officials. China would not have been completely unknown to the Taliban as the latter had their roots in the 'mujahideen' groups of the 1980s and China had supported them in their anti-Soviet 'Jihad'. China soon announced the beginning of direct flights between Kabul and Urumqi, the capital of Xinjiang Region bordering Afghanistan, and the opening of formal trade ties with Afghanistan.[58]

An interesting observation was made by Surya Ganagadharan about the aforesaid visit by the Chinese delegation to Kabul:

> The visit was never commented upon publicly by Beijing. Unofficial reports suggested that that the visit was China's way of saying thank you to the Taliban, who, in October 1998, had allowed in Chinese missile experts to recover and examine the remains of the cruise missiles the US had fired on Afghan terrorist bases in August that year. The Taliban also allowed the Chinese to take back an unexploded cruise missile. But it is difficult to accept the argument that the Chinese had sent a top team of diplomats to Kabul merely to say thank you.[59]

There were also reports about China agreeing to train the Taliban pilots at Jalalabad. Apart from all this, an agreement on military cooperation was also reportedly signed on 10 December 1998 between the senior commanders of the People's Liberation Army (PLA) and the Taliban military representatives.[60] A few weeks after the 9/11 attacks, *The Washington Times* carried a report on

28 September 2001, citing US intelligence sources, alleging that the Taliban had handed over pieces of US cruise missiles to the Chinese Government, in lieu of a military cooperation with Beijing. The Chinese Foreign Ministry spokesman later rejected the report as "totally groundless" and reiterated that the "Chinese Government has not established any kind of official relations with the Taliban."[61]

It was further reported that two Chinese state-run telecommunications companies—Zhongxing Telecom and Huawei Technologies—had been engaged since 1999 in installing a telephone system in Kabul. The system was said to be a switching network to handle up to 130,000 users. The report also pointed to al-Qaeda leader Osama bin Laden's statement issued just a month before in August, calling for "good relations" between Afghanistan and China. However, then Chinese Foreign Ministry spokesman Zhu Bangzao had stated earlier on 18 September that China's contacts with the Taliban were limited to "the working level" and that it "does not have any kind of formal relations with the Taliban". He was said to have referred to the reports about China building the telephone network and constructing a dam in Afghanistan as "unfounded rumors".[62]

At the end of October 2001, *The Washington Times* carried another report that quoted Jalaluddin Haqqani as having stated in his interview published in an Urdu newspaper on 22 October that "China is a good country. Taliban are in contact with it even now. China is also extending support and cooperation to the Taliban government, but the shape of this cooperation cannot be disclosed". The then Chinese foreign ministry spokesman, Sun Yuxi, was said to have dismissed Haqqani's statement as "a complete fabrication".[63]

However, former Taliban Ambassador to Islamabad Abdul Salaam Zaeef described in his autobiography, published in 2010, how the Chinese ambassador in Islamabad, Lu Shulin, "was the only one to maintain a good relationship" with the Taliban embassy in Islamabad and with Afghanistan, and how Zaeef had facilitated his visit to Kabul and Kandahar. Zaeef also mentioned that the Chinese ambassador was "the first foreign non-Islamic ambassador ever to see" Taliban chief Mullah Mohammad Omar.[64] The meeting probably took place in December 2000.

In the late 1990s, there were reports of growing social-political unrest in the Xinjiang Region before China initiated talks with the Taliban in February 1999. Ahmed Rashid had reported that on 29 January 1999, the Chinese authorities arrested some 29 Uygurs for allegedly masterminding the bloody anti-government riots in the city of Yining, which went on for two days in February 1997 in Xinjiang before it was suppressed by the Chinese Government. Since then, the region was witness to a steady rise in violence. The situation in the Yining city was reportedly still volatile when the Chinese delegation met the Taliban in February 1999.[65] Later, in August 2011, Chinese Ambassador to Kabul, Xu Feihong, claimed that there were over 200 cases of militant attacks in Xinjiang between 1990 and 2001.[66]

From China's point of view, it was the fear of the Taliban-style radical Islam spreading among its Muslim population in the Xinjiang Region bordering Afghanistan and cheap Afghan heroin flooding into the Chinese market that necessitated its engagement with the Taliban. Uygur militants were known to have fought along with the Afghan 'mujahideen'. China's use of the Karakoram Highway to transport assistance to the anti-Soviet jihad had also invariably opened the way for Uygur militants to Afghanistan, and especially Pakistan, where they had a notable presence in the Pashtun tribal areas.

The prospects of an abiding nexus between Uygur separatists and drug mafias destabilising the region further propelled China into engaging the Taliban who in turn were desperate for international recognition and legitimacy. It was probably for the first time since the Soviet withdrawal in 1988–89 that Afghanistan had again appeared in China's security calculus. However, this time the Sino-Afghan or the Sino-Taliban relations do not seem to have been fashioned by any larger geo-strategic calculus or great power politics, but by domestic security consideration. Besides having a nuclear testing site in Lop Nur, the Xinjiang Region was also said to have proven petroleum reserves and more was expected to be found in the Tarim Basin.

China's engagement with the Taliban was facilitated by Pakistan, which had enormous influence over the Taliban at the time and was one of the three countries to have recognised the Taliban regime. Pakistan had reportedly been pursuing China and the US to adopt a more modest approach towards the Taliban. According to Ahmed Rashid, "Pakistan has been trying to convince

Beijing that the Taliban, to which it gives substantial military and financial aid, are willing to clamp down on the drug trade and have no desire to fund or support Islamic Uygurs in their fight for independence."[67]

Whatever might have been the nature of relationship or the level of interaction between China and the Taliban at the time, the most notable aspect of it was that even as China reached out to the Taliban regime, it also endorsed the UN Security Council's partial as well as additional sanctions against the Taliban in 1999 and 2000, respectively.

With the international attention turning towards Afghanistan in the wake of the Taliban regime destroying nearly 1,500-year-old two giant statues of Lord Buddha in the central Bamyan Province in March 2001, it could not have been possible for China to keep up its informal engagement with the Taliban regime. China had reportedly turned down Pakistan's offer to convene a meeting with the Taliban foreign minister in July 2001.[68] However, China was opposed to any military action in Afghanistan by external powers as it believed that there was no military solution to the Afghan problem. It advocated a more active role by the UN. Perhaps, the determinants of China's Afghan policy in the post-Cold War era had shifted from confrontation to accommodation, to a combination of such non-militaristic means as diplomatic coercion and engagement.

NOTES

1 'Question of the Representation of China in the United Nations (concluded)' and 'Restoration of the Lawful Rights of the People's Republic of China in the United Nations (concluded)', Agenda Items 90 and 91, UN General Assembly (UNGA), Sixteenth Session, 1080th Plenary Meeting, 15 December 1961, at https://digitallibrary.un.org/record/744227?ln=ar&v=pdf; and 'Restoration of the Lawful Rights of the People's Republic of China in the United Nations (continued)', UNGA, Agenda Item 93, Twenty-Sixth Session, 1976th Plenary Meeting, 25 October 1971, at https://documents.un.org/doc/undoc/gen/nl7/102/97/pdf/nl710297.pdf.

2 'Foreign Affairs', Chapter IV, in *China Handbook: 1937–1945. A Comprehensive Survey of Major Developments in China in Eight Years of War*, Compiled by Chinese Ministry of Information, The MacMillan Company, New York, 1947, p. 181. Also see 'Treaty of Amity between the Republic of China and the Kingdom of Afghanistan', 2 March 1944, Treaty and Agreement Database, Ministry of Foreign Affairs, Taiwan, at https://no06.mofa.gov.tw/mofatreatys/IndexE.aspx. Faiz Mohammed Khan, also known as Faiz Mohammed Zikria or Zakaria, served as the Afghan Ambassador to Turkey from 1938 to 1948. He had earlier served as the education minister under King Amanullah Khan and as foreign minister under King Nadir Shah. See Ludwig W. Adamec, *Historical Dictionary of Afghanistan*, Second Edition,

Asian/Oceanian Historical Dictionaries, No. 5, The Scarecrow Press, Inc., Lanham, Maryland, 1997, p. 103.

3 Madhavi Thampi and Nirmola Sharma, *Catalogue of Materials Related to Modern China in the National Archives of India, 1939–1945*, Monograph No. 2, Institute of Chinese Studies, Delhi, June 2015, at https://www.icsin.org/uploads/2015/06/22/f78ab2f03bd28291b725f6819da48c4a.pdf. Also see, Shen-Yu Dai, 'China and Afghanistan', *The China Quarterly*, No. 25, January–March 1966, pp. 215–216, at https://www.jstor.org/stable/3082103.

4 Ibid.

5 Ko Po-nien, 'China's Peace Policy', *People's China*, No. 19, 1 October 1953, p. 12, at https://www.marxists.org/subject/china/peoples-china/1953/PC1953-19-OCR-sm.pdf.

6 India does not recognise the China–Pakistan 'Boundary Agreement' of 2 March 1963 and considers it as illegal and invalid. See "Appendix IX: Note Given by the Ministry of External Affairs, New Delhi, to the Embassy of China, March 2, 1963", in *Sino-Pakistan 'Agreement', March 2, 1963: Some Facts*, External Publicity Division, Ministry of External Affairs, Government of India, 16 March 1963, at https://www.claudearpi.in/wp-content/uploads/2021/01/1963-Agreement-GOI.pdf. China has been in illegal occupation of 37,555 sq kms of Indian Territory in Aksai Chin since the 1962 conflict. In addition, under the so-called 'Boundary Agreement' of 1963, Pakistan ceded 5,180 sq kms of Indian Territory in the Shaksgam Valley that was under Pakistan's illegal occupation to China. Pakistan has been in illegal and forcible occupation of 78,114 sq kms of Indian Territory (part of the former State of Jammu and Kashmir, reorganised in 2019 as Union Territories of Jammu & Kashmir and Ladakh) since 1947. See District Census Handbook–Leh, Census of India 2011, Directorate of Census Operations, Jammu and Kashmir, p. 8, at https://censusindia.gov.in/nada/index.php/catalog/498. Also see, "Text of Raksha Mantri Shri Rajnath Singh's Statement in Lok Sabha on September 15 Regarding Situation on Eastern Border in Ladakh", Press Information Bureau, Government of India, 15 September 2020, at https://www.pib.gov.in/PressReleasePage.aspx?PRID=1654484; Lok Sabha, "Question No.5459: Area of India Under Foreign Countries", Answer by Minister of State (MoS) for External Affairs Gen (Dr) V. K. Singh (Retd), 28 March 2018, at https://sansad.in/getFile/loksabhaquestions/annex/14/AU5459.pdf?source=pqals; Rajya Sabha, "Q. No. 2757: Illegal Occupation of Land by China And Pakistan", Answer by MoS for External Affairs V. Muraleedharan, 12 December 2019, at https://www.mea.gov.in/rajya-sabha.htm?dtl/32197/QUESTION_NO2757; Lok Sabha, "Q. No. 648: Shaksgam Valley", Answer by MoS for External Affairs V. Muraleedharan, 4 February 2022, at https://www.mea.gov.in/lok-sabha.htm?dtl/34811/QUESTION+NO648+.

7 Alfred D. Wilhelm, Jr., 'The Chinese at the Negotiating Table: Style and Characteristics', National Defense University Press, Washington, D.C., February 1994, p. 73, at https://apps.dtic.mil/sti/tr/pdf/ADA279207.pdf.

8 'On this Day in Chinese History; 20 January', *The Nanjinger*, 22 January 2024, at https://www.thenanjinger.com/the-nanjinger/diplomacy-talks/on-this-day-in-chinese-history-22-january/.

9 Mohammad Ayub Khan, *Friends Not Masters: A Political Autobiography*, Oxford University Press, London, 1967, pp. 126–127; J.N. Dixit, *India–Pakistan in War and Peace*, Routledge, London and New York, 2002, p. 127.

10 Shen-Yu Dai, 'China and Afghanistan', *The China Quarterly*, No. 25, January–March 1966, p. 216, at https://www.jstor.org/stable/3082103. .

11 Ibid.
12 Yaacov Vertzberger, "Afghanistan in China's Policy", *Problems of Communism*, Vol. XXXI, May–June 1982, p. 1.
13 Ibid.
14 Shen-Yu Dai, n. 10, pp. 216–217.
15 Ibid., p. 217.
16 Ibid.
17 Chronicle of Events, *People's China*, No. 16, 16 August 1957, p. 42, at https://www.marxists.org/subject/china/peoples-china/1957/PC1957-16.pdf.
18 Cultural News, *Peking Review*, Vol. 1, No. 25, 19 August 1958, p. 22, at https://massline.org/PekingReview/PR1958/PR1958-25.pdf.
19 China and the World, *Peking Review*, Vol. 1, No. 33, 14 October 1958, p. 19, at https://massline.org/PekingReview/PR1958/PR1958-33.pdf.
20 Ahmad Ali Kohzad (1907–1983) was the curator of the Kabul Museum and the founding director of *Anjoman-e Tarikh-e Afghanistan* or the Historical Society of Afghanistan. He was known for his pioneering work on Afghanistan's rich pre-Islamic heritage. See Nilly Kohzad, "My Grandfather, My Hero: Remembering The Historian Ahmad Ali Kohzad", RFE/RL, 30 December 2020, at https://www.rferl.org/a/ahmad-ali-kohzad-historian-legacy-afghanistan/31026493.html; and William Figueroa, 'Ahmad Ali Kohzad's visit to China (1958): A Voice from the Past', in Su Lin Lewis and Nana Osei-Oparein (eds.), *Socialism, Internationalism, and Development in the Third World: Envisioning Modernity in the Era of Decolonization*, Bloomsbury Academic, London, 2024, pp. 181–192, at https://www.bloomsburycollections.com/monograph?docid=b-9781350420175.
21 China and the World, *Peking Review*, Vol. 1, No. 39, 25 November 1958, p. 19, at https://massline.org/PekingReview/PR1958/PR1958-39.pdf.
22 'What's On in Peking – Highlights of Current Entertainment Exhibitions, etc.', *Peking Review*, Vol. 1, No. 28, 9 September 1958, p. 23, at https://massline.org/PekingReview/PR1958/PR1958-28.pdf.
23 'Afghan Ensemble in Peking', China and the World, *Peking Review*, Vol. III, No. 31, 2 August 1960, p. 27, at https://massline.org/PekingReview/PR1960/PR1960-31.pdf.
24 'Afghan Deputy-Premier Welcomed', China and the World, *Peking Review*, Vol. II, No. 36, 8 September 1959, p. 21, at https://massline.org/PekingReview/PR1959/PR1959-36.pdf.
25 "Afghan Deputy-Premier in Peking", China and the World, *Peking Review*, Vol. II, No. 37, 15 September 1959, p. 30, at https://www.massline.org/PekingReview/PR1959/PR1959-37.pdf.
26 "China–Afghanistan Joint Communiqué", *Peking Review*, Vol. II, No. 38, 22 September 1959, p. 21, at https://www.massline.org/PekingReview/PR1959/PR1959-38.pdf.
27 Ibid.
28 Ibid.
29 "Vice-Premier Chen Yi's Banquet Speech", *Peking Review*, Vol. III, No. 35, 30 August 1960, p. 7, at https://www.massline.org/PekingReview/PR1960/PR1960-35.pdf.
30 Shen-Yu Dai, n. 10, pp. 6–9; "Vice-Premier Chen Yi's Farewell Speech", *Peking Review*, Vol. III, No. 35, 30 August 1960, p. 9, at https://www.massline.org/PekingReview/PR1960/PR1960-35.pdf.
31 "Another Example of Peaceful Coexistence", Translation of the *Renmin Ribao* Editorial of 28 August 1960, *Peking Review*, Vol. III, No. 35, 30 August 1960, p. 10, at https://

www.massline.org/PekingReview/PR1960/PR1960-35.pdf.

32 "Vice-Premier Chen Yi's Farewell Statement", *Peking Review*, Vol. III, No. 35, 30 August 1960, p. 9, at https://www.massline.org/PekingReview/PR1960/PR1960-35.pdf. .

33 "Chairman Liu Reiterates China's Proposal for Complete Prohibition of Nuclear Weapons", *Peking Review*, Vol. VII, No. 45, 6 November 1964, p. 6, at https://www.massline.org/PekingReview/PR1964/PR1964-45.pdf.

34 "Afghan Royal Family in China", *Peking Review*, Vol. VII, No. 45, 6 November 1964, p. 6, at https://www.massline.org/PekingReview/PR1964/PR1964-45.pdf.

35 Ibid., p. 7.

36 "China-Afghanistan Joint Communiqué, 12 November 1964, Peking", *Peking Review*, Vol. VII, No. 47, 20 November 1964, p. 17, at https://www.massline.org/PekingReview/PR1964/PR1964-47.pdf.

37 "Afghan King and Queen Leave for Home", *Peking Review*, Vol. VII, No. 47, 20 November 1964, p. 3, at https://www.massline.org/PekingReview/PR1964/PR1964-47.pdf.

38 "Afghanistan-People's Republic of China Boundary Protocol", *International Legal Materials*, Vol. 4, No. 6, Cambridge University Press, November 1965, p. 1061, at https://www.jstor.org/stable/20689984.

39 "Afghanistan-People's Republic of China Agreement on Cultural Cooperation", *International Legal Materials*, Cambridge University Press, Vol. 4, No. 6, November 1965, p. 1070, at https://www.jstor.org/stable/20689985.

40 "Afghanistan-People's Republic of China Agreement on Economic and Technical Cooperation", *International Legal Materials*, Cambridge University Press, Vol. 4, No. 6, November 1965, pp. 1072–1073, at https://www.jstor.org/stable/20689986.

41 News Briefs, *Peking Review*, Vol. 15, No. 31, 4 August 1972, p. 19, at https://www.massline.org/PekingReview/PR1972/PR1972-31.pdf.

42 News Briefs, *Peking Review*, Vol. 15, No. 43, 27 October 1972, p. 21, at https://www.massline.org/PekingReview/PR1972/PR1972-43.pdf.

43 "A Major Victory for China's Foreign Policy of Peace", *Renmin Ribao* Editorial of 21 April 1966, *The Peking Review*, Vol. 9, No. 18, 29 April 1966, p. 11, at https://www.massline.org/PekingReview/PR1966/PR1966-18.pdf.

44 Yaacov Vertzberger, n. 12, p. 3.

45 Sreedhar, "Sino-Afghan Economic Relations", *China Report*, Vol. 12, Issue 5–6, 1976, p. 7.

46 "Solicitude for Afghan Drought and Flood Victims", *Peking Review*, Vol. 14, No. 33, 13 August 1971, p. 29, at https://www.massline.org/PekingReview/PR1971/PR1971-33.pdf.

47 The World Bank, *Afghanistan: The Journey to Economic Development*, Vol. I: The Main Report, Report No. 1777a-AF, 17 March 1978, p. 27, at https://documents1.worldbank.org/curated/en/110641468195844097/pdf/multi-page.pdf.

48 Ron Synovitz, "Afghanistan: History of 1973 Coup Sheds Light on Relations with Pakistan", *RFE/RL*, 18 July 2003, at https://www.rferl.org/a/1103837.html.

49 Sreedhar, n. 45, p. 9.

50 "Afghan Special Envoy Naim Visits China", *Peking Review*, Vol.17, No. 50, 13 December 1974, pp. 4–5, at https://www.massline.org/PekingReview/PR1974/PR1974-50.pdf.

51 Gargi Dutt, "China and the Development in Afghanistan", in K. P. Misra, (ed.), *Afghanistan in Crisis*, Vikas Publishing House, New Delhi, 1981, p. 43.

52 A.Z. Hilali, "China's Response to the Soviet Invasion of Afghanistan", *Central Asian Survey*, Vol. 20, No. 3, September 2001, p. 334.

53 *Far Eastern Economic Review*, Hong Kong, 8 May 1981. Also see, "Arming Afghan Rebels", *Foreign Report*, London, 13 August 1981, p. 3.

54 Y. Agranov, "The Afghan Revolution and Peking's Treacherous Course", *Far Eastern Affairs*, Moscow, No. 3, 1980, p. 13.

55 S.K. Ramazani, "Weapons Can't Replace Words", *Newsweek*, 27 September 1980, p. 17.

56 Yaacov Vertzberger, "Afghanistan in China's Policy", *Problems of Communism*, Vol. XXXI, May–June 1982, p. 14.

57 Robert Pear, "Arming Afghan Guerrillas: A Huge Effort Led by U.S.", *The New York Times*, 18 April 1988, at https://www.nytimes.com/1988/04/18/world/arming-afghan-guerrillas-a-huge-effort-led-by-us.html.

58 Hamid Wahed Alikuzai, *From Aryana–Khorasan to Afghanistan: Afghanistan History in 25 Volumes*, Trafford Publishing, United States of America, 2011, p. 345.

59 Surya Gangadharan, "The China–Taliban Equation", *Aakrosh*, Vol. 3, No. 6, January 2000. p. 58.

60 Ibid., pp. 67–68.

61 "Spokesperson on the US Report that China Was Supplied by the Taliban US Cruises Missiles Fired During Attacks Against the Taliban", Chinese Ministry of Foreign Affairs, Updated 2 October 2001, at https://www.fmprc.gov.cn/eng/gjhdq_665435/2675_665437/2676_663356/2679_663362/202406/t20240607_11406369.html.

62 "Chinese Firms Helping Put Phone System in Kabul", *The Washington Times*, 28 September 2001, at https://www.washingtontimes.com/news/2001/sep/28/20010928-025638-7645r/.

63 "Taliban Leader Cites Help by China", *The Washington Times*, 31 October 2001, at https://www.washingtontimes.com/news/2001/oct/31/20011031-030638-1656r/.

64 Abdul Salam Zaeef, *My Life with the Taliban*, Hachette India, 2010, p. 135.

65 Ahmed Rashid, "Taliban Temptation", *Far Eastern Economic Review*, Hong Kong, 11 March 1999, p. 22.

66 Xu Feihong, "A Unique Neighbor of Afghanistan: China's Xinjiang", Chinese Embassy in the Islamic Republic of Afghanistan, 27 August 2011, at http://af.china-embassy.org/eng/dsxx/remarks/t852487.htm

67 Ahmed Rashid, "Taliban Temptation", *Far Eastern Economic Review*, Hong Kong, 11 March 1999. p. 21.

68 "Total Ban on Poppy Cultivation", *POT Afghanistan Series*, New Delhi, Vol. 25, No. 33, 4 September 2000, p. 139.

*"We are closely linked and share weal and woe with Afghanistan."**

—Chinese Foreign Minister Wang Yi
December 2015

* * *

*"We [the SCO] will continue to manage regional affairs by ourselves, guarding against shocks from turbulence outside the region, and will play a bigger role in Afghanistan's peaceful reconstruction. We'll strengthen communication, coordination and cooperation in dealing with major international and regional issues."***

— Chinese President Hu Jintao
People's Daily, June 2012

* "Wang Yi Attends the Fifth Foreign Ministerial Conference of the Istanbul Process on Afghanistan", Chinese Ministry of Foreign Affairs, 9 December 2015, at https://www.fmprc.gov.cn/eng/gjhdq_665435/2675_665437/2676_663356/2678_663360/202406/t20240607_11406376.html.

** "Hu Says Regional Bloc to Seek Role in Afghanistan", *Shanghai Daily*, 7 June 2012, at https://archive.shine.cn/nation/Hu-says-regional-bloc-to-seek-role-in-Afghanistan/shdaily.shtml.

2

China and the Islamic Republic of Afghanistan
Modest to Active Engagement

Beijing despite its ties with the Taliban regime in Kabul had not protested when the United States launched Operation Enduring Freedom in Afghanistan in October 2001. Chinese President Jiang Zemin reportedly called US President George W. Bush and offered Beijing's cooperation on the issue of terrorism. China like many other countries plagued by separatist movements was also busy building a case for an acceptance of its own 'war on terror' against Uygur militants, especially those belonging to what China referred to as the East Turkistan Islamic Movement (ETIM), in its northwestern Xinjiang Region. It was perhaps looking at the US re-engagement in Afghanistan as an opportunity for both countries to work together. It was reported that in October 2002, Chinese ambassador to Brussels had met NATO's Secretary General Lord Robertson "to discuss the potential for building a closer relationship" between China and the NATO.[1]

In his message to President Bush on 11 September 2001, Chinese President Jiang had stated that "the Chinese government consistently condemns and opposes all manner of terrorist violence."[2]

The next day, he called up Bush and reportedly offered to cooperate with the United States on the issue of terrorism. At the UN Security Council, the same day, China as a permanent member voted in favour of Resolution 1368 (to combat terrorism). On September 20, Beijing offered 'unconditional support' to the US in fighting terrorism. On 21 September, visiting Chinese Foreign Minister Tang Jiaxuan reiterated China's cooperation, and US Secretary of State Colin Powell indicated that their discussions covered intelligence-sharing but not military cooperation. Tang while speaking to the media stated that both sides are cooperating on anti-terrorism and "such cooperation will continue into the future".[3]

Meanwhile, China's counter-terrorism experts participated in a counter-terrorism meeting held in Washington on 25 September 2001. Three days later, on 28 September, China voted in favour of Resolution 1373, reaffirming the need to combat terrorism. However, President Jiang in a phone call with British Prime Minister Tony Blair on 18 September said that the war against terrorism required conclusive evidence, specific targets to avoid hurting innocent people, compliance with the UN Charter, and a role for the Security Council. China had also reportedly sent its vice minister of foreign affairs to convince then Pakistan President Gen Pervez Musharraf to support the US in its war in Afghanistan. Later, testifying to the US Congress in February 2002, Powell acknowledged the Chinese assistance in the war against terrorism.[4] However, it was noteworthy that the Pentagon's June 2002 report on foreign contributions in the counter-terrorism war did not mention China among the 50 countries in the coalition.[5] This was very much in continuation of the Bush Administration's failure to fully engage the regional countries other than Pakistan after the overthrow of the Taliban regime.

Chinese Position on Terrorism

Post 9/11, China was clearly articulating its position on the issue of terrorism and the need for a stronger UN role in Afghanistan. On 12 November 2001, Chinese Foreign Minister Tang in his speech delivered at the meeting of the foreign ministers of the 'six-plus-two' countries at the UN had observed that "China closely follows the situation in Afghanistan and stands for a political solution through negotiation and dialogue." He argued that certain principles should be followed while dealing with Afghanistan: (i) Maintain the national sovereignty, independence, and territorial integrity of Afghanistan; (ii) The Afghan people should choose their own solution; (iii) The future government in Afghanistan should be broadly based, represent all ethnic interests, and co-exist with all countries, neighbors in particular, in amity; (iv) Regional peace and stability should be maintained; and (v) The UN should play a more active and constructive role. He also stated that "the 6+2 mechanism is important and effective in discussing and promoting a political settlement of the Afghan Issue, and should be given full play."[6]

Further articulating the Chinese position, Foreign Minister Tang in an interview to the Italian daily *La Stampa* on 24 November 2001 stated:

> China supports the war against all forms of terrorism and upholds the resolutions approved by the UN Security Council. We strongly believe that such actions must avoid harming innocents and shall be consistent with the principles of the UN Charter and other universally recognized norms of international law. This serves the interests of peace and long-term stability in the world and in the region. The war against terrorism is a delicate issue having long-term impact. In agreement with the European Union, China also thinks that the war against terrorism requires the strengthening of international cooperation and the full development of the role of the UN and of its Security Council.
>
> No double standard should be adopted in connection with anti-terrorism. No matter where and when terrorist acts occur or which form they take, what the target is, or who is involved or supports them, the international community should condemn them with equal severity and firmly counterstrike.
>
> It is worth noting that China is also a victim of terrorism. The terrorist forces of Eastern Turkestan have been trained by international terrorist organizations, which have supported and financed them. Such forces have staged many attacks both in China and abroad, causing innocent victims. *The Eastern Turkestan group is certainly a terrorist organization and fighting against it is part of the international war against terrorism* (emphasis added).[7]

On Afghanistan, while expressing China's support to what he described as "positive" and "constructive proposals" by the special envoy of the UN secretary general, Tang stated that the resolution of the Afghan issue must be consistent with the following principles:

1. Afghanistan's political independence and territorial integrity shall be guaranteed;
2. The Afghan people shall finally decide by themselves how to solve the problems of Afghanistan;

3. Afghanistan's future government shall have a broad base and represent the interests of each ethnic group, it shall pursue a peaceful foreign policy and abandon extremism, it shall entertain friendly relationships with all countries and specifically with neighboring ones;
4. The UN shall intervene in a more intensive and active fashion;
5. The solution of the Afghan issue shall serve the interests of peace and stability in the region.[8]

Similarly, in a report issued by the Chinese Information Office of State Council in January 2002 it was stated:

> The Chinese government opposes terrorism in any form; at the same time it opposes the application of double standards concerning the anti-terrorism issue. Any tolerance or indulgence toward the "East Turkistan" terrorist forces will not harm China and the Chinese people alone. Today, as the international community becomes more clearly and deeply aware of the harm brought about by terrorism, we hope that all peace-loving people throughout the world, regardless of ethnic status or religious belief, region or country, political or social system, will fully recognize the nature of the "East Turkistan" terrorist forces and the serious harm caused by them, see through all their disguises, and jointly crack down on their terrorist activities, leaving not a single opportunity for them to exploit to their advantage.[9]

Though China's cooperation with US in the wake of 9/11 attacks did not transform the Sino-US relations, it did help in tiding over the bilateral tension over the bombing of the Chinese Embassy in Belgrade in May 1999 and EP-3/F-8 aircraft collision crisis in April 2001. The visit by President Bush to Shanghai in October 2001 to attend the Asia-Pacific Economic Cooperation (APEC) Forum was seen as an opportunity to make advances in the bilateral relations. Though the Sino-US relations improved after 11 September but fundamental problems between the two countries remained. China was well aware of the fact that the Uighur militants were still in Afghanistan and in the north-western tribal areas of Pakistan. Initially, it appeared that the US invasion of Afghanistan had again provided an opportunity for China and the US and the NATO to explore ways of future cooperation as was the case in the wake of the Soviet invasion of Afghanistan in 1979, but that was not to happen.

Rebuilding of Bilateral Ties

China's approach towards the emerging Afghan reality was characteristically cautious. China endorsed the Bonn Agreement signed among diverse Afghan groups on 5 December 2001. The Chinese Foreign Ministry spokesman informed in December that since the 1980s, China has regularly provided humanitarian aid each year to the Afghan refugees in Pakistan and Iran through the UN High Commissioner for Refugees (UNHCR), International Committee of the Red Cross (ICRC), and other channels. Earlier, China had helped build Parwan Irrigation Works and Kandahar Hospital and carried out some 10 other projects.[10]

At a conference on reconstruction aid to Afghanistan held in Tokyo on 21 January 2002, China pledged $1 million, in addition to humanitarian goods worth $3.6 million. It was noteworthy that China was among the first countries that Hamid Karzai visited in January 2002, days after his appointment as the chairman of the Afghan interim administration on 22 December 2001. President Jiang Zemin promised to the visiting Afghan leader an additional reconstruction aid of $150 million spread over four to five years.[11] Of the $150 million, China provided $47 million by 2003 and $15 million in 2004. In March 2002, a Chinese delegation carrying the first batch of assistance arrived in Kabul as part of the urgent humanitarian assistance committed by Beijing during the January 2002 Tokyo Conference on Afghanistan. Under the exchange of letters signed by the visiting Chinese delegation with Afghan officials, it was said that China will provide Kabul with 20,000 sets of uniforms and boots for the police and 50,000 sets of uniforms and boots for the army, and stationery and office supplies for 80,000 civil servants.[12]

In January 2002, China also announced that it will reopen its embassy on 6 February, with then Vice Foreign Minister Wang Yi leading a delegation to Kabul to preside over the embassy reopening ceremony.[13] Earlier in the third week of December 2001, a team of six Chinese officials led by Zhang Min, China's former chargé d'affaires in Kabul before the closure of the embassy in February 1993, had visited Kabul via Bagram to inspect the Chinese embassy building and attend the 22 December inauguration of the Afghan Interim Administration.[14]

Thereafter, what was notable was a series of high-level visits between the two countries. Post-2001, Chinese Foreign Minister Tang Jiaxuan was the first senior Chinese official to visit Kabul on 15 May 2002. He met Karzai, and also his Afghan counterpart Abdullah Abdullah and former Afghan King Zahir Shah. Tang welcomed the idea of holding a *Loya Jirga* (a traditional assembly of tribal elders and chieftains) to elect the leader for the Afghan transitional government in June 2002. He remarked that "China hopes that the *Loya Jirga* could turn out to be a success and all parties in Afghanistan would bear in mind national and ethnic minorities, conscientiously abide by the Bonn Agreement and work for national reconciliation, peace and prosperity."[15]

In his meeting with Abdullah, Tang announced that China will send teams to study the rehabilitation of the Kabul Republic Hospital, the water conservancy project in Parwan and a hospital in Kandahar. He also assured his Afghan counterpart that "China will fulfill as soon as possible its pledges to provide Afghanistan with police uniforms and stationery and office supplies for 80 thousand people." He further stated, "Chinese businesses are ready for economic and technological cooperation with Afghanistan in various ways and at various levels." The two ministers also signed an agreement on economic and technological cooperation.[16] The next month, on 5 June 2002, Karzai made his second good-will visit to China and exchanged views with President Jiang. Karzai's visit came just days ahead of the Emergency *Loya Jirga*, which was convened in Kabul between 11 and 19 June to decide on the formation of the Afghan Transitional Administration.

Afghan Vice-President Niamatullah Shahrani visited China on 27 May 2003 and met his Chinese counterpart Zeng Qinghong. Besides reiterating cooperation against East Turkistan militants, China announced $15 million grant to Afghanistan; another $1 million in cash to support the Afghan Government budget; resumption of the China–Afghanistan Friendship Association; inter-college relations between Beijing University and Kabul University; and an economic and technical cooperation agreement.[17]

On 10 March 2004, Chinese Foreign Minister Li Zhaoxing met Afghan Foreign Minister Abdullah and stated that "Afghanistan was now in a critical period and the international community should continue to offer their attention and support in addition to the efforts made by the Afghan government and its people."[18] The same month, Chinese Ambassador Sun Yuxi, in a joint press conference with the then Afghan finance minister, Ashraf Ghani Ahmadzai, announced China's decision to write off about $18 million debt Afghanistan owed to China since 1965.[19] The debt was finally signed off during a meeting between Chinese Foreign Minister Li and Afghan Foreign Minister Abdullah held on the sidelines of the Berlin Conference on Afghanistan on 31 March 2004.

On the second day of the Berlin Conference (31 March–1 April 2004), Chinese Ambassador Sun in his address clearly identified "terrorist attacks, factional conflicts and drug-related crimes" as "three most outstanding security issues facing Afghanistan". He suggested five points to deal with security threats to Afghanistan: *first*, the speedy formation of the Afghan national army and the national police. He called for the establishment of a "unified national military force transcending ethnic and factional divisions". He informed that China has delivered some army and police uniforms and police vehicles to Afghanistan. Referring to the Chinese Foreign Minister Li's announcement just a day before, he added that China would build a shooting range in Afghanistan and help train the Afghan police in China; *second*, expand the scope of deployment of the International Security Assistance Force (ISAF) in Afghanistan. He stated that China also supports a greater role for provincial reconstruction teams; *third*, continued disarmament, demobilisation and reintegration (DDR) process aimed at disarming and reintegrating militias into the society; *fourth*, vigorous anti-drug campaign; and, *fifth*, addressing the fundamental and structural political and economic causes of security challenges in the country. He called for a "comprehensive and integrated solution" to deal with it.[20]

On 10 June 2004, about 11 Chinese workers engaged in a World Bank-funded road construction project in northern Kunduz Province were killed.[21] However, it did not deter China from bidding for huge mining contracts in Afghanistan. Later, in December 2006, Chinese workers engaged in another road construction project in Badghis Province came under attack but no casualty was reported.[22] In August 2005, Chinese Ambassador to Afghanistan Liu Jian, during an interview to the *Pajhwok Afghan News*, had stated that more than 100 Chinese businessman were involved in various reconstruction projects in Afghanistan. He stated that the Sino-Afghan trade volume, which was about $25 million in 2002, has increased as per the Afghan statistics to $380 million in 2004. Jian further stated that about 5,000 Afghans, mostly businessmen, had visited China in 2004 and that the number was likely to reach 7,000 by the end of 2005. He had also called for establishing a banking credit system between the two countries to further boost the bilateral economic ties.[23] Thereafter, on 4 November 2005, a protocol on establishing the SCO–Afghanistan Contact Group was signed in Beijing.

On 7 December 2004, China sent a special envoy to attend the inauguration of Hamid Karzai as the elected president of Afghanistan. Interestingly, in most of the meetings between the senior leaders and officials of the two countries, China, besides emphasising the principle of "good neighbourliness," appreciated Afghanistan's support for its "one-China policy" *vis-à-vis* Taiwan and the issue of cooperation against the activities of the East Turkistan militants. The perceived threat from ETIM was consistently projected as China's primary concern.

In October 2005, it was reported that an Afghan defence ministry delegation paid an eight-day official visit to China that began on 12 October. The delegation was led by Afghan Deputy Defence Minister Gen Hamayun Fauzi who was quoted as stating that China would be providing military equipment worth $2 million in accordance with a list handed over by the Afghan defence ministry to the Chinese Government. It was further stated that apart from supplying equipment, China also agreed to impart training and education to the Afghan defence ministry personnel.[24] Later, on 19 June 2006, Afghan Defence Minister Gen Abdul Rahim Wardak, who was accompanying President Karzai during his four-day state visit to China, met Chinese Defence Minister Cao Gangchuan. According to *Xinhua*, Cao, who was also vice chairman of the central military commission and state councilor, in his meeting with Gen Wardak stated that "China is committed to developing its military ties with Afghanistan, and will continue efforts to upgrade such relations".[25] Thereafter, on 24 June, spokesperson of the Afghan defence ministry, Gen Zahir Azimi, announced that an MoU was signed according to which China would impart training to 30,000 Afghan soldiers during the next four years and that China would allocate $3 million for the training.[26] On 31 October 2006, during Gen Wardak's good-will visit to Beijing, Chinese Defence Minister Cao again reiterated his commitment to strengthening cooperation between the armed forces of the two countries. Wardak was also reported to have visited Xinjiang Province and Shanghai during his visit.[27] On 12 November 2007, Chief of the Afghan National Army Gen Bismillah Mohammadi visited Beijing and met Chinese Defence Minister Cao and his Chinese counterpart Chen Bingde.

In December 2010, Afghan Deputy Defence Minister Gen Mohebullah Moheb was reported to have visited China. On 23 July 2012, Gen Wardak again visited Beijing and met Chinese Defence Minister and State Councilor Liang Guanglie who was quoted to have stated that "the military-to-military exchanges are increasing, the high-level interactions are going on and the pragmatic cooperation in terms of personnel training and military aid...are going ahead in a stable way." He added that "the Chinese side was willing to cement and enhance the current cooperation between the two militaries based on mutual respect and win-win reciprocity to advance the military ties in a sustainable way."[28] On 15 April 2013, Afghan Deputy Interior Minister Abdul Rahman Rahman was reported to have met China's Assistant Public Security Minister Li Wei to further discuss the security cooperation.

President Karzai's third visit to China in June 2006, this time as an elected president, led to the signing of the Treaty on Good Neighbourliness and Mutual Cooperation between the two countries on 19 June 2006.[29] The Treaty was ratified later by the Standing Committee of China's National People's Congress and the Afghan Parliament on 14 August 2008.[30] Karzai's June 2006 visit was particularly significant in view of the large number of agreements and MoUs, a total of 11 documents, which were signed between the two countries. The joint statement issued on the occasion was probably the most comprehensive one by the two countries. It clearly stated that "trade and economic relations are an important part of China-Afghanistan good-neighborliness and friendly cooperation," which was well reflected in the long list of agreements and MoUs envisaged in the document (see Appendix II):

- Agreement on Cooperation on Combating Trans-national Crime;
- Agreement on Trade and Economic Cooperation;

- Agreement on Economic and Technical Cooperation;
- Exchange Letter for China Granting Zero Tariff Treatment to Certain Goods Originated in Afghanistan;
- Agreement on Air Service;
- Protocol on Institutionalizing Consultations between foreign ministries of the two countries;
- MoU on Agricultural Cooperation;
- MoU on Cooperation in the Maintenance and Preservation of Cultural Heritage;
- Memorandum of Agreement between the Afghanistan Chamber of Commerce and Industry and the China Council for the Promotion of International Trade; and
- Memorandum of Agreement between the Afghanistan Investment Support Agency and the China Council for the Promotion of International Trade.

The joint statement announced that China would grant zero-tariff treatment to 278 items of Afghan exports to China as of 1 July 2006; train 200 Afghan professionals in the coming two years and offer 30 government scholarships to Afghanistan annually starting from 2007. While welcoming Afghanistan's engagement with the SCO within the context of "Contact Group Protocol," the Chinese side also "expressed readiness to enter into cooperation in pragmatic terms with the Afghan side within the framework of regional cooperation." The Afghan side too welcomed China's entry as an observer state into the SAARC.[31] By now, it was said that China was Afghanistan's third major trading partner after Japan and Pakistan with its export volume to Afghanistan totaling US$ 317 million in the fiscal year 2005–06.[32] In November 2006, China reportedly donated 20 jeeps, 20 pickup trucks, sets of security monitoring system and kitchenware worth $1 million to the Afghan Parliament.[33]

Chinese Foreign Minister Yang Jiechi in his speech at the Paris Conference on Afghanistan on 12 June 2008 articulated the Chinese position on the future of Afghanistan. While endorsing the newly formulated Afghanistan National Development Strategy (ANDS), he emphasised that: (i) We need a safe and secure Afghanistan; (ii) We need an Afghanistan that enjoys development; (iii) We need an Afghanistan that stays far away from drugs; and (iv) We need a sustainable Afghanistan.[34] Nine months later, at the UN co-sponsored International Conference on Afghanistan held in Hague on 31 March 2009, Chinese Vice Foreign Minister Wu Dawei announced Beijing's decision to provide US$ 75 million aid to Afghanistan in the next five years.[35]

Interestingly, then Afghan Foreign Minister Rangin Dadfar Spanta during his four-day visit to Beijing from 9 April to 12 April 2009 had called for the opening of the border with China through the Wakhan Corridor to strengthen security cooperation. Spanta made the suggestion while speaking at the China Institute of International Studies, the Chinese foreign ministry think tank, during his three-day visit. The *China Daily* reported that Spanta spoke of "a triangle of terrorism" — al-Qaida, the Taliban and external support—which "presents existential threats not only to Afghanistan but also to the region and the world's peace and stability." Arguing that the solution to the terrorism threat has to be "comprehensive, regional and international", he noted that it was his "personal wish" that the Wakhan Corridor connecting the two countries was opened.[36]

Commenting on Spanta's suggestion, then Chinese foreign ministry spokesperson Qin Gang stated that China "will study" Spanta's suggestion "with a serious and positive attitude towards conducting cooperation with Afghanistan in transportation and trade." On Spanta's talks with Chinese Foreign Minister Yang Jiechi, Qin stated that "China feels positive about developing trade and security cooperation with Afghanistan" and that it will continue to support "the peaceful reconstruction and economic development of Afghanistan."[37] Qin had earlier while announcing Spanta's forthcoming visit stated that China had offered assistance worth US$ 170 million to Afghanistan since 2002.[38] Spanta's suggestion assumed significance in the light of troops surge announced by the Barack Obama Administration just a few months before in March 2009 and the Western coalition's search for an alternative logistics route to Afghanistan.

China had earlier ignored the British request to contribute troops to the NATO-led International Security Assistance Force (ISAF) in Afghanistan. In November 2008, Chinese foreign ministry spokesperson Qin had stated that "Except for the U.N. peace-keeping missions approved by the U.N. Security Council, China never sends a single troop abroad. It's out of the question to send Chinese troops to ISAF in Afghanistan."[39] Meanwhile, there were reports suggesting that China was developing the logistical infrastructure on its side of the border with Afghanistan. First was the construction of a 75 km long road, which extended up to 10 kms from the border with Afghanistan. It was reported that the construction of the road, which began in the summer of 2009, was scheduled for completion in October 2010. The road was intended to facilitate frontier patrols and transportation of supplies to the border police units. Second was the construction of a supply depot for the border units. Third was the setting up of a mobile communications centre to facilitate the operation of mobile devices along the border with Afghanistan. It was said that an optical cable for web connection and internet access had been laid, and there were plans to construct a special line for the border police force.[40]

At a time when President Karzai was coming under intense criticism from the Western countries for his allegedly controversial role in the 2009 presidential election, Chinese Foreign Minister Yang met him on the sidelines of the Istanbul Summit on 26 January 2010 and assured him of China's continued assistance to Afghanistan. He stated:

> Under the leadership of President Karzai, the Afghan government and people have made arduous efforts for post-war reconstruction and achieved positive progress, which China highly appreciates. China supports the international community to work closely with the Afghan government and offer positive aid to the country for its reconstruction. China fully respects the will and initiative of the Afghan government and people and supports the UN's leading role in coordinating international efforts. China will continue to offer assistance within its ability for Afghanistan's peaceful reconstruction...[41]

Again, on 28 January 2010, Yang in his address at the London Conference on Afghanistan remarked that "Afghanistan's reconstruction process has gone through twists and turns, yet its future holds great promise." In his opinion, "the successful elections held by the Afghan people have opened a new chapter in the history of Afghanistan" and that "the international community should give continued attention to Afghanistan and offer greater support and assistance" which "is of particular importance to help Afghanistan strengthen its sovereignty, ownership and development capacity, thus laying the groundwork for a full transition to governance of Afghanistan by the Afghan people." While emphasising on Afghan ownership, Yang argued that "it is up to the Afghan people to shape the future of Afghanistan, but the help and support of the international community is indispensable."[42]

On the role of the regional countries, Yang was of the view that, "the neighboring countries should take advantage of their geographical proximity and play a unique role in assisting with Afghan reconstruction, and the international community should take concrete actions to support such regional cooperation." He also emphasised on the UN role, a known Chinese position, and stated that "there are now quite a number of mechanisms in the world regarding the issue of Afghanistan, and we should make good use of these mechanisms." He added that "We should encourage them to enhance coordination and work together to play an active role under the leadership of the United Nations. The United Nations Assistance Mission in Afghanistan has done an outstanding job in performing its missions in extremely challenging circumstances. China highly commends its work."[43]

Karzai paid his fourth visit to China, after his re-election, from 23 March to 25 March 2010. He met Chinese President Hu Jintao on 24 March in the Great Hall of the People, where Hu identified five priority areas for both the countries to build a "comprehensive cooperative partnership of good-neighbourliness, mutual trust and friendship for generations": (i) strengthen overall bilateral ties by engaging in more regular meetings and exchanges; (ii) promote further bilateral economic collaboration; (iii) deepen cooperation in the humanities in areas such as personnel training, education, culture and public health; (iv) enhance security and police collaboration by combating cross-border organized crimes and the three evil forces of terrorism, extremism and separatism; and (v) coordinate with each other in multilateral affairs. The two presidents oversaw the signing of three bilateral cooperation agreements on aid, tax reduction and personnel training. Hu emphasised that both the countries should work together against cross-border crimes and "the three evil forces of terrorism, extremism and separatism." Hu also expressed his concerns about security of Chinese citizens working in Afghanistan and urged Karzai to ensure a sound environment for bilateral cooperation.[44]

Later, President Hu, in his address at the second Bonn Conference on

Afghanistan held on 5 December 2011, again proposed a five-point proposal as the way forward:

> First, the international community should firmly support an "Afghan-led and Afghan-owned" process of peace and reconstruction; second, the international community should firmly support Afghanistan in capacity building so that it can take over the responsibility of safeguarding national peace and stability as early as possible; third, the international community should firmly support Afghanistan in advancing national reconciliation through its own efforts and help create a favorable environment for reconciliation; fourth, the international community should firmly support Afghanistan in developing the economy. During the transition period and beyond 2014, the international community should continue to honor its commitments and provide support and assistance with no strings attached to bolster Afghanistan's capacity for sustainable development; fifth, the international community should firmly support Afghanistan in developing external relations. The international community should fully respect and accommodate the legitimate concerns of countries in the region. We should support the United Nations in continuing to play a leading role in coordinating international assistance to Afghanistan. The role of the Shanghai Cooperation Organization and other existing international organizations and cooperation mechanisms should be brought into full play.[45]

The first China–Pakistan–Afghanistan trilateral dialogue at the level of director generals from the foreign ministries of the three countries was held on 28 February 2012 in Beijing. The dialogue was chaired by then Director General of the Department of Asian Affairs in the Chinese Foreign Ministry Luo Zhaohui. Pakistan was represented by then Additional Secretary in the Pakistan Foreign Ministry Alamgir Babar and Afghanistan was represented by then Director General of the First Political Department in the Afghan Foreign Ministry Amanullah Jayhoon. It is not known if any joint statement was issued at the end of the meeting. Later, it was reported that the officials from the three countries agreed to explore the prospects of trilateral cooperation in the field of connectivity, resource development and combating the three forces of terrorism, separatism and extremism.[46] As early as September 2013, the then chief of staff of the Afghan presidential office, Abdul Karim Khurram, was quoted by *Xinhua* as stating that "This is our desire and we have wished it many times that China should play a role in the peace process of Afghanistan. We certainly would welcome it."[47]

On 8 June 2012, during Karzai's fifth visit to Beijing to attend the SCO summit, Hu Jintao met Karzai in the Great Hall of the People (like in March 2010) and came out with his five-point suggestions for both sides: (i) to deepen political mutual trust and maintain close high level contacts; (ii) to expand cooperation in areas including economy and trade, contracted projects, resource and energy development, agriculture and infrastructure based on mutual benefit and common development; (iii) to expand cultural and people-to-people exchanges; (iv) to enhance security cooperation and jointly combat the "three forces" of terrorism, separatism and extremism as well as trans-national crimes, including drug trafficking and (v) expand multilateral coordination and cooperation within the framework of the SCO and the South Asian Association for Regional Cooperation (SAARC).[48]

Prior to the above meeting, the same day, China and Afghanistan upgraded their relationship by establishing a Strategic and Cooperative Partnership (see Appendix III), building on the June 2006 Treaty of Good Neighbourliness and Friendly Cooperation. In the joint statement issued on the occasion, it was stated that the Strategic and Cooperative Partnership "will be an enduring and comprehensive relationship between the two nations which will serve the fundamental interests of two countries and peoples, facilitate the efforts to consolidate the traditional friendship of the two countries, expand cooperation in various fields, including political, economic, cultural and security." It was also stated that "cooperation in the political, economic, cultural and security fields, as well as on regional and international affairs, are the five pillars" of the China-Afghanistan Strategic and Cooperative Partnership.[49]

Growing violence in Xinjiang, particularly the riots of July 2009, had heightened the Chinese concerns regarding the impact of an unstable Afghanistan on security situation in Xinjiang. In retrospect, it is quite clear that China was accelerating its process of diplomatic engagement on the Afghan issue both at the bilateral and multilateral levels. As the process of security transition entered into its final phase and the distance and difference between Kabul and Washington continued to grow on a wide range of issues—from the US role in opening negotiations with the Taliban representatives based in

Qatar to the terms and conditions of the Bilateral Security Agreement—China further raised its diplomatic support for Kabul and its initiatives.

At the SCO Summit held in Beijing from 6 June to 7 June 2012, China also backed Afghanistan's observer status and discussed the evolving situation in Afghanistan. Chinese President Hu laid emphasis on strengthening cooperation through SCO to turn it into "a fortress of regional security and stability" and urged the members to fully implement the Shanghai Pact on fighting the "three evil forces" of terrorism, separatism and extremism, establish and perfect the security cooperative mechanism and take consistent actions to strike on the "three evil forces." In November 2012, at the Vice Foreign Ministerial Level Consultation on Regional Security of the SCO in Moscow, which was also attended by Jan Kubis, the Special Representative of the UN Secretary General for Afghanistan, China pushed for a greater role of the SCO on the Afghanistan issue and stated that China "support[ed] the international community's efforts in Afghanistan's peaceful reconstruction, and [was] willing to contribute to maintaining security and stability in Afghanistan and promoting its economic growth."[50]

On 22 September 2012, Zhou Yongkang, a senior member of the Standing Committee of the Politburo of the Communist Party of China (CPC), and former minister of public security (responsible for counter-terrorism, counter-insurgency, intelligence and internal security), paid an unannounced four-hour-long visit to Kabul. The media reported it as the most important visit by a senior Chinese leader since 1966 when the then Chairman of the PRC, Liu Shaoqi, had visited Afghanistan. It was also reported in the media that the two sides signed a formal security liaison agreement which provided for Chinese support for Afghan efforts "to counter terrorism and maintain national security" and expressed Chinese willingness "to provide help within its ability to improve Afghanistan's security capacity-building."[51] It was further stated that China will be training 300 Afghan police officers over the next four years.[52]

After June 2012, Karzai visited China in September 2013 to attend the Euro-Asia Economic Forum. Chinese President Xi Jinping met President Karzai on 27 September 2013 in the Great Hall of the People. Xi described China and Afghanistan as "traditionally friendly neighbours" and pointed out that with the signing of the Strategic and Cooperative Partnership in 2012 relations between the two countries "have entered a new stage" and that China "firmly adheres to the policy of friendship towards Afghanistan and is ready to deepen strategic cooperative partnership with the Afghan side." Xi thereafter proposed the following for developing the China–Afghanistan relations:

> First, to maintain high-level exchanges as well as contacts between the governments, legislative bodies and political parties, to strengthen strategic communication on major issues, to enhance political mutual trust. Second, to boost cooperation in the fields of economy, trade, project contracting, resources and energy development, infrastructure construction. China supports competent Chinese companies to invest in Afghanistan and will continue to offer help within its ability for peace and reconstruction as well as economic and social development in Afghanistan. Third, to strengthen security cooperation, to join hands (in) combating the 'three evil forces', drug trafficking and transnational crime. Hope the Afghan side will take effective measures to create a safe environment for bilateral cooperation. Fourth, to expand people-to-people and cultural exchanges. China is ready to continue to train all kinds of talented people for Afghanistan. Fifth, to enhance communication and coordination within the UN and other frameworks, to support the SCO for playing a greater role on the Afghanistan issue.[53]

Xi also stressed that the year 2014 is a "critical one for Afghanistan to achieve transition" and reiterated China's support for "the development path chosen by the Afghan people in accordance with their own national conditions, supports Afghanistan for achieving smooth transition and for improving and developing relations with other countries in the region." Xi also reiterated Beijing's support for an "Afghan-led, Afghan-owned" reconciliation process. During this visit, extradition treaty was also signed between the two countries.[54] The signing of the extradition treaty clearly indicated China's growing concern about security in its Xinjiang Region after 2014. A MoU on cooperation between Shanxi Normal University and Kabul University too was signed.

On 27 September 2013, President Karzai also met Chinese Premier Li Keqiang who on the occasion stated, "China and Afghanistan are traditionally friendly neighbours and there are neither historical grievances nor realistic contradictions between both sides, only friendship and cooperation." Li also stated that China is "ready to deepen bilateral strategic cooperative partnership with Afghanistan, to strengthen trade and investment cooperation, to promote the construction of energy resources and other major projects". Premier Li further stated that "security and stability as well as improvement of people's livelihood in Afghanistan are two 'wheels'. China is ready to work with the international community to push for balanced turning of the two 'wheels' in order to promote peace, stability and development of the region."[55]

Just before President Karzai's visit to Beijing, Chinese Foreign Minister Wang Yi had met the then Afghan Foreign Minister Zalmai Rassoul on 25 September 2013 at the UN headquarters in New York. During the meeting, he had reiterated China's firm support to the "Afghan-led and Afghan-owned" reconciliation process and stated that "China is ready to play a constructive role" in this regard.[56]

The third trilateral dialogue at the level of director generals was held in Kabul on 9 December 2013. The dialogue was chaired by Sultan Ahmad Bahin, Director General of Third Political Department of the Afghan Ministry of Foreign Affairs, and attended by Luo Zhaohui, Director General of Asian Affairs Department of the Chinese Ministry of Foreign Affairs, and Muhammad Iftikhar Anjum, Director General of Afghanistan Division of the Pakistan Ministry of Foreign Affairs.

It was stated that the three sides agreed to cooperate on maintaining security in Afghanistan and in the region; both China and Pakistan expressed support for the 'Afghan-led and Afghan-owned' reconciliation process and the efforts of the Afghan High Peace Council in this regard; the three sides "decided to explore possibilities of enhancing trilateral cooperation in various fields" and "supported the role played by Shanghai Cooperation Organization for peace and stability in the region"; "highlighted the importance of countering the common threats of terrorism, extremism and separatism"; the three sides "agreed to verify and share information on security threats to Chinese companies and personnel working on different projects in Afghanistan and Pakistan".

Besides the abovementioned, the three sides welcomed the outcomes of the Istanbul Conference on Afghanistan held in Almaty on 26 April 2013, the First Track-II Trilateral Dialogue held in Beijing in August 2013 and the first joint visit of Afghan and Pakistani parliamentarians to China in September

2013. The Chinese and Afghan sides welcomed Pakistan's offer to host the Second Track-II Trilateral Dialogue in Islamabad in 2014, and the Afghan and Pakistani sides welcomed China's readiness to host the next meeting of the Istanbul Process in 2014. The Afghan and Pakistani sides welcomed China's offer to host the second joint parliamentary delegation as well as the second joint media delegation from Afghanistan and Pakistan in 2014. The Chinese and Pakistani sides supported the Afghan proposal to establish a trilateral association of journalists, as well as a trilateral friendship group of parliamentarians. The Chinese side also agreed to host the next trilateral meeting in 2014.[57]

On 22 February 2014, Chinese Foreign Minister Wang Yi led a Chinese delegation to Kabul. During his one-day visit, he met a plethora of Afghan leaders and senior government officials. Apart from meeting his Afghan counterpart, Zarar Ahmad Osmani, he met Afghan President Hamid Karzai, then Afghan National Security Advisor Rangin Dadfar Spanta and the UN Secretary General's Special Representative for Afghanistan Jan Kubis. Interestingly, he also interacted with Zalmay Rassoul, Abdullah, Ashraf Ghani Ahmadzai and Abdul Qayum Karzai, all four leading candidates for the April 2014 presidential election.

In his press conference with Afghan Foreign Minister Osmani, Wang particularly focused on the upcoming Fourth Ministerial Conference of the Istanbul Process which China is hosting in Tianjin on 29 August 2014. He stated that China "expects to work closely with all parties including Afghanistan to make sure that practical outcomes will be achieved" from the conference. He described the Istanbul Process as "the only international mechanism on the Afghan issue led by the countries in the region" and added that the "member countries, adjacent or close to Afghanistan, all have connections with Afghanistan in both historical exchanges and realistic interests."[58]

Commenting on the Afghan transition, Wang stated that "with the accelerated withdrawal of the US and NATO troops and the upcoming of Afghan presidential election, Afghanistan is now experiencing a triple transition in politics, security and economy, which brings about both challenges and opportunities. At this point, the holding of the fourth Foreign Ministers' Conference of the Istanbul Process on the Afghan issue is of great practical significance." He also stated that the Chinese side "hopes to pool consensus from all parties by holding this conference and make concerted efforts to assist Afghanistan in realizing the triple transition."[59]

Calling Afghanistan "an important neighbouring country of China" and also "a country exerting unique and important influence in this region," Wang Yi clearly acknowledged that "Afghanistan's peace and stability has a bearing on the security of western China, and more importantly, bears on the peace and development of the entire region." Hinting at the urgency of political reconciliation as Western forces drawdown, Wang pointed out that as "harmony boosts everything," it is "only by allowing all factions to participate in the reconciliation process can Afghanistan realize its lasting peace and stability." He stated that "the Chinese side expects that Afghanistan can achieve broad and inclusive political reconciliation as soon as possible, and is willing to continue to play a constructive role in this regard."[60]

While supporting sustained international engagement in Afghanistan, Wang pointed out that, "The aid of the Chinese side, though limited, is very sincere with no political conditions attached." Probably emphasising on the need for Afghanistan and Pakistan to mend their ties, Wang noted that "The Chinese side supports Afghanistan in improving its relations with all countries, especially with neighboring countries; supports Afghanistan in actively participating in regional cooperation, including conducting cooperation with the Shanghai Cooperation Organization (SCO)." Wang also invited Afghanistan to join the "Economic Belt along the Silk Road."[61] In his meeting with President Karzai, he stated that 2014 is "a crucial year of Afghanistan's transition", and that "his visit to Afghanistan this time is to deliver a clear message that China attaches great importance to China-Afghanistan relations, and will continue to stick to the friendly policies towards Afghanistan and firmly support the domestic political reconciliation and reconstruction process in Afghanistan."[62]

Reports quoting diplomatic cables exposed by *Wikileaks*, show how the US efforts to gain Chinese cooperation for opening up alternate overland transit supply routes for the Western troops and delivery of non-lethal aid to Afghanistan were earlier rebuffed by China.[63] It is pertinent to mention here that in May 2010, Robert Blake, the US Assistant Secretary of State for South and Central Asian Affairs, had visited Beijing and expressed the hope that China would contribute more to the ongoing process of reconstruction in Afghanistan. In his meeting with Hu Jintao, the Chinese media reported, Blake "suggested that Beijing provide more aid in agriculture, education and training of officials." Though Hu agreed that China should "actively contribute to helping Afghanistan with people's livelihood, economic growth and social stability,"[64] but nothing substantive in terms of bilateral cooperation on the Afghanistan issue emerged from the initiative. However, the two countries had been discussing the Afghan situation. Later, on 17 May 2012, the Joint China–US Training Programme for Afghan diplomats was launched at the China Foreign Affairs University in Beijing.[65]

Low Trade and Increased Economic Investment

The Karzai Government opened up Afghanistan's energy and mineral sectors to foreign investment in 2006–2007. China's interests in Afghanistan grew subsequently. In 2007, China followed Pakistan, European Union (EU), US and India (in that order) as the fifth largest trading partner of Afghanistan. Chinese telecom companies like Huawei Technology Company Ltd. and Zhong Xing Telecommunication Equipment Company Limited (ZTE) had provided equipment to the Afghan Ministry of Communications and Information Technology (MCIT),[66] and in November 2012, Afghan Telecom and ZTE signed a contract of US$ 32 million to implement part of MCIT plans to apply GSM and 3G services with $100 million investment during 2012–14. The Afghan Telecom was supposed to receive 700 telecommunication towers from ZTE. Many development projects sponsored by the EU and even USAID were being executed through Chinese companies and workers.

During 2002–2010, China provided Afghanistan aid worth 1.3 billion Yuan (US$ 203 million) and waived debt worth US$ 19.5 million. While signing the Strategic and Cooperative Partnership with Afghanistan in June 2012, China pledged additional assistance of 150 million Yuan (US$ 23.7 million). Altogether, Chinese assistance was a small fraction (about 0.60 per cent) of the total global assistance that Afghanistan had received since 2002. On an average, Chinese assistance to Afghanistan amounted to approximately

US$ 22–23 million per year which was about 1.1–1.47 per cent of the total assistance China committed annually at that time around the world.[67]

China was engaged in reconstruction and developmental work as well. It rebuilt the Republic Hospital in Kabul, renovated the Parwan irrigation project, established a Confucius Institute in Kabul University[68] and provided training to Afghan officials and technicians. Chinese Ambassador Deng Xijun, while addressing the students of the Confucius Institute at Kabul University on 20 October 2013, stated that the Institute had enrolled 174 Afghan students in five years and 50 of them had studied in China for a two-year course with scholarship sponsored by the Chinese Government. Out of 33 graduates, some had been employed by local Chinese companies, some worked for the Chinese Embassy in Kabul and others had become lecturers teaching Chinese language at Kabul University. The agreement to establish Confucius Institute was signed with the Kabul University on 9 January 2008.[69]

In August 2011, the Chinese Ambassador to Kabul, Xu Feihong, stated that about 600 Afghan officials and technical personnel and 140 anti-narcotics police officers had reportedly received training in China.[70] Apart from the above, China was also building a multi-purpose centre in the presidential palace, and a National Education Centre of Science and Technology as well as a teaching building and a guest house for Kabul University. In 2011, China donated 100 ambulances to the Afghan ministry of public health. Chinese media agencies such as *Xinhua News Agency*, *China Central Television* (CCTV) and *China Radio International* (CRI) had set up offices in Afghanistan. To encourage trade from Afghanistan, it had progressively withdrawn tariff from about 278 items and signed off old Afghan debts as stated earlier in the chapter. Despite this, the volume of trade between the two countries remained very modest. In 2010, the bilateral trade stood at $715.7 million, a rise of about 94 per cent from the previous year, and Chinese imports from Afghanistan were worth just $7.9 million.[71] In 2011, according to the Chinese customs data, the total bilateral trade stood at $234.4 million, a rise of 31 per cent on the previous year, and Chinese imports from Afghanistan were worth just $4.4 million.[72] In the coming years too, the Chinese imports from Afghanistan remained abysmally low (see Table II below).

Table II: China–Afghanistan Trade: 2015 to 2021
(In US$ Million)

YEAR (January to December)	*2015*	*2016*	*2017*	*2018*	*2019*	*2020*	*2021*
Exports to Afghanistan	361,819,889	431,292,877	541,205,962	667,589,880	599,799,484	500,680,466	472,113,930
Imports from Afghanistan	11,770,644	4,534,101	3,427;619	24,079,054	29,279,265	54,512,300	49,513,779
Total Trade	373,590,533	435,826,978	544,633,581	691,668,934	629,078,749	555,192,766	521,627,709

Source: Website of the General Administration of Customs, People's Republic of China.

Even before the US media reported findings by the US geologists (June 2010)[73] about the vast untapped mineral wealth of Afghanistan to the tune of US$ 3 trillion, China had already gainfully engaged itself in the Afghan mining sector. In late 2007, China emerged as the largest source of foreign direct investment (FDI) when state-owned Metallurgical Corporation of China (MCC) Limited, a subsidiary of super conglomerate China Metallurgical Group Corporation, in collaboration with two other Chinese mining groups, Jiangxi Copper, the biggest copper producer in the country, and Zijin Mining Group, China's leading gold mining company, won the contract bid for exploring Aynak copper mines in the Logar Province south of Kabul.

The Aynak mine was projected to have some of the largest untapped reserves of copper in the world. The $3.5 billion copper mining contract was the first largest ever Chinese investment in Afghanistan.[74] This project was likely to be expanded to include building railways, investment in coal mines and a coal-fired power plant (400 MW), which would lead to potential Chinese investment up to US$ 10 billion.[75] In late 2008 and early 2009, through additional agreements, China secured a commitment from the Afghan Government to secure the project area, agreed to develop an ancillary 400-MW thermal power plant, and in return the Afghan Government agreed to provide water supply, and other minerals, including coal and limestone, required as inputs for copper production. Subsequently, in mid-2010, an agreement for a proposed regional shared-use railroad was finalised.[76] According to some estimates, this would have enabled the Afghan Government to earn about $808 million from the Chinese as payment for the rights for exploitation of its resources, and about $70 million per year as taxes over a period of about 10 years.[77]

However, China's direct investments were vulnerable as evident from the local media reports suggesting that the Chinese workers had to withdraw from the Aynak site in September 2012 due to security reasons.[78] The Taliban influence and activity had been rising in Logar Province since 2011. The project could not pick up as it remained vulnerable to growing insecurity in the region.[79]

On 28 December 2011, the state-owned China National Petroleum Corporation (CNPC) became the first foreign firm to sign a deal to jointly explore oil blocks with Afghanistan's Watan Group in the Amu Darya Basin in the north-western provinces of Sar-e Pul and Faryab. [80] The deal was signed by General Manager of CNPC International Lu Gongxun and Afghan Minister of Mines Wahidullah Shahrani, in the presence of Chinese Ambassador Xu Feihong and senior Afghan government officials, including the governors of Sar-e Pul and Faryab provinces.[81] The inauguration ceremony of the oil exploration project was held six months later, on 24 June 2012, in the presence of Chinese Ambassador Xu, Afghan First Vice President Mohammad Qasim Fahim, Finance Minister Omar Zakhilwal, Mines Minister Shahrani, and governors of Sar-e pul, Faryab and Jowzjan provinces.

Under this deal, the CNPC and the Watan Group were to jointly explore for oil in three fields in the Amu Darya Basin—Kashkari, Bazarkhami and Zamarudsay, which were estimated to hold around 87 million barrels of oil. The CNPC was to pay a 15 per cent royalty on oil, a 20 per cent corporate tax and give up to 70 per cent of its profit from the project to the Afghan Government. The Afghan Ministry of Mines reportedly stated in October 2011 that the deal was likely to result in government revenues of about US$5 billion over the next 10 years. According to another source, the CNPC had also offered to build an oil refinery, which was said to be a money spinner for it could have helped Afghanistan earn about US$ 7 billion over the next 25 years.[82] It seemed very assuring from Afghanistan's point of view which regarded such projects as critical to its economic revival and growth. However, Chinese bids, which perhaps initially appear overly generous, are often later re-negotiated with host governments on terms relatively more favourable to Chinese state-owned corporations. The same could be noted in the case of renegotiation between the Chinese consortium and the Taliban interim government on the Aynak copper mining project.

Chinese companies engaged in Afghanistan had often come under criticism for lack of respect for Afghan laws. In November 2007, it was reported that the Afghan finance ministry had alleged that ZTE had not paid taxes in the past three years and was operating without obtaining a proper license. The allegation came immediately after ZTE had signed a $64.5 million contract with the Afghan Ministry of Communications for extending the fibre optic cable network in the country.[83]

In the case of Aynak Copper Mine, there were reports about Chinese firm wanting to re-negotiate the contract. Chinese deals were also characterised by "a lack of transparency," "miscommunication of partnership terms," "lax environmental standards," and "disputes with local communities over working conditions, biased hiring and procurement practices and inadequate assistance for villages displaced by mining."[84] Later, post-2014, in view of the undesirable effects of the fragile security situation in the country, China had to mind its involvement in huge investment projects.

China's 'Peace' Forays on Afghanistan

By 2014–2015, Beijing had emerged as a key stakeholder in Afghanistan's political future. With the formation of the Ashraf Ghani-led National Unity Government (NUG) and the withdrawal of the bulk of Western forces by the end of 2014, Beijing had cautiously moved to the centre of the Afghan reconciliation process. President Ghani's early outreach to Beijing was very much a part of his efforts to fundamentally transform Kabul's traditionally adversarial equation with Pakistan's powerful military establishment. As Kabul sought to engage Rawalpindi hoping it would bring the Quetta-based Taliban leadership to the negotiating table, enlisting Beijing's support given its leverage over the Pakistan Army was accorded a high priority. Beijing responded pledging full support to the NUG and particularly Ghani's quest for peace with both Pakistan and the Taliban. Beijing subsequently made several efforts towards facilitating direct talks between the Afghan Government and the Pakistan-based and backed Taliban leadership.

By 2014, Beijing had started appointing special envoys on Afghan affairs to strengthen its communication with Kabul.[85] It had increased its interaction with party leaders across the Afghan political spectrum. Chinese ambassadors were actively exploring the prospect of building inter-party relations between the CPC and the relatively moderate Afghan Islamist parties, including Shiite Islamist parties. The press releases put out by the Chinese Embassy repeatedly stated that inter-party exchanges were an important part of the Sino-Afghan relations and that the embassy is willing to make consistent efforts to enhance the inter-party ties of the two sides.

In his interactions with leaders of various Afghan political parties held during 2011–2013, then Chinese Ambassador Xu Feihong spoke of inter-party exchanges and relations in his meetings with Sibghatullah Mojadeddi, former Afghan President and leader of Jabha-e Milli; Abdul Rashid Dostum, leader of Junbish-e Milli; Sayyed Hussain Anwari, leader of the breakaway faction of Shiite Harakat-e Islami; Pir Sayyed Ahmad Gailani, leader of Mahaz-e Milli Islami; Ajmal Sohail, leader of Liberal Party of Afghanistan; Ahmed Zia Massoud, leader of National Front of Afghanistan and former Afghan Vice President.[86] In February 2015, the Chinese Embassy along with Afghanistan–China Friendship Association and Afghan Institute for Strategic Studies held the introduction ceremony of President Xi's first of the four-volume book, *The Governance of China*, in Kabul. In August 2015, China also conducted a tour for the Afghan Ulema Council delegation to its predominantly Muslim Xinjiang Region.

Beijing hosted the Fourth Ministerial 'Heart of Asia' Conference of the Istanbul Process, supposedly the largest regional platform on Afghanistan, in October 2014. China had also reportedly hosted secret meetings between the Taliban and the Afghan government representatives. Interestingly, given its growing global profile and lingering security concerns too, Chinese aid and assistance to Afghanistan had been notably negligible.

However, China along with the US was not only mediating between Pakistan and Afghanistan but also as part of the quadrilateral effort was working towards reviving a direct dialogue between the Afghan Government and the Taliban leadership. Chinese and American representatives were very much part of the first ever official meeting held between the Afghan government officials and the Taliban representatives at Murree near Islamabad on 7 July 2015. The Murree talks though collapsed as reports about Taliban leader Mullah Mohammad Omar having died two years ago in 2013 appeared just before the second round of meeting was expected to take place. The Taliban had immediately confirmed Mullah Omar's death, but it strongly resisted attempts to continue with the Murree talks.

Soon thereafter, the next Taliban chief, Mullah Akhtar Mohammad Mansour, was killed in May 2016 in a US drone attack close to the Pakistan–Iran border. Further complicating the scenario was the establishment of *Wilayah Khorasan* or 'Khorasan Province' by so-called Islamic State of Iraq and Syria (ISIS), also known as Daesh, largely comprising Afghanistan–Pakistan region, in January 2015. Former Pakistani and Afghan Taliban fighters owing allegiance to the ISIS chief Abu Bakr al-Baghdadi had quickly established their strong presence in at least three districts of the eastern Nangarhar Province. Though the pro-ISIS fighters were confronting the Taliban fighters in the east, there were also reports of the two joining forces against the Afghan government forces in the northern Kunduz Province.[87]

The growing presence of the Taliban and various foreign militant groups in northern Afghanistan particularly provinces bordering China's restive Xinjiang Region could not have gone unnoticed in Beijing. Areas that once served as the buffer for China's Turkic Muslim borderlands against the Islamist turbulence south of the Hindukush were fast becoming home to several foreign militant groups pushed out of Pakistan's tribal areas. Most of them later settled along with their families in northern and eastern Afghanistan.

The Operation *Zarb-e-Azb* initiated by the Pakistan Army in June 2014 to flush out select foreign and local militants based in North Waziristan had led to influx of thousands of militants into bordering provinces of Afghanistan with several of them pledging allegiance to the ISIS. According to an estimate, more than 7,000 foreign militants had moved into Afghanistan.[88] Interestingly, Pakistan expected a badly stretched Afghan National Army (ANA) to confront, apprehend, and finally handover Pakistani militants that had crossed over onto the Afghan side of the Durand Line.

Beijing's security concerns began to grow as Afghanistan entered into the final stages of security transition from Western to Afghan forces in 2014. Meanwhile, with strategic northern Afghan city of Kunduz collapsing under sustained Taliban offensive in September 2015, becoming the first provincial capital to fall into Taliban hands since 2001, and district after district falling to the Taliban in the southern Helmand Province, Afghanistan's security institutions had been scrambling for a working strategy to minimise or rather absorb the impact of the Taliban onslaught. The ANA, which had suffered heavy casualties during the 2015 fighting season, had started retreating from certain areas to be able to focus more on securing key populations centres and highways.

Interestingly, Beijing, which had long opposed the Western military presence in Afghanistan, now wary of possible security vacuum, appeared supportive of much smaller but critical presence of the American troops beyond 2014. As Kabul struggled with three simultaneous transitions—security, political and economic—Beijing began to further widen and enhance its diplomatic engagement with Afghanistan.

Enhanced Diplomatic Engagement

As mentioned earlier, Chinese Foreign Minister Wang Yi's visit to Kabul in late February 2014, just before the April presidential election, was particularly significant in terms of setting the stage for Beijing's continued engagement with the post-transition Afghanistan. In his meeting with Afghan Foreign Minister Osmani on 22 February, Wang called for maintaining the momentum of high level exchanges and expanding economic and security cooperation between the two countries.[89]

In a joint press conference with his Afghan counterpart, Wang linked the security of western China and the entire region to peace and stability in Afghanistan. He argued that for establishing lasting peace and stability in the country, it is important that all Afghan factions are allowed to participate in the reconciliation process. He stated that China is willing to play a constructive role in this regard.[90]

Probably keeping in view the tense relations between Afghanistan and Pakistan, Wang also conveyed China's support to Kabul's endeavour to improve its ties with the neighbouring countries.[91] In his meeting with President Karzai, Wang clearly stated that as Afghanistan undergoes crucial security transition, China would continue to support the political reconciliation and economic reconstruction efforts in Afghanistan.[92]

In his interaction with Afghan National Security Adviser Spanta, Wang was said to have stated that "security cooperation…has become an important content of China-Afghanistan strategic and cooperative partnership." It was also said that "the Chinese side admired the Afghan side in cracking down the 'East Turkistan Islamic Movement' (ETIM) and other terrorist forces and appreciated the efforts the Afghan side has made for ensuring the safety and security of Chinese personnel and institutions in Afghanistan."[93] With the US-led coalition force withdrawing in large numbers in 2014, China had been worried about the security of its project personnel in Afghanistan. It is to be noted that just six months before the Chinese foreign minister's visit, three self employed Chinese nationals were killed in capital Kabul.[94]

Deputing Special Envoy

Meanwhile, with none of the presidential candidates securing the mandatory 50 per cent vote in the first round of election held in April 2014, a runoff election between the two leading candidates, Ashraf Ghani and Abdullah Abdullah, was held in June. As serious differences between the two over the final outcome of the runoff vote threatened to plunge the country into a major political crisis, a wary Beijing dispatched its newly-appointed first special envoy on Afghan affairs, Sun Yuxi, to Kabul on 24 July 2014. Sun, who earlier served as the Chinese ambassador in Kabul, met both President Karzai and the leading presidential candidates. Later, while interacting with media the following day, he stated that a government that reflects national solidarity should be formed and the new government must focus on national reconciliation and economic reconstruction. He also expressed support for an Afghan-led and owned reconciliation process and assured China's constructive role in this regard.[95]

Interestingly, according to a report published in the BBC, Amb Sun had been associated with Afghanistan since 1981, when as a young diplomat he was part of the Chinese efforts to provide arms to the Afghan 'mujahideen' fighting the anti-Soviet jihad. In his interview to the BBC, after being appointed as the special representative to Afghanistan, Sun stated that with the US withdrawing its forces, Afghanistan is "facing a critical period" and that China is "ready to do more" and wants to "play a bigger role." On Chinese efforts to bring about national reconciliation in Afghanistan, he stated that "We would welcome the Taliban in any neutral venue such as in China. We will make negotiations happen but the process must be Afghan-owned and Afghan-led – the agenda must be proposed by President Ashraf Ghani." Elaborating further on the Chinese initiatives to bring regional countries together on the issue, he referred to the China–Afghanistan–Pakistan "tripod" and the broader 'six-plus-one' group involving US, Russia, China, India, Pakistan and Iran, plus Afghanistan. He added that China's "larger strategy is also economic development – the construction of the Silk Road which includes Pakistan and Afghanistan."[96]

China the 'Mediator'

Post-2014, the most significant moment in China–Afghanistan ties came when the newly-elected Afghan president, Ashraf Ghani, visited Beijing for the Fourth 'Heart of Asia' Ministerial Conference of the Istanbul Process held on 31 October 2014. Ghani first met President Xi Jinping who received him in the Great Hall of the People on 28 October 2014. According to the statement issued by the Chinese foreign ministry giving details about the meeting:

> Xi Jinping emphasized that since the establishment of the new Afghan government, China-Afghanistan relations have embraced new development opportunities. I would like to, together with you, chart the course for the development of bilateral relations in the new era. Both sides should keep high-level exchanges, enhance exchanges between governments, legislative bodies and political parties, and strengthen communication on major issues. China will intensify its support for the peaceful reconstruction in Afghanistan, helping Afghanistan formulate national plans for economic and social development, train various talents, and develop agricultural, hydropower and infrastructure construction, and promoting projects such as the Mes Aynak copper mine and the Amu Darya basin for substantive progress so as to boost economic development and improve people's livelihood in the local regions.[97]

While welcoming China's support to his government, President Ghani noted:

> Afghanistan views China as *a reliable strategic partner*, admires China's long-term stability and development, and believes that China is able to

> help Afghanistan speed up development. Afghanistan is willing to develop Afghanistan-China long-term strategic cooperative partnership on the basis of the Five Principles of Peaceful Co-existence. (Emphasis added)
>
> The Afghan side stands ready to enhance bilateral cooperation in oil, gas, mineral products, infrastructure construction, people's livelihood and other fields, and welcomes Chinese enterprises to invest and will do its utmost to ensure safety of the Chinese institutions and personnel. Afghanistan firmly supports China in fighting against terrorist forces, does not allow any forces to use its territory for anti-China activities and is willing to enhance coordination and cooperation with China.[98]

Chinese Premier Li Keqiang too met President Ghani in the Great Hall of the People. In his meeting with Ghani, he stated that China is "willing to take an active part in building Afghanistan's infrastructure including railway, road, water conservation, and electricity." President Ghani, on his part, pointed out that "further deepening Afghanistan-China strategic cooperative partnership serves as the consensus among various parties in Afghanistan and the core principles of the diplomacy of the country." He also reiterated Afghanistan's active support for the 'Silk Road Economic Belt' proposed by China.[99]

On 31 October 2014, Beijing hosted the much-awaited Fourth 'Heart of Asia' Ministerial Conference, a clear indication of its growing concern as well as interest in the post-2014 Afghanistan.[100] The significance of the event was further enhanced by the fact that it was the first major international conference on Afghanistan since the NUG was formed in September 2014. Chinese Premier Keqiang in his extremely detailed address described the Istanbul Process as "a unique regional cooperation mechanism on Afghanistan," and called on the member countries to "vigorously support Afghanistan's peace process and its reconstruction." He put forth five points to help settle the Afghan conflict: first, Afghanistan must be governed by the Afghan people; second, promote political reconciliation; third, speed up economic reconstruction; fourth, explore the path of development; and finally, provide stronger external support.[101]

While candidly admitting that "peace and stability in Afghanistan have a direct bearing on China's security and stability," the Chinese premier elaborated on the assistance extended to Afghanistan:

> Since 2001, China has exempted Afghanistan's matured debts, provided 1.52 billion RMB yuan of grant assistance, and built a number of major projects to the benefit of the Afghan people's livelihood. That included the Kabul Republic Hospital, Parwan Hydraulic Project Rehabilitation Work, the National Education Center of Science and Technology, and the complex of the Chinese Language Department of Kabul University. China has also trained more than 1,000 Afghan professionals in various fields. China will continue to provide necessary assistance and support to Afghanistan, do what it can as a neighbor and fulfill due responsibilities of a big developing country.
>
> ...China is ready to step up cooperation with Afghanistan in such areas as infrastructure, agriculture, water conservancy and the exploration and utilization of mineral resources. China has decided to offer Afghanistan grant assistance of 500 million RMB yuan this year, and 1.5 billion RMB yuan in the coming three years. China will also train 3,000 Afghan professionals in various fields and offer 500 scholarships in the next five years. China will continue to expand security training and assistance to Afghanistan.[102]

President Ghani's address at the Fourth Ministerial Conference was signified by the fact that it was his first international address since coming to power in September 2014. He used the occasion to reach out to the wider regional as well as the international audience, which was well represented in the conference. He articulated the domestic priorities and foreign policy approaches of his government in the light of the four critical and simultaneous transitions facing Afghanistan: First, the political transition; second, the security transition; third, the economic transition; and fourth, also the most significant transition in his view, changing the culture of the state and the relation between the citizen, as the principal, and the state, as the agent. He also made it clear that establishing peace in the country was his highest priority. It was during this address that he for the first time invited the political opposition including the Taliban to join the inter-Afghan dialogue and asked for international support for an 'Afghan-led and Afghan-owned' peace process.[103]

Of particular note was the conceptualisation of his foreign policy in his address at the conference. Arguing that since geography has placed Afghanistan at the heart of Asia and history has made it a "pivotal intersection of contending powers and ideas," country's foreign policy therefore is "intrinsically connected" with its domestic policy. He added, "Recognising that we are at the intersection of five circles of international relations, our goal is to provide the platform for collaboration of these states, organizations, powers and networks of virtue." He defined the five circles in his foreign policy as:

> Our immediate six neighbors form our *first circle*. The Islamic world forms our *second circle*. North America, Europe, Japan, Australia, and members of NATO-ISAF form our *third circle*. Asia, being transformed into a continental economy, forms our *fourth circle*. And international development organisations, the UN, multinational firms, and international civil society and non-governmental organisations form our *fifth circle*.[104]

Chinese Foreign Minister Wang Yi in his address clearly identified five aspects to China's approach towards Afghanistan:

> First, help Afghanistan with the construction of a series of major projects, improving its national economy and people's livelihood. Second, encourage China-funded enterprises to invest and develop in Afghanistan, strengthening its capability of self-development. Third, train professionals in various fields for Afghanistan, helping to improve its capacity of state governance. Fourth, promote the conduction of dialogues among different sides in Afghanistan, playing a constructive role in its reconciliation process. Fifth, support Afghanistan in its improvement of relations with neighboring countries and its integration into the regional cooperation process.[105]

While emphasising the need for Afghan reconciliation, Chinese foreign minister further stated:

> China holds that *political reconciliation is the important foundation for Afghanistan's peaceful reconstruction* and the fundamental resolution for Afghanistan to achieve long-lasting peace and stability. Currently, Afghanistan's political reconciliation process is *facing new opportunities.* (Emphasis added)
>
> We *sincerely call on Afghanistan's political factions including the Taliban to seize the opportunity, make decisions, discard past grievances and look into the future*, and participate in the political reconciliation process as soon as possible to jointly discuss major plans for Afghanistan's peace and development. China firmly supports the Afghan reconciliation process, and is willing to continue to play its constructive role in the process (emphasis added).[106]

China Hosts Taliban

Around the same time, reports about a Taliban delegation from its political office in Doha having secretly visited China for a meeting with Afghan representatives in early November 2014, immediately after Beijing hosted the Fourth Ministerial Conference of the Istanbul Process on 31 October 2014, began to appear in media. It was said that the Taliban visit was in response to a visit undertaken by a Chinese delegation to the Taliban office in Doha. There were also reports that Qari Din Mohammad and Abbas Stanakzai from the Doha office were likely to soon visit Pakistan for 'follow-up discussions' with the Chinese officials.[107]

The purpose of Chinese facilitation was to help establish initial or preliminary contacts between the new government in Kabul and the Taliban, probably part of an early understanding between Beijing, Rawalpindi and Kabul. It is worth noting here that within days of the Fourth Ministerial Conference of the Istanbul Process, it was reported by *Reuters* that Beijing was keen on establishing a "peace and reconciliation forum" to assist Afghanistan with its reconciliation process.[108] Though Beijing had to give up on its idea of floating such a platform, it was clear that Beijing would be the new facilitator of the Afghan peace process. It also showed the line of trust between Beijing and the Taliban that could be traced back to the late 1990s when the two had first come into direct contact.

Rawalpindi's Response

After visiting Beijing, it was no surprise that Ghani visited Pakistan. In fact, Sartaj Aziz's visit to Kabul a week before President Ghani left for Beijing, followed by his remarks at the Fourth Ministerial Conference of the Istanbul Process, both in the latter half of October 2014, had clearly set the stage for President Ghani's visit to Pakistan.

In his address at the Fourth Foreign Minister, Aziz declared that "Pakistan fully supports China's constructive contribution and Premier Li's five point proposal for Afghanistan's peace and economic development." He described President Ghani's statement as "comprehensive", and had appreciated him for his "bold vision" and "reform agenda" and also "strong leadership". He also welcomed the "historic transfer of power from one elected President to another elected President" and described National Unity Government as "both a testimony to the statesmanship of the new Afghan leadership, and an essential framework for ensuring a stable and unified Afghanistan." Emphasising the need for an "inclusive intra-Afghan" reconciliation process, Aziz expressed support for President Ghani's call to the armed opposition for talks with the government. He suggested that "the international community should also be unanimous in calling upon all Afghan stakeholders to seek a peaceful solution, as a return to the 1990s would be unacceptable." He stressed that the reconciliation process "must be a truly Afghan-owned and Afghan-led process."[109]

Assured of strong support from Beijing, President Ghani visited Pakistan on 14–15 November 2014. In an unprecedented move, Ghani upon his arrival straightaway went to meet Pakistan Army Chief General Raheel Sharif at the General Head Quarters (GHQ) in Rawalpindi, prior to meeting the civilian leadership in Islamabad. A confident Ghani, convinced of full support from both Washington and Beijing, sought to achieve a major breakthrough in thawing relations with Pakistan's powerful military-intelligence apparatus. Pakistan Prime Minister's Advisor on National Security and Foreign Affairs Sartaj Aziz, Foreign Secretary Aizaz Ahmad Chaudhry, Defence Secretary Gen (Retd) Alam Khattak and Director General of the Inter-Services Intelligence (ISI) Gen Rizwan Akhtar were also present on the occasion. President Ghani reportedly stated that "Afghanistan wants to bolster security and defence ties with Pakistan including cooperation in training and border management" and also "assured of Afghan cooperation to jointly curb the menace of terrorism."[110]

President Ghani later held both one-on-one and delegation-level talks with Pakistan Prime Minister Nawaz Sharif. In the meeting, Sharif was said to have "outlined his vision of a strong, comprehensive and enduring partnership between Pakistan and Afghanistan" and "underscored the importance of multi-tiered bilateral engagement, including at the political, security, economic, leadership, and people-to-people levels." On his part, Ghani "affirmed the importance Afghanistan attached to forging a 'special relationship' with Pakistan" and emphasised the "importance of mutual trust and understanding, close political and security engagement, a comprehensive economic strategy, and increased regional economic cooperation" between the two countries.[111] Thereafter, several visits were made by Pakistan Army Chief Gen Raheel Sharif and Director General, ISI, Gen Rizwan Akhtar, particularly following the deadly attack on the Army Public School in Peshawar on 16 December 2014.

Meanwhile, on 5 November 2014, President Ghani signed the 'Agreement between the People's Republic of China, the Republic of Tajikistan and the Islamic Republic of Afghanistan on the Trijunction Point of Their Boundaries'. It was signed in the presence of Chinese Ambassador Deng Xijun and Tajikistan's Ambassador Sharafuddin Imamov. Afghanistan's Chief Executive Abdullah Abdullah and Acting Foreign Minister Zarar Ahmad Osmani also attended the signing ceremony held in Kabul.

First Trilateral Dialogue

To further strengthen the evolving understanding between the three countries, Chinese Assistant Foreign Minister Liu Jianchao visited Kabul to initiate the first round of China–Afghanistan–Pakistan Trilateral Dialogue held in February 2015. Prior to the dialogue, in his meeting with Afghan Deputy Foreign Minister Hekmat Khalil Karzai, he stated that China "sincerely hopes that the national unity government of Afghanistan could stay united" and "hopes that the Afghan side will arrive at a broad and inclusive political reconciliation at an early date" and that China is "willing to continuously play a constructive role for this goal."[112]

Jianchao, thereafter, met President Ghani during which he referred to the "significant consensus" reached during latter's visit to Beijing in October 2014 on taking the partnership forward. He reiterated China's support for an 'Afghan-led and Afghan-owned' reconciliation process for which China is "willing to play a constructive role." President Ghani too stated that Afghanistan "is willing to work with China to expand cooperation in economy and trade, infrastructure construction, connectivity, water resources, counter-terrorism and other fields" and that it "welcomes and expects China to play a greater role in the reconciliation process of Afghanistan."[113]

Later, along with Afghan Deputy Foreign Minister Hekmat Karzai and Pakistan Foreign Secretary Aizaz Ahmad Chaudhry, Jianchao co-chaired the trilateral dialogue held in Kabul on 9 February 2015. According to the statement put out by the Chinese foreign ministry, China as the "common friend and neighbor" of both Afghanistan and Pakistan would like the two countries "to increase mutual strategic trust as well as enhance mutually beneficial cooperation." All the three countries agreed "to continue to deepen counter-terrorism and security cooperation." China announced that it will "invite five delegations of senators, media, diplomats, friends and think-tanks from Afghanistan and Pakistan to visit China in 2015." It was further stated that China has "agreed to support relevant proposals such as strengthening highway and rail link between Afghanistan and Pakistan including the Kunar Hydroelectric Dam, pushing forward connectivity, and enhancing economic integration."[114]

Interestingly, on 12 February 2015, just three days after the trilateral dialogue, Chinese Foreign Minister Wang Yi made an official visit to Pakistan. In a joint press conference with Sartaj Aziz, Advisor on National Security and Foreign Affairs to the Pakistan Prime Minister, he stated that the Afghan issue can be tackled by enhancing support in four ways:

> First, *support the effective administration of the Afghan National Unity Government.* The international community should respect the development path that the Afghan people have chosen according to their own national conditions.
>
> Second, *support the reconciliation between the Afghan government and various political forces including the Taliban.* He stated that *broad-based inclusive reconciliation, on the "Afghan-led and Afghan-owned" basis,* is the right direction for Afghanistan. He added, "If the political forces in Afghanistan are in need, the Chinese side is always ready to provide necessary convenience for the reconciliation process." Third, support the economic and social reconstruction of Afghanistan. *To solve the issue of Afghanistan, reconciliation is the key and reconstruction is the root.* Fourth, support *Afghanistan's integration in regional cooperation* (emphasis added).[115]

As for Pakistan's role, the visiting Chinese foreign minister observed that Pakistan and Afghanistan "enjoy impartible natural connections in various aspects such as history, culture, nationality and religion" and that "Pakistan has always played a unique and irreplaceable role in dealing with the issue of Afghanistan". He also asserted that both China and Pakistan "are willing to strengthen communication and coordination with Afghanistan and work with the international community to make unremitting efforts to realize the successful transition of Afghanistan."[116]

Interestingly, immediately after the trilateral dialogue, there were unconfirmed reports of Afghan authorities capturing and handing over some Uygur militants to the Chinese authorities. Chinese Uygur militants who had long been trained and sheltered in Pakistan were said to have crossed over from Pakistan into Afghanistan under pressure from Operation *Zarb-e-Azb* launched by Pakistan Army in June 2014 in its North Waziristan region.[117] Kabul had been seeking military assistance from Beijing since long, as evident from the visits of several delegations from the Afghan defence ministry since 2005, but it had not elicited any concrete response from Beijing.

The Urumqi Meeting

Buoyed by the outcomes of Chinese President Xi Jinping's visit to Pakistan in April 2014, with Beijing pledging $46 billion for building the China–Pakistan Economic Corridor (CPEC), Prime Minister Nawaz Sharif visited Kabul on 12 May 2015. During his visit, he assured Kabul that "the enemies of Afghanistan cannot be friends of Pakistan" and all militant "sanctuaries when found, will be eliminated by direct action, and will be monitored by the existing mechanism," further adding that "any effort by any militant or group to destabilize Afghanistan will be dealt with severely and such elements will be outlawed and hunted down."[118]

Later, it was reported by the *Wall Street Journal* that a three-member Taliban delegation from the Quetta Shura had travelled to China and met former Secretary of the Afghan High Peace Council (HPC) Secretariat and then Defence Minister-designate Masoom Stanakzai in Urumqi, capital of China's southwestern Xinjiang region, on 19–20 May 2015. Chinese officials and the ISI representatives were said to be present during the meeting. Mohammad Asem, a former lawmaker considered close to Chief Executive Abdullah, was also to have participated in the meeting. Taliban delegation comprised of Mullah Abdul Jalil (Head of the Taliban Committee on Internal Affairs), Mullah Mohammad Hassan Rahmani (former head of Kandahar Province) and Mullah Abdul Razaq (former interior minister).[119]

The Taliban however rejected the reports about the Urumqi meeting as rumour. In a statement issued on 24 May 2015, Taliban stated that "the policy of Islamic Emirate with regards to political interactions and steps is very clear. We do not deem it necessary to meet or establish political links with anyone secretly. If we have ever travelled anywhere or met with anyone, we have informed the media on the matter. We do not believe in secret talks."[120] However, Sartaj Aziz, Advisor on National Security and Foreign Affairs to Pakistan Prime Minister, later confirmed the talks held at Urumqi.[121]

Increased Bilateral Interaction

The next important bilateral interaction between Beijing and Kabul took place when foreign ministers of the two countries met on the sidelines of the Shanghai Cooperation Organisation (SCO) conference held in Moscow on 4 June 2015. Describing China and Afghanistan as strategic partners, Chinese Foreign Minister Wang Yi once again assured his Afghan counterpart Salahuddin Rabbani that China "will continue to support Afghanistan in strengthening anti-terrorism capacity building" and will "launch bilateral and multilateral security cooperation with Afghanistan."[122]

Soon President Ghani met President Xi for the second time on the sidelines of the SCO Summit held in the Russian city of Ufa on 10 July 2015. According to the statement issued by the Chinese foreign ministry, Xi "emphasised that *strengthening security cooperation is in line with the common interests* of both China and Afghanistan" and that China is "willing to continue to provide the Afghan side with *assistance in security materials, technology, equipment and training*." While reiterating China's support for an "Afghan-led and Afghan-owned" reconciliation process, Xi pointed out that "achieving broad and inclusive national reconciliation in Afghanistan is a realistic way to solve the Afghan issue" and that China is "willing to work with all parties concerned to play a constructive role in resolving the Afghan issue at an early date."[123]

As the relationship soured between Afghanistan and Pakistan in the wake of reports of Mullah Omar's death, leading to the collapse of July 2015 Murree talks, and with President Ghani lashing out at Pakistan as series of suicide bombings hit the capital Kabul in the first week of August, China began to make efforts to put the peace process back on track. On 8 September 2015,

Chinese Foreign Minister Wang Yi spoke on telephone to both Sartaj Aziz, Advisor to the Pakistan Prime Minister, and Hanif Atmar, the Afghan National Security Advisor. According to the statement issued by the Chinese foreign ministry, while acknowledging that recently "new and complicated factors have emerged in the process," China "hopes that Pakistan and Afghanistan will cherish and earnestly safeguard the improvement and development momentum in their relations and enhance coordination and cooperation on the Afghan reconciliation process and other issues." The statement added, "China stands ready to continue playing a constructive role to this end and work with relevant parties for the early and long-lasting peace in Afghanistan."[124]

Amidst continuing tension between Afghanistan and Pakistan, Chinese Vice President Li Yuanchao visited Kabul on 3 November 2015 to commemorate the 60th anniversary of the establishment of diplomatic ties between the two countries. In his address at the reception held to mark the occasion, Yuanchao attributed "sound and steady growth" of bilateral ties to four reasons:

> First, leaders of successive generations of both countries have kept our relations on the right track from a strategic perspective; second, both countries have been committed to the Five Principles of Peaceful Coexistence, treated each other with respect and as equals; third, we have engaged in win-win cooperation, and the livelihood projects China has undertaken in Afghanistan have brought the two peoples closer; fourth, we have had close coordination in regional and international affairs to uphold the common interests of our two countries and all developing countries.[125]

Referring to his meeting with President Ghani earlier in the day, he informed that the two sides have agreed that there is a need to: first, maintain high-level visits and meetings; second, effectively implement bilateral development cooperation projects; third, deepen counter-terrorism, defence and security cooperation; and fourth, support Afghanistan in improving its internal and external environments. He also announced humanitarian supplies worth 10 million yuan and provision of $1million in emergency aid to help Afghanistan deal with massive destruction caused by the earthquake in its north. This was in addition to assistance being provided by the Red Cross Society of China for disaster relief. He reiterated China's commitment to provide grant worth 1.5 billion yuan in three years' time. He declared that China will provide 500 million yuan to build affordable housing in 2015. He further offered Chinese assistance in drawing up an infrastructure development plan for Afghanistan.[126]

Interestingly, in his meeting with Chief Executive Abdullah, the visiting Chinese vice-president specifically referred to the two key stalled Chinese projects in Afghanistan and also spoke about the security of its personnel working in the country. According to the statement issued by the Chinese foreign ministry:

> The two sides should strive for early progress of the Mes Aynak copper project and the Amu Darya basin oil project, which will help build up Afghanistan's capacity of independent economic growth and set an example for Afghanistan's attraction of foreign investment.
>
> The Chinese side is ready to offer more government scholarships to Afghan students traveling to China, and train more health and agriculture workers for Afghanistan. The two sides shall make joint efforts to combat terrorism and extreme forces.
>
> The Chinese side hopes that the Afghan side would take further steps to protect Chinese institutions and nationals in Afghanistan and create a safe environment for bilateral cooperation in various fields.[127]

Reinforcing Trilateral and Quadrilateral Initiatives

Chinese Foreign Minister Wang Yi visited Islamabad the very next month in December 2015 to participate in the Fifth Ministerial Conference of the 'Heart of Asia' Istanbul Process. Various meetings held on the sidelines made more headlines than the outcome of the conference itself. Islamabad became the venue and the conference provided the opportunity to help break stalemate between Afghanistan and Pakistan. Wang Yi met President Ghani who reluctantly agreed to visit Islamabad for the conference. Wang Yi also participated in the second round of the China–Pakistan–Afghanistan Trilateral Dialogue and also the Afghanistan–Pakistan–China–United States Quadrilateral meeting to help resume talks between the Afghan Government and the Taliban.

Quite ironically, the *Islamabad Declaration* issued at the end of the 'Heart of Asia' Conference agreed to "taken necessary actions to deny terrorists' access to financial and material resources, to dismantle their sanctuaries and training facilities, and to curtail their ability to recruit and train new terrorists" and urged "all Afghan Taliban groups and all other armed opposition groups to enter into peace talks with the Afghan Government."[128] On the same day, Afghan President Ghani, Pakistan Prime Minister Nawaz Sharif and Chinese Foreign Minister Wang Yi met for the Second Trilateral Dialogue in Islamabad to explore ways to revive the stalled reconciliation process. According to the press release, "The three sides shared the view that advancing the reconciliation process in Afghanistan is the important condition to realize long-term security of the country." It added that based on 'Afghan-led, Afghan-owned' principle, both China and Pakistan will provide all support and help for resuming and advancing peace talks in Afghanistan.[129]

Thereafter, Afghanistan–Pakistan–United States Trilateral Meeting was held where the three countries agreed "to accelerate diplomatic and political efforts to put an end to the conflict in Afghanistan" and "develop a lasting solution that meets the needs of all Afghans." The press release added, "All three countries will work to create conditions that encourage participation of Taliban groups in a peace process that demonstrates to them that they have a real option of political engagement. All efforts for dialogue between the Government of Afghanistan and Taliban groups will be explored and encouraged. All will pursue with urgency confidence building measures that reduce the level of violence in Afghanistan, and allow for full participation and talks by all participants." Both Afghanistan and Pakistan expressed their commitment "to preventing their territories to be used by any violent extremist group or third party and acknowledge that those who refuse to join a political resolution of the conflict in Afghanistan must be opposed with all means available."[130]

Thereafter, a quadrilateral (2+2) meeting comprising Afghan President Ghani, Pakistan Prime Minister Sharif, Chinese Foreign Minister Wang and the US Deputy Secretary of State Antony J. Blinken was held to discuss the Afghan reconciliation process. According to the statement issued: "The meeting expressed full commitment to enabling an Afghan-led and Afghan-owned political process that promotes a dialogue between the Afghan Government and Taliban groups, including on *reduction and renunciation of violence*. It was agreed that reconciliation remains the most viable option to end violence and promote stability in Afghanistan and the region." The meeting also "affirmed full support to the democratically elected National Unity Government of Afghanistan" and "agreed that *authority of the Afghan State and the legitimacy of Afghanistan's constitution* must be fully respected by the international community."[131] Virtually nothing was stated of what was expected of the Taliban.

Later, the Quadrilateral Coordination Group (QCG) comprising the same four countries held its first meeting in Islamabad on 11 January 2016. The delegations were led by Afghan Deputy Foreign Minister Hekmat Khalil Karzai, Pakistan's Foreign Secretary Aziz Ahmad Chaudhry, the US Special Representative for Afghanistan and Pakistan Amb Richard G. Olson, and China's Special Envoy for Afghanistan Amb Deng Xijun. The meeting "emphasized the immediate need for direct talks between representatives of the Government of Afghanistan and representatives from Taliban groups" and "adopted terms for the work of the QCG and agreed to continue regular meetings to advance the peace and reconciliation process in Afghanistan."[132]

The agenda for the first meeting of the QCG was clearly set by host Pakistan Government. Sartaj Aziz, Foreign Affairs Advsior to Nawaz Sharif, in his opening statement not only spelt out the agenda of the meeting but also suggested the way forward. According to Aziz, the first and foremost task before the Quadrilateral is to "define the overall direction of the reconciliation process along with the goals and targets it would like to set with a view to creating a conducive environment for holding direct talks between Afghan government and Taliban groups." He called for undertaking a "realistic assessment of the opportunities as well as anticipated obstacles" in the process. He was of the view that specific tasks should be assigned to the member countries based on the "principle of shared responsibility". He expressed hope that the meeting will help "evolve an efficient procedural framework" for the functioning of the Quadrilateral.[133]

Aziz argued that 'pre-conditions' should not be attached to the reconciliation process as it will prove counterproductive. Instead, there is a need to "create conditions to bring the Taliban groups to the negotiation table and offer incentives to them that can persuade them to move away from using violence as tool for pursuing political goals." In his opinion, confidence building measures could help in encouraging Taliban to join the negotiation process.[134]

Aziz pointed out that the "threat of the use of military action against irreconcilables cannot precede the offer of talks to all the groups and their response to such offers." He added that "Distinction between reconcilable and irreconcilables and how to deal with the irreconcilables can follow once the avenues for bringing them to the talks have been exhausted." He cautioned the Quadrilateral against setting unrealistic targets and deadlines. Finally, he suggested that the work of the Quadrilateral should be kept out of media glare to the extent possible. Taliban meanwhile continued to refuse to enter into any dialogue with the NUG.[135]

Interestingly, the Third China–Pakistan–Afghanistan Trilateral Dialogue on the topic, "Quest for peace in Afghanistan: Role of Neighbouring Countries," was also held the same day. It was jointly organised by the Pakistan–China Institute and the Konrad Adenauer Stiftung of Germany.[136] In his keynote address to the gathering, Sartaj Aziz, Advisor on Foreign Affairs to the Pakistan Prime Minister, argued that the Afghan reconciliation process will have to take into account following two fundamentals:

> One, the process has to be Afghan-led and Afghan-owned as an externally imposed settlement is neither desirable nor it would be sustainable. The role of Pakistan, China and the United States is basically to facilitate the process.
>
> Two, political reconciliation by nature is a complex process requiring time, patience and sense of accommodation by the concerned parties with a view to arriving at a win-win solution.[137]

As agreed during the first meeting, the second round of the QCG meeting was held just a week later in Kabul on 18 January 2016. The meeting, however, could not go beyond discussing the roadmap for initiating peace talks with the Taliban groups. Though three more rounds of meeting were held in the same year—the third round on 6 February in Islamabad, fourth round on 23 February in Kabul, and the fifth round on 18 May in Islamabad—the QCG failed to make any forward movement as the Taliban refused to participate in the talks. With Russia and the US later directly engaging the Taliban representatives based in Doha, the Beijing-led trilateral process with Afghanistan and Pakistan too had to take a backseat.

On 26 January 2016, Afghan foreign minister visited Beijing and met his Chinese counterpart Wang Yi. The two later agreed on a six-point consensus: (i) enhance high-level exchanges, (ii) China will help the country formulate infrastructure plan and blueprint for its future development, (iii) China welcomes Afghanistan to take part in "Belt and Road" construction and both sides agreed to discuss and sign the intergovernmental cooperation document on jointly building the "Belt and Road", (iv) Since Afghanistan is at the forefront of anti-terrorism, both sides agreed to boost bilateral and multilateral cooperation in anti-terrorism, (v) the two countries will strengthen people-to-people and cultural exchanges. China will earnestly fulfill its commitments of providing training and government scholarship for Afghan personnel. Both sides will support exchanges between their colleges, universities, think-tanks and local governments; and (vi) both sides agreed to intensify cooperation in international and regional mechanisms related to Afghanistan, support the positive role of the Istanbul Process, and hold discussions on expanding the trilateral cooperation among China, the US and Afghanistan. Afghanistan expressed hope to become a formal member of the SCO and join the Asian Infrastructure Investment Bank at an early date.[138]

In the joint press meet held following the meeting between the two foreign ministers, Wang stated that "China will continue to serve as a supporter, mediator and facilitator of peace talks" on the Afghan issue. On the QCG mechanism, he stated that it is aimed at "creating necessary external conditions for the Afghan government to resume talks with the Taliban. We hope that the quadrilateral coordination group continues its efforts and strive for an early reconciliation roadmap acceptable to all parties." He added that "China is willing to strengthen communication on the matter with countries concerned such as Russia, Iran and India to make joint efforts and joint contributions to reconciliation."[139] However, in the absence of the Taliban representatives, the QCG despite holding five rounds of meeting was clearly not making any headway.

On 3 June 2016, the Russian foreign ministry stated that "The national reconciliation process has come to a standstill. The attempts of the quadrilateral contact group (Afghanistan, Pakistan, the United States and China) to encourage the Taliban to pursue reconciliation with Kabul have failed so far. Russia supports the inter-Afghan dialogue on the unconditional understanding that the armed opposition must renounce the use of violence and break all ties with terrorist organisations, primarily ISIS and al-Qaeda."[140] It was also quite clear that both the Taliban and Pakistan were not keen on taking the QCG mechanism forward.

The Chief Executive Abdullah Abdullah, led a delegation to China from 15 to 18 May 2016. During his visit, he met President Xi Jinping, Prime Minister Li Keqiang and Vice President Li Yuanchao. Abdullah also visited Urumqi. According to the joint statement issued, China expressed its firm support to the National Unity Government in Afghanistan and to the 'Afghan-led, Afghan-owned' peace and reconciliation process. The Afghan side was said to have "reaffirmed its commitment to the one China policy and firm support for China's positions on issues related to Taiwan, Tibet, and Xinjiang and stated that Afghanistan would not allow its territory to be used by any forces for any separatist activities against China."[141] Interestingly, the joint statement referred to latest developments in the South China Sea and China's position on it, issues most unrelated and irrelevant to Afghanistan.

The Chinese side announced that in 2016, it will provide RMB 500 million aid gratis to the Afghan Government for mutually agreed projects; start the feasibility study on construction of low-cost affordable housing in Afghanistan; implement the Kabul University main building and auditorium project; provide approximately RMB 50 million non-emergency humanitarian aid in kind; continue to support Afghanistan in capacity building through training programmes for Afghan professionals; and will work with the Afghan side to formulate a national infrastructure plan and set priority areas. Interestingly, in the joint statement, both the countries expressed concern over the delay in the implementation of the Mes Aynak copper mine project and the Amu Darya basin oil project, and agreed to carry out further consultations to make 'practical progress' in this regard. It was also stated that China would like to "explore flexible and diversified cooperation forms with the Afghan side"; the Afghan side will provide "necessary facilitation for Chinese enterprises" and "ensure the safety of the relevant projects and personnel"; the two sides will "cooperate actively and step up their work to complete the access protocol for Afghan saffron, the access assessment for pine nuts, pomegranate and realize the export of these products to China at an early date, and work on facilitating the export of other fresh and dry fruits to China in the future."[142]

After the collapse of the QCG mechanism and the trilateral format with Pakistan and Afghanistan in 2016, Beijing reinvented the trilateral with Afghanistan and Pakistan by adding "practical cooperation" to it. The First China–Afghanistan–Pakistan Trilateral Practical Cooperation Dialogue was held in Beijing on 27 May 2017. It was co-chaired by Director-General of the Department of Asian Affairs of the Chinese Foreign Ministry Xiao Qian, Director-General of Department of Macro-Fiscal Policies of the Afghan Ministry of Finance Khalid Payenda, and Director General of Afghanistan Division of the Pakistan Ministry of Foreign Affairs Mansoor Ahmad Khan. According to the Chinese foreign ministry, the three countries "agreed to actively carry out such activities as trainings, exchanges, workshops and forums" and "explore trilateral cooperation in infrastructure, energy, education, health, agriculture and other fields, and strengthen human resources training, so as to help Afghanistan improve its capacity building." It was also stated that the countries appreciated the CPEC and its role in facilitating regional connectivity within the framework of the BRI.[143]

On 8 June 2017, President Ghani and President Xi met in Astana. According to the statement issued by the Chinese foreign ministry, President Xi noted that the two countries "have intensified exchanges at all levels, deepened cooperation in such areas as economy, trade and people-to-people and cultural exchanges, and made positive progress in the joint construction of the 'Belt and Road'". Xi added that both sides "should actively implement the practical cooperation agreements including the Memorandum of Understanding on Jointly Promoting the Construction of the 'Belt and Road'" and also "cooperation in anti-terrorism and security."[144] About six months later, on 1 December 2017, Afghanistan's Chief Executive Officer Abdullah met Chinese Premier Le Keqiang in Sochi. During the interaction, the Chinese premier stated that "expanding economic and trade, as well as other practical cooperation between China and Afghanistan cannot be done without a safe and stable external environment." He further stated that "China is willing to work with Afghanistan and Pakistan to strengthen dialogue and cooperation, and make joint efforts to strive for a stable and safe regional environmental construction, in a bid to promote the realization of long-term stability and peace in the region at an early date."[145] That was quite a straight message from the Chinese premier that Kabul needs to work closely with Beijing and Islamabad to create conducive environment, without which there can be no practical cooperation between China and Afghanistan. Chinese premier's statement assumes significance in the light of the fact that by 2016–17, both the US and Russia were actively exploring prospects of engaging the Taliban.

Former Taliban finance minister Agha Jan Motasim, was removed from the UN sanctions list in 2016 to kick start talks with the Taliban.[146] The growing influence of the ISIS in Afghanistan 2015 onwards was a major factor driving engagement with the Taliban. Russia was particularly concerned about regional militant Islamist groups pledging loyalty and allegiance to ISIS, which had established its Afghan chapter, the IS-K, in January 2015. With the security situation deteriorating in northern Afghanistan and IS-K gaining foothold in the northern Jowzjan and Kunduz provinces bordering Central Asia, Russia began to widen the ambit of its consultations with the regional countries.

Emergence of Moscow Format

By 2015–16, Russia had begun holding trilateral consultations on the Afghan situation with special representatives from China and Pakistan. The third round of trilateral consultations held on 27 December 2016 was significant as it expressed serious concerns over the increased activities of the IS-K, emphasised the need for a flexible approach towards de-listing of certain Taliban elements from the UN sanctions list, and most importantly, decided to expand the consultation format by inviting Afghanistan to it. According the Russian foreign ministry press release:

> The parties pointed to the worsening security situation in the Islamic Republic of Afghanistan and were *especially worried about intensifying activities by extremist groups in that country, including the Afghan branch of ISIS*.
>
> The participants agreed to continue efforts to assist in furthering the national reconciliation process in Afghanistan, based on the key role of

> the Afghans themselves and in line with the principles of integrating the armed opposition into peaceful life. *Russia and China, as permanent members of the UN Security Council, reaffirmed their readiness for flexible approaches to the prospect of excluding certain individuals from the list of sanctioned persons* as part of efforts to promote a peaceful dialogue between Kabul and the Taliban movement.
>
> The participants *agreed to continue consultations in an expanded format* and therefore would like to see Afghanistan take part (emphasis added).[147]

Shortly thereafter, on 15 February 2017, Russia launched a wider regional platform on Afghanistan, involving special representatives and senior officials from six countries: Russia, Afghanistan, Pakistan, China, Iran and India. According to the Russian foreign ministry press release, the participants "discussed regional approaches to the development of security" in Afghanistan and "agreed to step up efforts to promote the intra-Afghan peace process while maintaining the leading role of Kabul and observing the previously agreed upon principles of integrating the armed opposition into peaceful coexistence." Significantly, the participants also agreed to expand the negotiation format by inviting the CARs in the next meeting.[148]

Meanwhile, in early 2017, a Russian delegation led by Deputy Chief of the General Staff of the Russian Armed Forces Col Gen Sergey Istrako visited Rawalpindi to discuss "prospects for regional cooperation aiming to neutralise threats posed by international terrorist groups." It was stated that "The Pakistani side organised a presentation on the security situation in Pakistan" and "presented the results of Operation Zarb-e-Azb (Sharp Strike)...conducted in North Waziristan since 2014." The Russian delegation also visited Miramshah, the capital of North Waziristan, to see areas cleared of the terrorists by the Pakistan Army.[149]

On 14 April 2017, Moscow hosted the next round of the regional consultation on Afghanistan in an expanded format that included deputy foreign ministers and senior officials from all five CARs: Kazakhstan, Kyrgyzstan, Tajikistan, Turkmenistan and Uzbekistan, besides Afghanistan, China, India, Iran, Pakistan and Russia. A total of 11 countries were represented in the expanded format, which henceforth came to be referred as the "Moscow Format Consultations on Afghanistan". Russia had also invited US but according to the Russian foreign ministry press release, it did not attend the meeting "for unclear reasons". It was stated that the "main issue on the agenda was the coordination of regional efforts to assist the process of national reconciliation in the interests of restoring peace" in Afghanistan "as soon as possible." The participants "expressed a shared concern over the growing terrorist activity in the country" and "pointed out that there is no military solution to the Afghan crisis and that it can only be settled through the restoration of national accord by political means, in keeping with UN Security Council resolutions." The press release added that the participants "outlined their support for the efforts taken by the Kabul government and the socio-political forces to restore peace in Afghanistan" and "issued an appeal to the Taliban to abandon the use of force to resolve the internal Afghan conflict and to launch a direct dialogue with the government to work towards national reconciliation."[150]

Soon thereafter, on 25 April 2017, former Afghan President Karzai visited Moscow and met Foreign Minister Sergey Lavrov. In his opening remarks, Lavrov clearly stated that Russia is "willing to use any format to rally the support of external players" to facilitate Afghanistan's national reconciliation process. However, Lavrov also noted that "regrettably, the geopolitical games that are being played around Afghanistan have nothing to do with sincere concern for the future of the Afghan people" and "Russia-hating tendencies are being used in this dirty play."[151] A month later, in May, Russian foreign ministry provided detailed replies to various allegations made in Afghan and Western sources about Russia providing assistance to both Taliban and ISIS.[152]

Second China-led Trilateral Practical Cooperation Dialogue

The second China–Afghanistan–Pakistan Practical Cooperation Dialogue was held in Kabul from 26 to 27 September 2017. The dialogue was chaired by Mustafa Aria, Director General of Development Cooperation from the Ministry of Finance of Afghanistan, and was attended by Xiao Qian, Director General of the Asian Department of the Ministry of Foreign Affairs of China and Mansoor Ahmad Khan, Director General of the Afghanistan Department of the Ministry of Foreign Affairs of Pakistan. The three sides "agreed that the aim of the trilateral practical cooperation is to support the peaceful reconstruction and economic development of Afghanistan, to further strengthen the relations and to promote cooperation among the three countries within the "Belt and Road" and the Regional Economic Cooperation Conference on Afghanistan (RECCA) frameworks." The three sides also "agreed to enhance communication, coordinate China and Pakistan's assistance to Afghanistan on the basis of fully taking into account Afghanistan's priorities, carryout trilateral cooperation projects, gradually strengthen the mechanism building for trilateral cooperation, and to provide security for the trilateral cooperation projects" and that "policy communication, infrastructure, human resources, livelihood building and people to people exchange are the five key cooperation fields, and will steadily promote concrete cooperation."[153]

First China-led Trilateral Foreign Ministers' Dialogue

In December 2017, China upgraded the trilateral format with Pakistan and Afghanistan to the foreign ministers' level as well. The First China–Afghanistan–Pakistan Foreign Ministers' Dialogue was held in Beijing on 26 December 2017. In a joint press meet with the Afghan Foreign Minister Salahuddin Rabbani and Pakistan Foreign Minister Khawaja Muhammad Asif, Chinese Foreign Minister Wang Yi stated that "the China-Afghanistan-Pakistan Foreign Ministers' Dialogue seeks no replacement of the existing mechanisms and does not target any party except the three countries. China, Afghanistan and Pakistan are neighbors to each other, and it is perfectly natural and necessary for them to strengthen dialogue and cooperation."[154]

Elaborating on the dialogue mechanism, Wang said that the purpose is "to help Afghanistan and Pakistan to conduct dialogue, build mutual trust and improve relations between both sides" and "to coordinate the existing cooperation among China, Afghanistan and Pakistan, and strengthen political, economic and security cooperation among the three parties so as to achieve common development and security and commit to peace and stability in the region." He added that "such gestures comply with the common demand of the three countries and conform to the common interests of the three countries." Wang asserted that "the trilateral dialogue neither targets any party outside of the three countries, nor wants to be interfered or influenced by other countries or forces" and that it is "ready to coordinate and cooperate with other mechanisms, give play to respective strengths and create synergy to make joint contributions to promoting peace and stability in Afghanistan and the region."[155] Wang also informed that the three countries have reached a series of consensus, which were basically a reiteration of what Beijing had been stating for several years.

> The first is that the three parties will, under the framework of trilateral Foreign Ministers' Dialogue, take *political mutual trust and reconciliation, development cooperation and connectivity*, and *security cooperation and counter-terrorism* as three main topics to actively push forward trilateral cooperation in line with the principles of mutual respect, equal consultation, mutual benefit and win-win results;
>
> The second is that the three parties agreed that China-Afghanistan-Pakistan cooperation commits to realizing the following four goals: supporting Afghanistan's peaceful reconstruction and reconciliation process, helping Afghanistan and Pakistan to improve and develop relations, promoting common security in the three countries and the region, as well as pushing forward regional connectivity and international cooperation under the Belt and Road Initiative.
>
> The third is that Afghanistan and Pakistan agreed to improve bilateral relations as soon as possible, in a bid to achieve harmonious co-existence. The two countries agreed to solve issues of respective concerns through comprehensive dialogue and consultation. The Pakistani side put forward the Pakistan-Afghanistan Action Plan on Strengthening Unity, hoping to set up five liaison working groups in politics, military, intelligence, economy and refugee. The Afghan side expressed its willingness to fully echo it. Such gestures were supported and welcomed by China. This is an important progress made at the Dialogue.
>
> The fourth is that the three sides reaffirmed their commitments to advancing the "Afghan-led and Afghan-owned" reconciliation process of Afghanistan, and called on the Afghan Taliban to join the process. The Afghan government expressed that it will put forward more attractive options for reconciliation at an early date. China and Pakistan welcome it, stand ready to fully support the Afghan government in carrying out peace talks with the Taliban, and will continuously offer convenience to this end.
>
> The fifth is that Afghanistan and Pakistan reaffirmed to support the joint construction of the Belt and Road Initiative proposed by China. The two countries stand ready to align respective development strategies with the building of the Belt and Road Initiative, and meanwhile, actively discuss

> trilateral cooperation under the "Belt and Road" framework.
>
> The sixth is that China and Pakistan will carry out projects to aid Afghanistan in health care, human resources, agriculture and other livelihood areas. The three parties will actively conduct friendly exchanges in such fields as youths, think tanks and media, and will also give play to the location advantage of Xinjiang Uygur Autonomous Region of China to carry out cooperation between Xinjiang and relevant regions in Afghanistan and Pakistan.
>
> The seventh is that the three sides will enhance coordination and cooperation in counter-terrorism, and combat all terrorist organizations and individuals without any discrimination according to the consensus reached under the mechanism of China- Afghanistan-Pakistan trilateral vice-ministerial consultation on counter-terrorism and security.
>
> The eighth is that Afghanistan and Pakistan agreed to promote communication between the two Ulema Councils, so as to jointly make clear the stance of religious circles of both sides on no tolerance of terrorist acts to the outside, and jointly prevent the spread of religious extremism, which the Chinese side appreciates.[156]

Wang Yi also spoke about the need to extend the CPEC to Afghanistan. In this regard, he stated:

> *China and Pakistan stand ready to, together with Afghanistan, discuss extending the CPEC to Afghanistan in a proper manner under the principle of mutual benefit and win-win results, and gradually connect the CPEC with the China-Central Asia-West Asia Economic Corridor through Afghanistan in the long run.* With regard to specific cooperation projects and ways of cooperation, we will determine them through trilateral consultation on an equal footing with an incremental approach, starting from the easier to the more difficult ones and from small to big ones (emphasis added).[157]

Third China-led DG-Level Trilateral Practical Cooperation Dialogue

The Third Trilateral Practical Cooperation Dialogue, held on 28 May 2018 in Beijing, was chaired by Director-General of the Department of Asian Affairs of the Foreign Ministry Wu Jianghao, and attended by Director General of Regional Cooperation of the Ministry of Foreign Affairs Amir Mohammad Ramin of Afghanistan and Director of Afghanistan Division of the Ministry of Foreign Affairs Agazzi of Pakistan. The three participants "agreed to reinforce policy communication and mechanism construction, speed up the advancement of projects of human resources and people-to-people and cultural exchanges, discuss carrying out pilot projects in such areas as people's livelihood construction and infrastructure, and promote the extension of China-Pakistan Economic Corridor to Afghanistan, in a bid to promote mutual benefit, win-win results and regional connectivity among the three parties."[158]

Russia at Tashkent High-Level Conference on Afghanistan

Meanwhile, Russia continued to raise the issue of threat from the increased presence of IS-K in northern Afghanistan bordering CARs. In his remarks at the Tashkent International Conference on Afghanistan held on 27 March 2018, Russian Foreign Minister Lavrov stated:

> The situation in Afghanistan continues to deteriorate. In the absence of an intra-Afghanistan political process the Taliban fully or partially controls almost a half of the country, waging active hostilities and organising sabotage. The expanding penetration of the Islamic State, first of all in the northern provinces that have borders with CIS countries, is a matter of special concern. The group establishes strongholds where they train people from Central Asia, Russia and other states. We regard this as a direct threat to regional and international security.[159]

Lavrov indirectly criticised the US approach towards resolving the Afghan conflict stating that that "the conflict cannot be resolved by force, no matter which strategies foreign capitals may approve". He added, "Ideas of a military solution are disconnected from historical experience and today's reality" and "it is possible to achieve true peace and stability only by launching a constructive dialogue between the Afghan government and Taliban." He further stated:

> We are convinced that a comprehensive approach to a settlement is necessary through a search for balance between Afghan parties' interests as well as taking into account the approaches of Afghanistan's neighbours and other countries in the regions. We consider it to be a priority to actively involve such important organisations as the SCO and the CSTO, which have already proven their positive role in the Afghan issues in practice.

> We welcome the growing understanding of the importance of the regional context in the Afghan settlement process. As has been demonstrated many times, "recipes from afar" that fail to take into account local traditions and specifics do not help but rather harm. We believe that it is necessary to more actively engage the resources of organisations with Central Asian states as members. The principle of regional representation and honest and equal partnership between all key actors, which is the foundation of the Moscow format as well as the SCO-Afghanistan Contact Group, suits the goal of launching an intra-Afghan peace dialogue best. [160]

Xi–Ghani Meeting in Qingdao

President Ghani met Chinese President Xi Jinping on 10 June 2018 in Qingdao. The Chinese foreign ministry in its press release stated:

> Both countries should maintain high-level exchanges, intensify exchanges at all levels including government departments, legislative institutions, political parties and militaries, strengthen local cooperation, and deepen practical cooperation in economy and trade. China is willing to continue to provide assistance for Afghanistan's economic and social development within China's due capacity, and supports Afghanistan in participating in the "Belt and Road" construction and speeding up the realization of connectivity with countries in the region. Both sides should enhance cooperation in counter-terrorism and security.[161]

Abdullah–Keqiang Meeting in Dushanbe

Afghan Chief Executive Abdullah Abdullah met Chinese Premier Li Keqiang on the sidelines of the 17th SCO Council of Heads of Government held on 12 October 2018 in Dushanbe. According to the Chinese foreign ministry press release, Li stated that "China will continue to support the Afghan government in safeguarding national security and stability and promoting the Afghan-led and Afghan-owned political reconciliation and will continue to play a constructive role to this end"; "China is willing to help Afghanistan boost reconstruction and improve its people's livelihood by aligning the two countries' development strategies and deepening bilateral practical cooperation"; and "China also encourages more capable Chinese enterprises to participate in Afghanistan's infrastructure construction so as to boost the country's connectivity with other countries in the region." Li added that "China will enhance anti-terror cooperation and personnel training with Afghanistan, and promote trilateral cooperation among China, Afghanistan and Pakistan."[162]

Second Moscow Format Consultations on Afghanistan

The second round of Moscow Format Consultations was held on 9 November 2018. Besides 11 countries that had participated in the first round of meeting held in April 2017, a five-member Taliban delegation from their political office in Doha led by Sher Mohammad Abbas Stanekzai, and a delegation from the Afghan government-appointed High Peace Council (HPC) led by its Deputy Chairman Haji Din Mohammad, too participated in the consultations. The other four members of the Taliban delegation were Salam Hanafi, Shahabuddin Delawar, Zia-ur-Rahman Madani and Sohail Shaheen. The US was represented by an official from its embassy in Moscow. The Afghan Government was not officially represented and had instead sent a delegation from the HPC. In this regard, the Afghan foreign ministry had issued a statement:

> Today's Moscow Meeting, is not a follow up of the previous meetings (Moscow Format) held among sovereign states where the Government of Afghanistan also participated, as in today's meeting the Taliban have also been invited. In accordance with the principles and decisions of the Tashkent Meeting and that of the Kabul Process, Government of the Islamic Republic of Afghanistan and the Taliban must directly sit around the negotiation table. We emphasize the accepted principles of the Kabul and Tashkent meetings that is based on national and international consensus on the mechanism of dealing with the peace process and thus have not sent any representative to the Moscow Meeting. *The High Peace Council participates in this meeting hosted by Russia, as a National but non-government institution*, with a view to discuss the dynamics and details of initiating direct negotiations. As per the understanding between Afghanistan and Russia, the Government of the Islamic Republic of Afghanistan hopes that this meeting leads to direct talks between the Government of Afghanistan and the Taliban and that the *Taliban are not allowed to instrumentlaize this meeting* (emphasis added).[163]

In his remarks delivered at the meeting, Russian Foreign Minister Lavrov stated: "Afghanistan's problems can only be settled politically, through the attainment of national accord and with the involvement of all parties to the conflict".

Referring to the potential threat from the ISIS presence in Afghanistan, he stated that "ISIS as the spearhead of terrorists, supported by its foreign patrons, has tried to turn Afghanistan into a bridgehead for, its expansion into Central Asia and the whole of our vast region". He added, "Our countries and the multilateral organisations active in the region must help the people of Afghanistan foil these plans and root out the terrorist threat…We hope that responsible politicians will not be guided by personal or group considerations but by the interests of the people of Afghanistan." He further cautioned that "We must not think in terms of geopolitical games, which can only make Afghanistan an area of international rivalry with grave consequences for the people of Afghanistan and their neighbours."[164]

It was reported that taking full advantage of the regional platform, the Taliban delegation in its address referred to their group as the "Islamic Emirate of Afghanistan" 61 times. The delegation stated that "Peace in Afghanistan and withdrawal of foreign troops are tied with each other, because withdrawal of foreign troops practically paves the way for peace" and called for the complete withdrawal of the Western forces, release of all the Taliban detainees, and removal of the Taliban from the UN sanctions list, among other things.[165] Meanwhile, the head of the HPC delegation in his speech urged the Taliban group to positively respond to the offers of the Afghan Government regarding peace process, emphasising that the ongoing conflict is only claiming the lives of ordinary Afghans.

Interestingly, the Taliban spokesperson Zabihullah Mujahid had clearly stated a day before the meeting that "The representatives of Islamic Emirate will clarify the policy of Islamic Emirate about ending the occupation of Afghanistan to the participants"; "This conference is not about holding negotiations with any party whatsoever; rather it is about finding a peaceful solution to the issue of Afghanistan"; "There will not be any sort of negotiations taking place with the delegation of Kabul administration"; "This conference will not be chaired by the Kabul administration"; "With participation in the meeting, the international status of the Islamic Emirate will be strengthened even further"; and that "Such diplomatic efforts of the Islamic Emirate showcase the active, clear and independent diplomacy and policy of the Islamic Emirate in the political field."[166]

It was noteworthy that in absence of any official participation or representation from the Afghan Government, no joint statement was issued at the end of the meeting.

Second China-led Trilateral Foreign Ministers' Dialogue

On 15 December 2018, the second China–Afghanistan–Pakistan Trilateral Foreign Ministers' Dialogue was held in Kabul. It was held at a time when the US and the Taliban had entered into direct negotiations in Doha. The dialogue was attended by China's State Councilor and Foreign Minister Wang Yi, Afghan Foreign Minister Salahuddin Rabbani, and Pakistan Foreign Minister Makhdoom Shah Mahmood Qureshi.

According to the joint statement issued, the three sides "agreed to promote China-Afghanistan-Pakistan trilateral cooperation under the framework of jointly building the Belt and Road Initiative"; "reiterated their strong resolve to fight terrorism in all its forms and manifestations, and without any distinction"; "agreed to jointly continue their efforts for building political mutual trust and support reconciliation, development cooperation and connectivity, security cooperation and counter-terrorism as the three areas of the trilateral cooperation"; reiterated their support to the Afghan-owned, and Afghan led inclusive peace process that is fully supported regionally and internationally, as the most viable way to bring peace in Afghanistan"; appreciated the efforts of President Ghani "especially for the comprehensive peace plans that came out of the second Kabul Process and the Geneva Conferences on Afghanistan…called on the Afghan Taliban to join the peace process at an early date."[167]

The joint statement further stated that the three sides "will continue to implement and expand the 'soft' projects such as exchange and capacity building programs and explore 'hard' projects of livelihood facilities and connectivity." China "expressed its readiness to support Afghanistan and Pakistan in building immigration reception center and drinking water supply schemes at each side of the Ghulam Khan Khel crossing point, and to explore cold storages at Chaman and Spin Boldak." China "supports enhanced coordination between Afghanistan and Pakistan on major energy and connectivity projects including the construction of Quetta-Kandahar railway and Kabul-Peshawar Motorway and Railway." The three sides "agreed to counter terrorist' logistical capabilities including financing, recruitment, training, and strengthen trilateral cooperation for counter-terrorism capacity building, deny terrorist use of the internet and to take joint steps for deradicalization, as well as work together to break the nexus between narco-trade and terror financing." To advance their cooperation in the fields of counter-terrorism, the three sides signed a MoU on Counter-Terrorism.[168]

Wang Yi in his remarks "stressed that the accelerating evolution of the current international and regional situation has brought new opportunities and challenges to the security and development of the three countries and to trilateral cooperation." He hoped that the three sides will "gather new consensus on promoting realization of the inclusive political reconciliation in Afghanistan at an early date" and on "enhancing the momentum of improvement of Afghanistan-Pakistan relations, advancing practical cooperation and connectivity, and deepening counter-terrorism cooperation and other aspects."[169]

Wang Yi latter briefed the media and referred to the following six aspects of the "new and extensive consensus" reached by the three countries:

> First, we believed that further strengthening trilateral cooperation is of great practical significance for promoting common development and security of the three countries and safeguarding regional peace and stability.
>
> Second, we believed that the reconciliation process in Afghanistan faces important opportunities. The three sides are willing to strengthen coordination and push the Taliban back to the negotiating table and the political mainstream at an early date.
>
> Third, Afghanistan and Pakistan agreed to further improve bilateral relations, well implement the Action Plan for Peace and Solidarity.
>
> Fourth, the three sides agreed to strengthen cooperation among China, Afghanistan and Pakistan and will actively explore hardware projects for people's livelihood and transportation infrastructure construction on the basis of continuing software projects including personnel exchanges and training programs. At the early stage, *the Chinese side will help Afghanistan and Pakistan build amenities including reception centers, drinking water, and cold storage on the ports of both sides. Afghanistan and Pakistan introduced*

> *the situation of cross-border infrastructure projects such as the Peshawar-Kabul railway and the Quetta-Kandahar railway.*
>
> Fifth, the three sides agreed to jointly promote the undertaking of the Belt and Road Initiative and promote regional connectivity and economic development. *China and Pakistan support Afghanistan in leveraging its geographical advantages to become a hub connecting countries in the region and benefit from regional cooperation projects including the China-Pakistan Economic Corridor.* The three sides agreed to go on expanding trilateral cooperation under the framework of the Belt and Road Initiative.
>
> Sixth, the three sides agreed to earnestly implement the Memorandum of Understanding on Anti-terrorism Cooperation signed during the dialogue, strengthen dialogue on counter-terrorism policies, advance practical cooperation in counter-terrorism, intensify exchanges and cooperation in counter-terrorism within the multilateral frameworks, *and firmly crack down on the East Turkistan Islamic Movement* and other terrorist organizations (emphasis added).[170]

Third China-led Trilateral Foreign Ministers' Dialogue

The third round of China–Afghanistan–Pakistan Trilateral Foreign Ministers' Dialogue was held on 7 September 2019 in Islamabad. The dialogue was attended by China's State Councilor and Foreign Minister Wang Yi, Afghan Foreign Minister Salahuddin Rabbani and Pakistan Foreign Minister Makhdoom Shah Mahmood Qureshi.

According to the joint statement issued, the three sides "particularly underlined the need for an inclusive, Afghan-led and Afghan-owned peace process leading to a comprehensive agreement for durable peace and stability in Afghanistan." The three sides also "agreed to explore 'China-Afghanistan-Pakistan plus' cooperation, as well as working towards promoting trade and connectivity projects between Afghanistan and Pakistan, such as Kabul-Peshawar Motorway" and "welcomed the progress made on implementation of projects agreed under the China-Afghanistan-Pakistan Practical Cooperation Dialogue (CAPPCD)." China expressed its "readiness to support construction of refrigeration storages, clinic centers, drinking water supply schemes and immigration reception centers at crossing points between Afghanistan and Pakistan to facilitate the movement of people and trade activities among the two countries." The three sides also "welcomed the plans to hold a trilateral friendly cricket tournament among junior cricket teams of the three countries in Beijing in October 2019" and "agreed to arrange a capacity building workshop of young diplomats from the three countries under the Junior Diplomats Exchange Program to be held in Pakistan in October 2019." The three Foreign Ministers further "agreed to organize an Archaeologists' Exchange Program, explore cooperation among the Red Crescent Societies of the three countries, besides regularly undertaking exchange projects in the areas of media, think-tanks, sports, joint training etc."[171]

Wang in his remarks suggested three principles that should be followed in any future political arrangement for Afghanistan:

> First, it should have broad representation and inclusiveness to make all factions and ethnic groups in Afghanistan equally involve in the political life and share state power. Achieving this will build a united political foundation for the future of Afghanistan.
>
> Second, it should unswervingly stick to counter-terrorism and never let Afghanistan once again become a haven for terrorist organizations. Achieving this will maintain a stable security for the future of Afghanistan.
>
> Third, it should follow a foreign policy of peace and friendship, thus to live in peace with various countries in the world, especially with neighboring countries of Afghanistan, and play a constructive role in regional peace and stability. Achieving this will forge a favorable external environment for the future of Afghanistan.[172]

Taliban Delegation's Visit to Beijing

After the US President Donald Trump called-off talks with the Taliban on 7 September 2019,[173] following a Taliban car bomb attack near the NATO headquarters in Kabul in which two NATO troops, an American and a Romanian, were among the 12 people killed, a nine-member Taliban delegation led by Mullah Baradar visited Beijing and met Chinese Special Representative Deng Xijun on 22 September 2019. The Taliban spokesperson Suhail Shaheen tweeted that "The Chinese special representative said the US-Taliban deal is a good framework for the peaceful solution of the Afghan issue and they support it." Chinese Foreign Ministry spokesman Geng Shuang confirming the Taliban delegation's visit stated that "China's relevant foreign ministry official exchanged opinions with Baradar regarding the situation in Afghanistan and promoting Afghanistan's peace and reconciliation process," Geng said.[174]

The September 2019 visit was the second visit by the Taliban delegation to Beijing in the year. Chinese foreign ministry spokesman Lu Kang had confirmed earlier in June that a Mullah Baradar-led Taliban delegation from Doha had recently visited Beijing and Chinese officials met them to discuss the Afghan peace process and counter-terrorism issues. He stated that "China pays great attention to the evolving situation in Afghanistan" and it has "always played a positive role in the Afghan peace and reconciliation process." Lu added, "Both sides believe that this exchange was beneficial and agreed to keep in touch about and cooperate on continuing to seek a political resolution for Afghanistan and fighting terrorism."[175]

Karzai–Wang Yi Meeting

On 3 December 2019, Foreign Minister Wang Yi met former President Karzai who was visiting Beijing for the 2019 Imperial Springs International Forum. According to the Chinese foreign ministry press release, Wang during his meeting with Karzai stated that "the situation of Afghanistan and its process of peace and reconciliation are at a critical juncture" and it is imperative that both the US-Taliban peace talks and the intra-Afghan dialogue make progress and yield results. He was of the opinion that "the US and the Taliban should resume peace talks as soon as possible to produce results and peace, bringing about an orderly and complete withdrawal of the US and other foreign troops. The intra-Afghan dialogue should also be launched as soon as possible." Karzai on his part stated that "the Chinese side has maintained close communication with the Afghan side and actively promoted its process of peace and reconciliation, which has been welcomed by all parties" and "the Afghan side sincerely appreciates the Chinese side's efforts to facilitate the intra-Afghan dialogue and is willing to strengthen coordination with the Chinese side to promote an early launch of the dialogue."[176]

Post US–Taliban Doha Agreement

On 25 May 2020, three months after the signing of US–Taliban deal in Doha, Foreign Minister Wang while speaking at the press conference of the Third

Session of the 13th National people's Congress made five points regarding Afghanistan: first, the need to consolidate the unity of the government formed by Ghani and Abdullah; second, the need to establish a framework for intra-Afghan talks on the country's future political architecture; third, the need for US troop withdrawal to proceed in an orderly and responsible manner; fourth, the need to prevent any regrouping of terrorist forces; and, fifth, the need to mobilise greater international support and collaboration for the reconciliation process.[177]

Third China–Afghanistan–Pakistan Trilateral Vice Foreign Ministers' Strategic Dialogue was held in virtual mode due to COVID-19 restrictions on 7 July 2020. According to the joint press release:

> China and Pakistan appreciated the efforts by the Afghanistan government and relevant parties in expediting the exchange of the prisoners to pave the way for the start of the Intra-Afghan Negotiations and call for violence reduction and humanitarian ceasefire. China and Pakistan will enhance cooperation with the Afghan government in support of the "Afghan-led, Afghan-owned" peace reconciliation process, the launch of Intra-Afghan Negotiations at an early date, *support the preservation of the gains since 2001*, and looked forward to the early restoration of peace and stability in Afghanistan.
>
> Afghanistan and Pakistan agreed to further strengthen dialogue and work for continuous improvement of bilateral relations including through the effective implementation of the Afghanistan-Pakistan Action Plan for Peace and Solidarity (APAPPS). China will continue to play a constructive role in improving Afghanistan-Pakistan relations.
>
> The three sides agreed that *the return of Afghan refugees should be part of peace and reconciliation process and underlined the role of international community for a time-bound and well-resourced roadmap for the return of Afghan refugees* to their homeland with dignity and honour.
>
> The three sides urged for *an orderly, responsible and condition based withdraw* [*sic*] *of the foreign troops from Afghanistan to avoid potential terrorist resurgence* (emphasis added).[178]

China on Opening of Intra-Afghan Talks at Doha

On 12 September 2020, Chinese foreign minister Wang Yi in his address delivered online during the inauguration of intra-Afghan talks at Doha proposed "three proposals and expectations":

> First, keep to the fundamental direction of political settlement. History has shown that the Afghan issue can only be resolved by political means.
>
> Second, uphold the basic principle of an Afghan-led process. The future of Afghanistan must be in the hands of its own people, and the negotiations must be "Afghan-led, Afghan-owned"'. No external force should exploit the process for their selfish interests.
>
> Third, pursue the goal of a broad-based and inclusive framework. The future arrangements for Afghanistan need to be broadly representative and inclusive. Under such arrangements, all political parties and groups, ethnic groups and religious sects in Afghanistan will be able to participate on an equal footing and share state power.

He concluded stating that "China will continue to be a supporter, mediator and facilitator" for Afghan peace and reconciliation process and that the withdrawal of foreign troops "should proceed in a responsible and orderly way to ensure a stable transition in Afghanistan."[179]

China at 9th Ministerial Conference of Heart of Asia–Istanbul Process

At the 9th Foreign Ministers' Conference of the Istanbul Process on Afghanistan, held on 30 March 2021 in Dushanbe, Chinese Foreign Minister Wang Yi in his address proposed cooperation in three areas.

> First, sustaining the momentum of peace talks and reconciliation in Afghanistan. The Afghan issue can only be resolved by political means, and the future of Afghanistan should be kept in the hands of the Afghan people.
>
> Second, adding impetus to reconstruction and development in Afghanistan. While Afghanistan has made big strides in economic and social development in recent years, it lacks internal drivers of growth. Currently, *the implementation of the China-Afghanistan MOU on Belt and Road cooperation is well underway, and China has provided several billion yuan in grant to Afghanistan.*
>
> Third, keeping to the overall direction of counter-terrorism cooperation regarding Afghanistan.
>
> Foreign troops should withdraw from Afghanistan in a responsible and

> orderly way, so as to prevent the various terrorist forces from ramping up and creating trouble (emphasis added).[180]

Before Taliban Takeover

On 11 May 2021, Chinese Foreign Minister Wang elaborated China's position on the current Afghan situation when holding talks with visiting foreign ministers of countries including Uzbekistan and Tajikistan at the China+Central Asia (C+C5) Foreign Ministers' Meeting in Xi'an City, Shaanxi Province. He put forward the following propositions:

> The peace and reconciliation process in Afghanistan should firstly implement the principle of "Afghan-led and Afghan-owned". This is in line with the requirements of the UN Security Council's relevant resolutions and is the political prerequisite for peace and reconciliation in Afghanistan.
>
> Second, Afghanistan should form inclusive political arrangements to make sure that all ethnic groups and parties could participate in political life in the future and enjoy equal political rights..
>
> Third, Afghan national governance structure in the future should conform to the country's unique national conditions and development needs, and should not simply copy foreign models.[181]

Wang Yi pointed out that "regional countries and the international community hope that the future Afghan government could implement the moderate Muslim policy and avoid extremist tendencies, oppose all forms of terrorism and not allow the resurgence of terrorist forces in Afghanistan, develop good-neighborliness and friendship with neighboring countries and become a positive factor in promoting regional peace and stability." He concluded stressing that "as close neighbors of Afghanistan, Central Asian countries should make due contribution to the final settlement of the Afghan issue, and the Shanghai Cooperation Organization should also play its due role for the long-term peace and stability in Afghanistan."[182]

Fourth China-led Trilateral Foreign Ministers' Dialogue

On 3 June 2021, Chinese Foreign Affairs Minister Wang Yi, Afghan Foreign Minister Haneef Atmar and Pakistan Foreign Affairs Minister Shah Mahmood Qureshi met via video link for the Fourth Trilateral Foreign Ministers' Dialogue.

The long joint statement issued by the three sides has been summarised below:

> Underscored that as insecurity in Afghanistan will directly impact the stability and economic prosperity of the entire region, there is a need for joint efforts and response to eliminate the current challenges in our region;
>
> Noted that the start of withdrawal of foreign troops from Afghanistan, and believed that while this move has complex impacts on Afghanistan peace and reconciliation process, it will also provide opportunities for the Afghanistan and the region to truly take the future of their countries and nations into their own hands
>
> Called for responsible and orderly withdrawal of foreign troops to avoid deterioration of the security situation in the region or giving terrorist forces the opportunity to re-emerge and grow;
>
> Underlined the importance of a peaceful resolution to the conflict in Afghanistan and called on all parties in Afghanistan for an early declaration of a comprehensive ceasefire and an end to the senseless violence, in order to create the conditions needed for negotiation between the Islamic republic of Afghanistan and the Taliban;
>
> Believed that the UNSC resolution 2513 must be observed, while looking forward to and welcoming the early return of the Taliban to the political mainstream of Afghanistan;
>
> Reiterated that they do not support the establishment of any government imposed by force in Afghanistan;
>
> Supported Afghanistan to be an independent, sovereign and democratic state that enjoys security and stability, achieves development and prosperity, and lives in harmony with its neighbors;
>
> Maintained that resolution of the Afghan issue should fully reflect the "Afghan-led, Afghan-owned" principle. The Afghan government could play a leading role in Afghanistan's peace and reconciliation process to draw up a plan jointly with all parties that reflects extensiveness and inclusiveness;
>
> Supported all multilateral efforts that are conducive to building political consensus in Afghanistan, and the international community and to promoting Afghanistan's peace and reconciliation process; and
>
> Believed that Afghanistan's neighboring countries as the most direct stakeholders in relation to Afghanistan's domestic situation should play a more important, constructive role in this regard.[183]

China and Afghanistan "recognized that Pakistan has continued to host with dignity and honor millions of Afghan refugees for decades" and "emphasized that a time-bound and well-resourced return of Afghan refugees...and their re-integration in the Afghan society should be part of the comprehensive peace agreement." On the other hand, China and Pakistan "reaffirmed their firm support for the peaceful reconstruction of Afghanistan and readiness to expand economic and trade ties with Afghanistan, support Afghanistan in enhancing its capacity for independent development."[184]

Wang Yi in his remarks at the trilateral meeting stated that "the accelerated unilateral withdrawal of [Western] troops" from Afghanistan "poses a challenge to and also offers an opportunity for Afghanistan and other countries in the region". He added that "the challenge lies in whether the withdrawal will lead to changes in the talks among Afghans, wars and strife" and "the opportunity is that the pull-out of external military forces from Afghanistan will create conditions and open up prospects for the Afghan people to truly take control of their own future and destiny." He also put forth five ideas and propositions:

> First, adhere to the fundamental "Afghan-led, Afghan-owned" principle. We support all parties in Afghanistan *to jointly build an extensive and inclusive political structure for the future, which pursues a moderate Muslim policy and continues to firmly combat terrorism internally, and promotes peace diplomacy on all fronts externally*, especially being in friendly terms with neighboring countries.
>
> Second, maintain the momentum of intra-Afghan talks. The peace and reconciliation process in Afghanistan is at a critical moment, the opportunity for peace talks should not be missed, and the reconciliation process should not be reversed.
>
> Third, *bring the Taliban back into the political mainstream*. The international community has reached an important consensus that all parties in Afghanistan should strictly abide by the UN Security Council Resolution 2513.
>
> Fourth, the international community and the countries in the region should provide full support. China, Afghanistan and Pakistan should work together to push for the orderly withdrawal of the U.S. troops and the fulfillment of its due obligations, so as to prevent the deterioration of the security situation in Afghanistan and avoid the return of terrorist forces. Going

> forward, we will support the Shanghai Cooperation Organization in playing a bigger role in the peace and reconciliation in Afghanistan.
>
> Fifth, strengthen sincere cooperation among China, Afghanistan and Pakistan. Since last year, *Pakistan has played a unique role in facilitating the signing of the peace agreement between the United States and Taliban and the initiating of intra-Afghan negotiations*. China hopes that Pakistan will continue to make good use of its own advantages and make new and constructive efforts (emphasis added).[185]

Wang Yi–Atmar Meet

On 14 July 2021, Chinese Foreign Minister Wang Yi and Afghan Foreign Minister Haneef Atmar met in Dushanbe. According to the Chinese foreign ministry press release, Wang in his meeting with Atmar said that "China and Afghanistan are good neighbors connected by common mountains and rivers. China attaches great importance to the China–Afghanistan strategic partnership, and will work with Afghanistan to prepare for the high-level contact between the two countries so as to release positive signals of peace." He stated that "the hasty drawdown" of the US and NATO forces have "escalated tensions and wars in Afghanistan, bringing the Afghan issue to crossroads." China holds an 'Afghan-led and Afghan-owned' principle and "supports the building of an inclusive political structure in Afghanistan through dialogues and negotiations." He was of the view that "the pressing task at present is to prevent civil wars and to resume negotiations within the Afghans, in order to work out solutions for political reconciliation and, in particular, prevent any terrorist forces from inflating and Afghanistan from becoming the home of terrorists." He added that "the Taliban should stand clear of any and all terrorist forces."[186]

Last Xi–Ghani Talks

On 16 July 2021, President Xi had a phone conversation with President Ghani. According to the details provided by the Chinese foreign ministry, Xi stated that China believes that "political dialogue is the fundamental way to achieve national reconciliation and lasting peace in Afghanistan" and it will "continue to support the 'Afghan-led, Afghan-owned' principle, the peace and reconciliation process in Afghanistan, and an early peaceful reconstruction of the country." Xi added, China "is glad to see that the Afghan government and relevant parties in Afghanistan have reached positive consensus during the recent dialogue in Tehran. China hopes that both sides engaged in the dialogue will put the interests of the Afghan people first, and agree on a political solution through negotiation at an early date. China will, as always, play a constructive role in the process." Ghani on his part stated that "The Afghan government is dedicated to seeking a political solution to the current crisis." He added that "Afghanistan looks forward to China continuing to play an important role in pushing for a political settlement of the Afghan issue."[187]

Last Chinese Communication with Ghani Regime

On 6 August 2021, some nine days before Kabul fell to the Taliban, External Security Commissioner of the Chinese Foreign Ministry Cheng Guoping met with Afghan Ambassador to China Javid Ahmad Qaem and "exchanged views on China-Afghanistan relations, the situation in Afghanistan, and counterterrorism and security cooperation between the two countries." According to the official press release, Guoping stated, referring to the 16 July telephonic conversation between President Xi and President Ghani, that the two leaders had "reached new consensus on further enhancing bilateral cooperation." He added that "China is willing to work with Afghanistan to implement the important consensus reached by the two heads of state, play the role of the China-Afghanistan inter-departmental and inter-regional security cooperation mechanism, deepen cooperation in counterterrorism, security and other fields, and push forward the China-Afghanistan strategic and cooperative partnership."[188]

Taliban an "Important Military and Political Force"

In between the last telephonic conversation between President Xi and President Ghani on 16 July and Beijing's last official interaction with the Ghani regime on 6 August when the Afghan ambassador to Beijing met the Chinese External Security Commissioner, a Taliban delegation was received by Chinese Foreign Minister Wang Yi on 28 July 2021 in Tianjin. The Chinese Foreign Ministry press release referred to Mullah Abdul Ghani Baradar, who led the Taliban delegation, as the 'Head of the Taliban Political Commission' and mentioned that the Taliban delegation included heads of the Taliban Religious Council and the Taliban Publicity Committee.

According to the press release, Wang Yi said that "China, as Afghanistan's largest neighbor, has always respected Afghanistan's sovereignty, independence and territorial integrity, adhered to non-interference in Afghanistan's internal affairs and pursued a friendly policy toward the entire Afghan people." Criticising the hasty withdrawal of the US and NATO troops from Afghanistan, he stated that it "actually marks the failure of the U.S. policy toward Afghanistan" and that "the Afghan people now have an important opportunity to achieve national stability and development."[189]

Chinese foreign minister, for the first time, stated that "the Afghan Taliban is *an important military and political force in Afghanistan* and is expected to play an important role in the country's peace, reconciliation and reconstruction process." He stated that China hopes that the Afghan Taliban "will put the interests of the country and nation first, hold high the banner of peace talks, set the goal of peace, build a positive image and pursue an inclusive policy". He added that "All factions and ethnic groups in Afghanistan should unite as one, truly implement the 'Afghan-led and Afghan-owned' principle, push for early substantive results in the peace and reconciliation process, and independently establish *a broad and inclusive political structure* that suits Afghanistan's national realities."[190]

Wang Yi subsequently stressed that the ETIM "is an international terrorist organization designated by the UN Security Council that poses a direct threat to China's national security and territorial integrity" and "combating the ETIM is a common responsibility for the international community." He added that China hopes that the Afghan Taliban "will make a clean break with all terrorist organizations including the ETIM and resolutely and effectively combat them to remove obstacles, play a positive role and create enabling conditions for security, stability, development and cooperation in the region."[191]

According to the press release, Baradar said that "China has always been a reliable friend of the Afghan people and commended China's just and positive role in Afghanistan's peace and reconciliation process." He assured the Chinese side that the Afghan Taliban "has the utmost sincerity to work toward and realize peace" and that "It stands ready to work with other parties to establish a political framework in Afghanistan that is broadly-based, inclusive and accepted by the entire Afghan people and to protect human rights, especially the rights of women and children." He also stated that the Taliban "will never allow any force to use the Afghan territory to engage in acts detrimental to China" and that the Taliban hopes that "China will be more involved in Afghanistan's peace and reconciliation process and play a bigger role in future reconstruction and economic development". Subsequently, China's Assistant Foreign Minister Wu Jianghao met Baradar and his delegation "to exchange in-depth views on issues of common concern, which helped enhance mutual understanding and broaden consensus."[192]

Summing Up

Less than three weeks later, the Haqqani–Taliban fighters entered the capital, Kabul. From the abovementioned Chinese foreign ministry press release, which for the first time referred to the Taliban as "an important military and political force," and the timing of the Taliban delegation's visit, it was clear that Beijing was stepping up to deal with a Taliban-led political set-up in Kabul. While playing all sides, Beijing primarily stuck through and through to the trilateral format, trying to build a workable equation between Pakistan and Afghanistan, and integrating both into Xi Jinping's expansive 'Belt and Road' initiatives. Perhaps, it was intended to incentivise the Taliban into not allowing the Uighur militants to pose any security threat to China or to its interests spread across Central Asia. Following each of the four trilateral meetings with Pakistani and Afghan foreign ministers, Chinese foreign minister would repeatedly elaborate on the points of consensus reached between the foreign ministers of the three countries; however, none seems to have worked in practical terms. Chinese attempt at mediation between Pakistan and Afghanistan proved ineffective for it hardly had any impact on the situation on the ground. It neither led to any change in Pakistan's approach towards Afghanistan, nor in the Taliban's behaviour.

China as always would stress on its full support to the Afghan Government and to the latter's efforts at political reconciliation with the Taliban, but nothing seems to have translated into action on the ground even as the security situation inside Afghanistan rapidly deteriorated. Similarly, even as China continued to raise its diplomatic engagement with Afghanistan, often reiterating its economic support as well, it refrained from undertaking any new major infrastructure or reconstruction project in Afghanistan. The work on copper mine project in Logar, south of the capital Kabul, for which China won the contract over 17 years ago, in late 2007, largely remained suspended for security and various other reasons. China's overall aid and assistance to Afghanistan also remained notably modest.

Since Xi Jinping came to power and as the BRI unfolded, Chinese statements began to regularly refer to prospects of Afghanistan joining the BRI. China in its trilateral meetings with Pakistan and Afghanistan began stressing on the need for Afghanistan to join the CPEC. Otherwise, Chinese official statements would largely refer to traditionally friendly historical ties between the two countries, and how "China is ready" or "stands ready" to support Afghanistan in its economic endeavours but within its *limited* capacities. The official statements would generally close with the visiting Afghan leaders and ministers endorsing 'One-China' policy, the BRI, and the need to jointly fight the ETIM. Beijing's Afghan policy during the period remained low on economic assistance and investment but high on diplomatic posturing and optics.

Despite making regular references to China-centric trans-regional connectivity agendas in its talks with Kabul, Beijing never backed them up with financial instruments and resources required to implement them on the ground. Now, with the Taliban regime in Kabul, and claiming to be in full territorial control of Afghanistan, will the Chinese approach remain the same, low-cost and off the ground, or perhaps a more pertinent question would be, can China afford to keep it that way?

NOTES

1 Zuqian Zhang, "Beijing Calling", *NATO Review*, Autumn 2003, at http://www.nato.int/docu/review/2003/issue3/english/special.html.

2 "China Active in Global Counter-Terrorism", Chinese Ministry of Foreign Affair, 10 September 2002, at http://www.fmprc.gov.cn/ce/cegv/eng/zt/zgfk/t89060.htm.

3 "Remarks with Chinese Minister of Foreign Affairs Tang Jiaxuan after their Meeting", US Department of State, 21 September 2002, at https://2001-2009.state.gov/secretary/former/powell/remarks/2001/5005.htm.

4 Senate Foreign Relations Committee Hearing, Fiscal Year 2003, Foreign Affairs Budget, 5 February 2002.

5 "Fact Sheet: International Contributions to the War Against Terrorism", US Department of Defense, 14 June 2002.

6 "Foreign Minister Tang Jiaxuan Attended the Foreign Ministers' Meeting on the Afghan Issue", Chinese Ministry of Foreign Affairs, 14 November 2001, at http://www.fmprc.gov.cn/mfa_eng/wjb_663304/zzjg_663340/yzs_663350/gjlb_663354/2676_663356/2678_663360/t15825.shtml.

7 Francesco Sisci, "China Breaks its Silence", *Asia Times Online*, 28 November 2001, at http://www.atimes.com/china/CK28Ad01.html.

8 Ibid.

9 "East Turkistan Terrorist Forces Cannot Get Away with Impunity", State Council Information Office of China, 21 January 2002. It is interesting to note that exactly a year after the 9/11 attacks, the ETIM was added to the UN Sanctions List on 11 September 2002, at the request of Afghanistan, Kyrgyzstan, the US, and China. See "Security Council Committee Adds Name of an Individual and an Entity to its List", UN Press Release, SC/7502, 11 September 2002, at https://press.un.org/en/2002/sc7502.doc.htm.

10 "Spokesperson on China's Role in the Future Reconstruction of Afghanistan", Chinese Ministry of Foreign Affairs, 14 December 2001, at https://www.fmprc.gov.cn/eng/gjhdq_665435/2675_665437/2676_663356/2679_663362/202406/t20240607_11406373.html.

11 "President Jiang Zemin Meets Chairman Hamid Karzai of the Afghan Interim Government", Chinese Ministry of Foreign Affairs, 25 January 2002, at http://www.fmprc.gov.cn/mfa_eng/wjb_663304/zzjg_663340/yzs_663350/gjlb_663354/2676_663356/2678_663360/t15827.shtml.

12 "Afghanistan-China Relations Excellent: Karzai", *People's Daily Online*, 27 March 2002, at http://english.peopledaily.com.cn/200203/26/eng20020326_92826.shtml.

13 "The Embassy of the People's Republic of China in Afghanistan Will Officially Reopen on February 6", Chinese Ministry of Foreign Affairs, 29 January 2002, at https://www.fmprc.gov.cn/eng/gjhdq_665435/2675_665437/2676_663356/2679_663362/202406/t20240607_11406378.html.

14 "Chinese Diplomats Arrive in Kabul", *People's Daily Online*, 20 December 2001, at http://en.people.cn/200112/19/eng20011219_87036.shtml.

15 "Former Afghan King Met with Foreign Minister Tang Jiaxuan", Chinese Ministry of Foreign Affairs, 21 May 2002, at http://www.fmprc.gov.cn/eng/wjb/zzjg/yzs/gjlb/2676/2678/t15831.htm.

16 "Foreign Minister Tang Jiaxuan Held Talks with His Afghan Counterpart", Chinese Ministry of Foreign Affairs, 21 May 2002, at http://www.fmprc.gov.cn/mfa_eng/wjb_663304/zzjg_663340/yzs_663350/gjlb_663354/2676_663356/2678_663360/t15832.shtml.

17 "Vice President Zeng Qinghong Holds Talks with Afghan Vice President Nimartullah Shaharani", Chinese Ministry of Foreign Affairs, 28 May 2003, at https://www.fmprc.gov.cn/eng/gjhdq_665435/2675_665437/2676_663356/2678_663360/202406/t20240607_11406273.html.

18 "Li Zhaoxing Meets with Afghan Foreign Minister", Chinese Ministry of Foreign Affairs, 10 March 2004, at http://www.fmprc.gov.cn/mfa_eng/wjb_663304/zzjg_663340/yzs_663350/gjlb_663354/2676_663356/2678_663360/t72653.shtml.

19 "China to Write Off Huge Afghan Debt", *China Daily*, 28 March 2004, at http://www.chinadaily.com.cn/english/doc/2004-03/28/content_318619.htm.

20 "Statement by H.E. Sun Yuxi Deputy Head of the Chinese Delegation on Security, Rule of Law and Reforms–the Challenges Ahead at the International Conference on Afghanistan",

Chinese Ministry of Foreign Affairs, 1 April 2004, at https://www.fmprc.gov.cn/eng/gjhdq_665435/2675_665437/2676_663356/2680_663364/202406/t20240607_11406445.html.

21 "Mystery Surrounds Attack on Road Workers", *China Daily*, 13 June 2004, at http://www.chinadaily.com.cn/english/doc/2004-06/13/content_338972.htm. Also see, Sayed Salahuddin, "Bodies of Chinese Workers Flown to Afghan Capital", *Reuters*, 11 June 2004, at http://www.afghanistannewscenter.com/news/2004/june/jun122004.html.

22 "Unknown Militants Attack Chinese Construction Camp in Afghanistan", *Pak Tribune*, 6 December 2006.

23 Syed Anwer, "China Suggests Deepening Friendship, Trade with Afghanistan", *Pajhwok Afghan News*, 18 August 2005.

24 Ahmad Khalid Mowahid, "Beijing to Provide Kabul Military Equipment", *Pajhwok Afghan News*, 23 October 2005, at http://www.pajhwak.com/viewstory.asp?lng=eng&id=8023.

25 "China Pledges to Strengthen Military Ties with Afghanistan", *Xinhua*, 19 June 2006, at http://news.xinhuanet.com/english/2006-06/19/content_4715712.htm.

26 Ahmad Khalid Mowahid, "China to Train Afghan Soldiers on Logistics", *Pajhwok Afghan News*, 24 June 2006, at http://www.pajhwak.com/viewstory.asp?lng=eng&id=20374.

27 "China, Afghanistan Vow to Strengthen Military Co-op", *Xinhua*, 31 October 2006, at http://news.xinhuanet.com/english/2006-10/31/content_5271908.htm.

28 "Chinese DM Holds Talk with Afghan Counterpart", *People's Daily Online*, 24 July 2012, at http://english.peopledaily.com.cn/90786/7885062.html; "Defense Minister Liang Guanglie Holds Talk with Afghan Defense Minister Wardak", Chinese Embassy in the Islamic Republic of Afghanistan, 23 July 2012, at http://af.china-embassy.org/eng/zagx/sbgx/t1099454.htm.

29 "Treaty of Good-Neighbourly Friendship and Cooperation", Ministry of Foreign Affairs, Islamic Republic of Afghanistan, at http://www.mfa.gov.af/Documents/ImportantDoc/Afghanistan-China%20Frienship%20accord.pdf.

30 "Treaty of China-Afghanistan Friendship, Cooperation and Good-Neighbourly Relations Takes Effect", Chinese Ministry of Foreign Affairs, 14 August 2008, at http://www.fmprc.gov.cn/eng/wjb/zzjg/yzs/gjlb/2676/2678/t484518.shtml.

31 "Full Text of Joint Statement between China, Afghanistan", *People's Daily Online*, 21 June 2006. Also see Appendix II.

32 Qin Jize, "China, Afghanistan Sign Deals to Fight Terrorism", *China Daily*, 20 June 2006, at http://www.chinadaily.com.cn/china/2006-06/20/content_620943.htm.

33 "China Donates Stuffs Worth 1 Mln USD to Afghanistan", *People's Daily Online*, 10 November 2006, at http://english.people.com.cn/200611/10/eng20061110_320066.html.

34 "Foreign Minister Yang Jiechi Attends the International Conference in Support of Afghanistan", Chinese Ministry of Foreign Affairs, 13 June 2008, at http://www.fmprc.gov.cn/mfa_eng/wjb_663304/zzjg_663340/yzs_663350/gjlb_663354/2676_663356/2678_663360/t465642.shtml.

35 "Vice Foreign Minister Wu Dawei Attends International Conference on Afghanistan", Chinese Ministry of Foreign Affairs, 1 April 2009, at https://www.fmprc.gov.cn/eng/gjhdq_665435/3265_665445/3341_664690/3343_664694/202406/t20240611_11422629.html.

36 Zhang Haizhou, "Afghanistan Asks For Help to Combat Terrorism", *China Daily*, 11 June 2009, at https://www.chinadaily.com.cn/cndy/2009-06/11/content_8270288.htm.

37 "Foreign Ministry Spokesperson Qin Gang's Regular Press Conference on June 11, 2009",

Chinese Ministry of Foreign Affairs, 12 June 2009, at https://www.worldaffairsboard.com/index.php?threads/the-uks-fishing-for-china.29786/page-2#post-816214.

38 "China Slams Clinton's June 4 Comments", *China Daily*, 5 June 2009, at https://www.chinadaily.com.cn/china/2009-06/05/content_8250388.htm.

39 Russell Hsiao and Glen E. Howard, "China Builds Closer Ties to Afghanistan through Wakhan Corridor", *China Brief*, Jamestown Foundation, Vol. 10, Issue 1, 7 January 2010, at https://jamestown.org/program/china-builds-closer-ties-to-afghanistan-through-wakhan-corridor/.

40 Ibid.

41 "Afghan President Karzai Meets with Yang Jiechi", Chinese Ministry of Foreign Affairs, 26 January 2010, at http://www.fmprc.gov.cn/mfa_eng/wjb_663304/zzjg_663340/yzs_663350/gjlb_663354/2676_663356/2678_663360/t654227.shtml.

42 "Yang Jiechi Attends the London Conference on Afghanistan and Delivers a Speech", Chinese Ministry of Foreign Affairs, 20 January 2010, at http://www.fmprc.gov.cn/mfa_eng/wjb_663304/zzjg_663340/yzs_663350/gjlb_663354/2676_663356/2678_663360/t654971.shtml.

43 Ibid.

44 Richard Weitz, "Karzai's State Visit Highlights Beijing's Afghan Priorities", *China Brief*, Vol. 10, No. 8, 16 April 2010, at http://www.jamestown.org/uploads/media/cb_010_41.pdf.

45 "Remarks by H.E. Yang Jiechi Minister of Foreign Affairs of the People's Republic of China at the International Afghanistan Conference Bonn", Chinese Ministry of Foreign Affairs, 6 December 2011, at http://www.fmprc.gov.cn/mfa_eng/wjb_663304/zzjg_663340/yzs_663350/gjlb_663354/2676_663356/2678_663360/t884443.shtml.

46 "First Afghan-Pak-China Trilateral Dialogue Held in Beijing", *Bakhtar News Agency*, 3 March 2012, at https://www.bakhtarnews.af/en/first-afghan-pak-china-trilateral-dialogue-held-in-beijing/.

47 "Interview: Afghanistan Welcomes China's Role in Peace Process", *Xinhua*, 18 September 2013, at http://news.xinhuanet.com/english/world/2013-09/18/c_132731879.htm.

48 "Hu Jintao Holds Talks with His Afghan Counterpart Karzai", Chinese Ministry of Foreign Affairs, 8 June 2012, at http://www.fmprc.gov.cn/eng/wjb/zzjg/yzs/xwlb/t941392.htm.

49 For details, see "Joint Declaration between The People's Republic of China and The Islamic Republic of Afghanistan on Establishing Strategic and Cooperative Partnership", Chinese Ministry of Foreign Affairs, 8 June 2012, at http://www.fmprc.gov.cn/eng/wjb/zzjg/yzs/xwlb/t939517.htm.

50 For details, see "Vice Foreign Minister Cheng Guoping Attends Vice Foreign Ministerial Level Consultation on Regional Security of SCO", Chinese Ministry of Foreign Affairs, 15 November 2012, at http://www.fmprc.gov.cn/eng/zxxx/t991773.htm.

51 See "Top Chinese Security Official Makes Surprise Visit to Afghanistan", *Xinhua*, 23 September 2012, at http://news.xinhuanet.com/english/china/2012-09/23/c_131867386.htm. Also see, "Foreign Ministry Spokesperson Hong Lei's Regular Press Conference", Chinese Ministry of Foreign Affairs, 24 September 2012, at http://www.fmprc.gov.cn/eng/xwfw/s2510/2511/t973835.htm.

52 "China and Afghanistan Sign Economic and Security Deals", *BBC News*, 23 September 2012, at http://www.bbc.com/news/world-asia-china-19693005.

53 "Xi Jinping Holds Talks with President Hamid Karzai of Afghanistan Stressing to Deepen Bilateral Strategic Cooperative Partnership and to Support Peace and Reconstruction Process

in Afghanistan", Chinese Ministry of Foreign Affairs, 27 September 2013, at http://www.fmprc.gov.cn/eng/wjb/zzjg/yzs/gjlb/2676/2678/t1083933.shtml.

54 Ibid.

55 "Li Keqiang Meets with President Hamid Karzai of Afghanistan, Stressing to Strengthen China-Afghanistan Traditional Friendship and to Promote Peace, Stability and Development of the Region", Chinese Ministry of Foreign Affairs, 27 September 2013, at http://www.fmprc.gov.cn/eng/wjb/zzjg/yzs/gjlb/2676/2678/t1083929.shtml.

56 "Wang Yi: China is Ready to Play a Role in Achieving Smooth Transition in Afghanistan", Chinese Ministry of Foreign Affairs, 26 September 2013, at http://www.fmprc.gov.cn/mfa_eng/wjb_663304/zzjg_663340/yzs_663350/gjlb_663354/2676_663356/2678_663360/t1082833.shtml.

57 "The Third China-Afghanistan-Pakistan Trilateral Dialogue Held in Kabul", Chinese Embassy in the Islamic Republic of Afghanistan, 10 December 2013, at http://af.china-embassy.gov.cn/eng/sgxw/201312/t20131210_1179052.htm.

58 "Wang Yi: China Calls for Joint Efforts to Assist Afghanistan's Triple Transition", Chinese Ministry of Foreign Affairs, 22 February 2014, at http://www.fmprc.gov.cn/mfa_eng/wjb_663304/zzjg_663340/yzs_663350/gjlb_663354/2676_663356/2678_663360/t1131886.shtml.

59 Ibid.

60 "Wang Yi: China Hopes to See a United, Stable, Developing and Amicable Afghanistan", Chinese Ministry of Foreign Affairs, 22 February 2014, at http://www.fmprc.gov.cn/mfa_eng/wjb_663304/zzjg_663340/yzs_663350/gjlb_663354/2676_663356/2678_663360/t1131887.shtml.

61 Ibid.

62 "Afghan President Hamid Karzai Meets with Wang Yi", Chinese Ministry of Foreign Affairs, 23 February 2014, at http://www.fmprc.gov.cn/mfa_eng/wjb_663304/zzjg_663340/yzs_663350/gjlb_663354/2676_663356/2678_663360/t1131896.shtml.

63 Craig Whitlock, "China Rebuffed U.S. Request to Open Route for Afghanistan War Supplies, Cables Show", *The Washington Post*, 3 July 2011, at https://www.washingtonpost.com/national/national-security/china-rebuffed-us-request-to-open-route-for-afghanistan-war-supplies-cables-show/2011/06/30/AG8cdYvH_story.html.

64 Zhang Haizhou, "US Seeks Bigger Role for China in Afghanistan", *China Daily*, 5 May 2010, at http://www.chinadaily.com.cn/world/2010-05/05/content_9809311.htm.

65 "Joint China-U.S. Training Program for Afghanistan Diplomats Holds Opening Ceremony", Chinese Embassy in the Islamic Republic of Afghanistan, 17 March 2013, at http://af.china-embassy.org/eng/zagx/sbgx/t1099461.htm.

66 ZTE was entrusted with the job of installing digital telephone switches and CDMA WLL equipments in 11 Provinces and the total subscriber lines in this project was 91,000 CDMA and fixed lines. Huawei was providing similar equipment in 12 provinces and the total subscriber lines in this project were 113,000 CDMA and fixed lines.

67 A detailed analysis was provided by Steven A. Zyck, "The Role of China in Afghanistan's Economic Development & Reconstruction", Civil Military Fusion Centre, March 2012, p. 2.

68 "Remarks by H.E. Deng Xijun, Chinese Ambassador to Afghanistan at 'My Chinese Dream' Speech Competition, Kabul," Chinese Embassy in the Islamic Republic of Afghanistan, 21 October 2013, at http://af.china-embassy.org/eng/dsxx/remarks/t1091235.htm.

69 Ibid.

70 Xu Feihong, "China's Always with Afghanistan", Chinese Embassy in the Islamic Republic of Afghanistan, 27 August 2011, at http://af.china-embassy.org/eng/dsxx/remarks/t852489.htm.

71 Zhao Huasheng, "China and Afghanistan: China's Interests, Stances, and Perspectives", A Report of the CSIS Russia and Eurasia Programme, Centre for Strategic and International Studies, Washington, D.C., March 2012, p. 7, at https://csis-website-prod.s3.amazonaws.com/s3fs-public/legacy_files/files/publication/120322_Zhao_ChinaAfghan_web.pdf.

72 Gleb Bryanski and Chris Buckley, "China's Hu Sees Role for Regional Bloc in Afghanistan", *Euronews*, 6 June 2012, at http://www.euronews.com/newswires/1541922-chinas-hu-sees-role-for-regional-bloc-in-afghanistan/.

73 James Risen, "U.S. Identifies Vast Mineral Riches in Afghanistan", *The New York Times*, 13 June 2010, at https://www.nytimes.com/2010/06/14/world/asia/14minerals.html.

74 The four other companies short listed for final bid were: Strikeforce, part of Russia's Basic Element Group; the London-based Kazakhmys Consortium; Hunter Dickinson of Canada; and the US copper mining firm, Phelps Dodge.

75 "Speech by Ambassador Yang Houlan at Reception for National Day", Chinese Ministry of Foreign Affairs, 29 September 2008, at http://www.fmprc.gov.cn/eng/wjb/zwjg/zwbd/t515714.htm.

76 Michael Stanley and Ekaterina Mikhaylova, "Mineral Resource Tenders and Mining Infrastructure Projects Guiding Principles, Case Study: The Aynak Copper Deposit, Afghanistan", *Extractive Industries for Development Series 22*, The World Bank, September 2011, p. 64.

77 "Based on the Long-Term Win-Win—Hutchison MCC Acquisition Aynak Copper Mine in Afghanistan", *Xinhua*, 4 June 2008, at http://news.xinhuanet.com/fortune/2008-06/04/content_8311160.htm.

78 Sajad, "Chinese Mine Workers Leave Afghanistan Due to Instability", *The Khaama Press*, 8 September 2012, at https://www.khaama.com/chinese-mine-workers-leave-afghanistan-due-to-instability-766/.

79 "Afghan Mining Deal with China Facing Failure", *Deutsche Welle*, 31 July 2013, at http://www.dw.de/afghan-mining-deal-with-china-facing-failure/a-16989797.

80 See Mirwais Harooni, "Afghanistan Signs Oil Development Deal with China", *Reuters*, 26 December 2011, at http://business.financialpost.com/2011/12/26/afghanistan-signs-oil-development-deal-with-china/.

81 "Ambassador Xu Feihong Attended the Signing Ceremony of Sino-Afghan Oil Exploitation Cooperation Project", Chinese Embassy in the Islamic Republic of Afghanistan, 9 January 2012, at http://af.china-embassy.gov.cn/eng/sgxw/201201/t20120109_1178544.htm.

82 "China, Afghanistan Sign First Oil Contract", *Chinese Network Television* (CNTV), 29 December 2011, at http://english.cntv.cn/program/newsupdate/20111229/107468.shtm.

83 Mustafa Basharat, "Chinese Enterprise Faces Tax Evasion Scam", *Pajhwok Afghan News*, 2 November 2007, at http://www.pajhwak.com/viewstory.asp?lng=eng&id=26865.

84 Steven A. Zyck, no. 135, pp. 5–6.

85 In July 2014, Chinese foreign ministry appointed Sun Yuxi, the former ambassador to Afghanistan (April 2002–January 2005), as its first special envoy on Afghan affairs. In November 2015, Sun Yuxi was succeeded by Deng Xijun, another former ambassador to Afghanistan (September 2013–October 2015).

86 "Ambassador Xu Feihong Pays a Courtesy Call to the Chairman of Mahas [*sic*] Meli of Afghanistan", Chinese Embassy in the Islamic Republic of Afghanistan, 28 August 2011, at http://af.china-embassy.gov.cn/eng/sgxw/201108/t20110828_1178421.htm; "Ambassador Xu Feihong Meets with the Head Secretary of Islamic Movement of Afghanistan," Chinese Embassy in the Islamic Republic of Afghanistan, 31 August 2011, at http://af.china-embassy.gov.cn/eng/sgxw/201108/t20110831_1178431.htm; "Ambassador Xu Feihong Pays a Courtesy Visit to the Leader of Jonbesh Meli Islami of Afghanistan", Chinese Embassy in the Islamic Republic of Afghanistan, 10 September 2011, at http://af.china-embassy.gov.cn/eng/sgxw/201109/t20110910_1178438.htm; "Ambassador Xu Feihong Visits the Chairman of Hakerat [*sic*] Islami of Afghanistan", Chinese Embassy in the Islamic Republic of Afghanistan, 25 September 2011, at http://af.china-embassy.gov.cn/eng/sgxw/201109/t20110925_1178467.htm; "Ambassador Xu Feihong Meets Leader of Afghan Liberal Party", Chinese Embassy in the Islamic Republic of Afghanistan, 10 June 2013, at http://af.china-embassy.gov.cn/eng/sgxw/201307/t20130701_1178829.htm; "Ambassador Xu Feihong Pays a Farewell Call to Chairman of National Front of Afghanistan", 17 July 2013, at http://af.china-embassy.gov.cn/eng/sgxw/201307/t20130718_1178860.htm.

87 "Afghanistan Forces Defend Kunduz from Taliban", *BBC*, 7 May 2015, at http://www.bbc.com/news/world-asia-32620595.

88 "'Unprecedented' Surge of Militants Plagues Afghanistan, UN Told", RFE/RL, 24 June 2015, at http://www.rferl.org/content/afghanistan-unprecedented-surge-militants-un-told/27090111.html.

89 "Wang Yi Holds Talks with Foreign Minister of Afghanistan Zarar Ahmed Moqbel Osmani", Chinese Embassy in the Islamic Republic of Afghanistan, 23 February 2014, at http://af.china-embassy.gov.cn/eng/sgxw/201402/t20140225_1179130.htm.

90 "Wang Yi: China Hopes to See a United, Stable, Developing and Amicable Afghanistan", Chinese Ministry of Foreign Affairs, 22 February 2014, at http://www.fmprc.gov.cn/mfa_eng/wjb_663304/zzjg_663340/yzs_663350/gjlb_663354/2676_663356/2678_663360/t1131887.shtml.

91 Ibid.

92 "Afghan President Hamid Karzai Meets with Wang Yi", Chinese Ministry of Foreign Affairs, 23 February 2014, at http://www.fmprc.gov.cn/mfa_eng/wjb_663304/zzjg_663340/yzs_663350/gjlb_663354/2676_663356/2678_663360/t1131896.shtml.

93 "Wang Yi Meets with Afghan President's National Security Advisor Rangin Dadfar Spanta", Chinese Ministry of Foreign Affairs, 23 February 2014, at http://af.china-embassy.gov.cn/eng/sgxw/201402/t20140225_1179134.htm.

94 "Three Chinese Citizens were Killed in Kabul", Chinese Embassy in the Islamic Republic of Afghanistan, 9 August 2013, at http://af.china-embassy.gov.cn/eng/sgxw/201308/t20130811_1178922.htm.

95 "Special Envoy of the Chinese Foreign Ministry on Afghan Affairs Sun Yuxi Holds Press Conference for Chinese and Afghan Media", Chinese Ministry of Foreign Affairs, 26 July 2014, at http://www.fmprc.gov.cn/mfa_eng/wjb_663304/zzjg_663340/yzs_663350/gjlb_663354/2676_663356/2678_663360/t1178881.shtml.

96 "Viewpoint: Can China Bring Peace to Afghanistan?", *BBC News*, 1 December 2014, at https://www.bbc.com/news/world-asia-30273431.

97 "Xi Jinping Holds Talks with President Ashraf Ghani of Afghanistan, Stressing China Values

Developing China-Afghanistan Strategic Cooperative Partnership and Hopes Afghanistan Achieve Enduring Peace and Stable Development", Embassy of the People's Republic of China in the Islamic Republic of Afghanistan, 29 October 2014, at http://af.china-embassy.org/eng/zagx/sbgx/t1206560.htm.

98 Ibid.

99 "Li Keqiang Meets with President Ashraf Ghani of Afghanistan", Chinese Ministry of Foreign Affairs, 29 October 2014, at http://www.fmprc.gov.cn/mfa_eng/wjb_663304/zzjg_663340/yzs_663350/gjlb_663354/2676_663356/2678_663360/t1206032.shtml.

100 It was during the Third Ministerial Conference held in Almaty, Kazakhstan in April 2013 that China offered to host the Fourth Ministerial Conference. The conference was originally slated to be held on 29 August 2014 in the Tianjin city of China, but had to be postponed by two months due to the election crisis in Afghanistan.

101 "Speech by H.E. Li Keqiang, Premier of the State Council of the People's Republic of China, at the Opening Ceremony of the Fourth Ministerial Conference of the Istanbul Process on Afghanistan", Chinese Ministry of Foreign Affairs, 31 October 2014, at https://www.mfa.gov.cn/eng/xw/zyjh/202405/t20240530_11340792.html.

102 Ibid.

103 "Statement by President Ghani at the 4th Ministerial Conference of the Istanbul Process on Afghanistan ", Office of the President, Islamic Republic of Afghanistan, 31 October 2014, at http://president.gov.af/en/news/statement-by-president-ghani-at-heart-of-asia-istanbul-process-4th-ministerial-conference. The statement is also available at former President Ghani's official Facebook Page, at https://www.facebook.com/photo.php?fbid=10152565773238292&id=34246523291&set=a.10151533396518292.

104 Ibid.

105 "Wang Yi: China has Always Been Responsible Supporter, Contributor and Constructor on the Afghan Issue", Chinese Ministry of Foreign Affairs, 1 November 2014, at http://www.fmprc.gov.cn/mfa_eng/wjb_663304/zzjg_663340/yzs_663350/gjlb_663354/2676_663356/2678_663360/t1207125.shtml.

106 "Wang Yi: China is Willing to Play Constructive Role in Peaceful Reconciliation Process of Afghanistan", Chinese Ministry of Foreign Affairs, 1 November 2014, at http://www.fmprc.gov.cn/mfa_eng/wjb_663304/zzjg_663340/yzs_663350/gjlb_663354/2676_663356/2678_663360/t1207127.shtml.

107 Tahir Khan, "Afghan Reconciliation: Senior Taliban Negotiator Visits Pakistan", *The Express Tribune*, 22 February 2015, at http://tribune.com.pk/story/842260/afghan-reconciliation-senior-taliban-negotiator-visits-pakistan/.

108 Jessica Donati, "Exclusive – China Seeks Greater Role in Afghanistan with Peace Talk Push", *Reuters*, 11 November 2014, at http://in.reuters.com/article/us-afghanistan-china-idINKCN0IV1ED20141111.

109 "Statement by Adviser to the Prime Minister on National Security and Foreign Affairs [.] Fourth Ministerial Conference of the Heart of Asia-Istanbul Process Beijing, 31 October 2014", Pakistan Embassy, Beijing, 5 November 2014, at https://pakbj.org/upload/20250103/c54dfc5165e14eeda82f26c720058f8c.pdf.

110 Press Release No PR249/2014-ISPR, Inter Services Public Relations (ISPR), 14 November 2014, at https://www.ispr.gov.pk/front/main.asp?o=t-press_release&date=2014/11/14.

111 "Pakistan and Afghanistan Reaffirm Resolve to Transform Bilateral Relationship", Pakistan

Ministry of Foreign Affairs, 15 November 2014, at http://www.mofa.gov.pk/pr-details.php?mm=MjM2NA,,.

112 "Assistant Foreign Minister Liu Jianchao Meets with Deputy Foreign Minister Hekmat Khalil Karzai of Afghanistan", Chinese Ministry of Foreign Affairs, 8 February 2015, at https://www.fmprc.gov.cn/eng/gjhdq_665435/2675_665437/2676_663356/2678_663360/202406/t20240607_11406351.html.

113 "President Ashraf Ghani of Afghanistan Meets with Assistant Foreign Minister Liu Jianchao", Chinese Ministry of Foreign Affairs, 9 February 2015, at https://www.fmprc.gov.cn/eng/gjhdq_665435/2675_665437/2676_663356/2678_663360/202406/t20240607_11406352.html.

114 "First Round of China-Afghanistan-Pakistan Trilateral Strategic Dialogue Held in Kabul", Chinese Ministry of Foreign Affairs, 10 February 2015, at http://www.fmprc.gov.cn/mfa_eng/wjb_663304/zzjg_663340/yzs_663350/gjlb_663354/2676_663356/2678_663360/t1236606.shtml.

115 "Wang Yi: Addressing the Issue of Afghanistan Requires Reinforced Support in Four Aspects", Chinese Ministry of Foreign Affairs, 12 February 2015, at http://www.fmprc.gov.cn/mfa_eng/wjb_663304/zzjg_663340/yzs_663350/gjlb_663354/2676_663356/2678_663360/t1238074.shtml.

116 "Wang Yi: Addressing the Issue of Afghanistan Requires Reinforced Support in Four Aspects", Chinese Ministry of Foreign Affairs, 12 February 2015, at http://www.fmprc.gov.cn/mfa_eng/wjb_663304/zzjg_663340/yzs_663350/gjlb_663354/2676_663356/2678_663360/t1238074.shtml.

117 Hamid Shalizi, "Afghans Arrested Chinese Uygurs to Aid Taliban Talks Bid: Officials", *Reuters*, 20 February 2015, at http://in.reuters.com/article/afghanistan-taliban-china-idINKBN0LO18220150220.

118 "Prime Minister's Remarks at Joint Press Stakeout", Pakistan Ministry of Foreign Affairs, 12 May 2015, at http://www.mofa.gov.pk/pr-details.php?mm=Mjc4NQ,,.

119 Margherita Stancati, "Afghan Peace Envoy Met Taliban in Secret China Talks", *The Wall Street Journal*, 24 May 2015, at http://www.wsj.com/articles/afghan-peace-envoy-met-taliban-in-secret-china-talks-1432486585.

120 "We Strongly Reject Propaganda of Meeting with Representatives of Kabul Administration in China", *Shahamat*, 24 May 2015, at http://shahamat-english.com/we-strongly-reject-propaganda-of-meeting-with-representatives-of-kabul-administration-in-china/.

121 Baqir Sajjad Syed, "Afghan Govt, Taliban Negotiators to Meet in a Week, Says Aziz", *Dawn*, 23 June 2015, at http://www.dawn.com/news/1189909.

122 "Wang Yi Meets with Foreign Minister Salahuddin Rabbani of Afghanistan", Chinese Ministry of Foreign Affairs, 5 June 2015, at http://www.fmprc.gov.cn/mfa_eng/wjb_663304/zzjg_663340/yzs_663350/gjlb_663354/2676_663356/2678_663360/t1271722.shtml.

123 "Xi Jinping Meets with President Mohammad Ashraf Ghani of Afghanistan", Chinese Ministry of Foreign Affairs, 10 July 2015, at http://www.fmprc.gov.cn/mfa_eng/wjb_663304/zzjg_663340/yzs_663350/gjlb_663354/2676_663356/2678_663360/t1281508.shtml.

124 "Foreign Minister Wang Yi Holds Telephone Talks with Pakistani and Afghan Senior Officials at Request", Chinese Ministry of Foreign Affairs, 9 September 2015, at http://www.fmprc.gov.cn/mfa_eng/wjb_663304/zzjg_663340/yzs_663350/gjlb_663354/2676_663356/2678_663360/t1295880.shtml.

125 "Address by H.E. Li Yuanchao Vice President of the People's Republic of China at the Reception of the 60th Anniversary Of China-Afghanistan Diplomatic Relations", Chinese Ministry of Foreign Affairs, 4 November 2015, at http://www.fmprc.gov.cn/mfa_eng/wjb_663304/zzjg_663340/yzs_663350/gjlb_663354/2676_663356/2678_663360/t1311793.shtml.

126 Ibid.

127 "Li Yuanchao Met with Afghan Chief Executive Officer Abdullah Abdullah", Chinese Ministry of Foreign Affairs, 4 November 2015, at http://www.fmprc.gov.cn/mfa_eng/wjb_663304/zzjg_663340/yzs_663350/gjlb_663354/2676_663356/2678_663360/t1311791.shtml.

128 "The Islamabad Declaration", Heart of Asia-Istanbul Process: Enhanced Cooperation for Countering Security Threats and Promoting Connectivity in the Heart of Asia Region, Islamabad, Pakistan Ministry of Foreign Affairs, 9 December 2015, at http://www.mofa.gov.pk/documents/IslamabadDeclaration9Dec2015.pdf.

129 "China-Pakistan-Afghanistan Trilateral Meeting", Pakistan Ministry of Foreign Affairs, Press Release, 9 December 2015, at http://www.mofa.gov.pk/pr-details.php?mm=MzMyNQ,,.

130 "Statement of the Trilateral Meeting Among Afghanistan, Pakistan and the United States", Pakistan Ministry of Foreign Affairs, 9 December 2015, at http://www.mofa.gov.pk/pr-details.php?mm=MzMyNA,,.

131 "Statement of the Quadrilateral Meeting Among Afghanistan, Pakistan, China and the United States", Pakistan Ministry of Foreign Affairs, Press Release, 9 December 2015, at http://www.mofa.gov.pk/pr-details.php?mm=MzMyMw,,.

132 "Joint Press Release of the Quadrilateral Coordination Group on Afghan Peace and Reconciliation", US Department of State, 11 January 2016, at http://www.state.gov/r/pa/prs/ps/2016/01/251105.htm.

133 "Opening Statement of Mr. Sartaj Aziz, Adviser to the Prime Minister on Foreign Affairs at the First Meeting of the Quadrilateral Contact Group (QCG) of Afghanistan, China, Pakistan and the United States on Afghan Reconciliation Process", Pakistan Ministry of Foreign Affairs, 11 January 2016, at https://mofa.gov.pk/opening-statement-of-mr-sartaj-aziz-adviser-to-the-prime-minister-on-foreign-affairs-at-the-first-meeting-of-the-quadrilateral-contact-group-qcg-of-afghanistan-china-pakistan-and-the-united-stat/.

134 Ibid.

135 Ibid.

136 According to a report published in the *Express Tribune*, the panellists at the conference included Dr Muhammad Khan of the National Defence University of Pakistan; Dr Andrew Small, author of *The China-Pakistan Axis: Asia's New Geopolitics*; Pakistan Senator Afrasiab Khattak; Deputy Leader of the National Islamic Front of Afghanistan Sayed Hamed Gailani; and Prof Li Xiguang of Tsinghua University, Beijing. See "Trilateral Dialogue: Curtain Raiser Opens the Dialogue", *Express Tribune*, 10 January 2016, at http://tribune.com.pk/story/1024803/trilateral-dialogue-curtain-raiser-opens-the-dialogue/.

137 "Keynote Address by Mr. Sartaj Aziz, Adviser to the Prime Minister on Foreign Affairs at the Third China-Afghanistan-Pakistan Trilateral Dialogue", Pakistan Ministry of Foreign Affairs, 11 January 2016, at https://mofa.gov.pk/keynote-address-by-mr-sartaj-aziz-adviser-to-the-prime-minister-on-foreign-affairs-at-the-third-china-afghanistan-pakistan-trilateral-dialogue/.

138 "Wang Yi Holds Talks with Foreign Minister Salahuddin Rabbani of Afghanistan", Chinese Ministry of Foreign Affairs, 26 January 2016, at https://www.fmprc.gov.cn/eng/gjhdq_665435/2675_665437/2676_663356/2678_663360/201601/t20160128_509558.html.

139 "Wang Yi: China is Always Trustworthy and Reliable Partner of Afghanistan on its Way to Peace", Chinese Ministry of Foreign Affairs, 26 January 2016, at https://www.fmprc.gov.cn/eng/gjhdq_665435/2675_665437/2676_663356/2678_663360/201601/t20160128_509561.html.

140 "Foreign Ministry Comment on Developments in Afghanistan", Russian Ministry of Foreign Affairs, 3 June 2016, at https://mid.ru/en/maps/af/1529468/.

141 "Joint Statement between the People's Republic of China and the Islamic Republic of Afghanistan", Chinese Ministry of Foreign Affairs, 18 May 2016, at https://www.mfa.gov.cn/eng/zy/gb/202405/t20240531_11367329.html.

142 Ibid.

143 "China, Afghanistan and Pakistan Hold the First Round of Trilateral Practical Cooperation Dialogue", Chinese Ministry of Foreign Affairs, 28 May 2017, at https://www.fmprc.gov.cn/eng/gjhdq_665435/2675_665437/2676_663356/2678_663360/201706/t20170601_509637.html.

144 "Xi Jinping Meets with President Mohammad Ashraf Ghani of Afghanistan", Chinese Ministry of Foreign Affairs, 8 June 2017, at https://www.fmprc.gov.cn/eng/gjhdq_665435/2675_665437/2676_663356/2678_663360/201706/t20170612_509645.html.

145 "Li Keqiang Meets with Chief Executive Officer Abdullah Abdullah of Afghanistan", Chinese Ministry of Foreign Affairs, 1 December 2017, at https://www.fmprc.gov.cn/eng/gjhdq_665435/2675_665437/2676_663356/2678_663360/201712/t20171205_509663.html.

146 Praveen Swami, "Key Taliban Leader Removed from U.N. Sanctions List", *The Hindu*, 29 July 2016, at https://www.thehindu.com/news/international/key-taliban-leader-removed-from-un-sanctions-list/article3663060.ece.

147 "Press Release on Trilateral Consultations on Afghanistan in Moscow", Russian Ministry of Foreign Affairs, 27 December 2016, at https://mid.ru/en/maps/af/1540097/.

148 "Press Release on Six-party Consultations on Afghanistan in Moscow", Russian Ministry of Foreign Affairs, 15 February 2017, at https://mid.ru/en/maps/af/1542268/.

149 "Comment by the Information and Press Department on a Misinformation Campaign by Some Afghan Media Outlets", Russian Ministry of Foreign Affairs, 8 April 2017, at https://mid.ru/en/maps/af/1545141/.

150 "Press Release on Regional Consultations on Afghanistan in Moscow", Russian Ministry of Foreign Affairs, 14 April 2017, at https://mid.ru/en/maps/af/1545411/.

151 "Foreign Minister Sergey Lavrov's Opening Remarks at Talks with Former President of Afghanistan Hamid Karzai, Moscow, April 25, 2017", Russian Ministry of Foreign Affairs, 25 April 2017, at https://mid.ru/en/maps/af/1546069/.

152 "Comment by the Information and Press Department on Repeated Accusations of Russian Support for the Taliban", Russian Ministry of Foreign Affairs, 23 May 2017, at https://mid.ru/en/maps/af/1547291/; "Comment by the Information and Press Department on the Activities of 'Unidentified' Aircraft in Afghanistan", Russian Ministry of Foreign Affairs, 30 May 2017, at https://mid.ru/en/maps/af/1547595/.

153 "The Joint Press Release of the Second Round China-Afghanistan-Pakistan Practical Cooperation Dialogue", Pakistan Embassy, Beijing, 27 September 2017, at http://www.pakbj.org/index.php?m=content&c=index&a=show&catid=12&id=143.

154 "Wang Yi: China-Afghanistan-Pakistan Foreign Ministers' Dialogue Seeks No Replacement of

the Existing Mechanisms", Chinese Ministry of Foreign Affairs, 26 December 2017, at https://www.fmprc.gov.cn/eng/gjhdq_665435/2675_665437/2676_663356/2678_663360/201712/t20171228_509666.html.

155 Ibid.

156 "Wang Yi Talks about Eight Major Consensus Reached at the 1st China-Afghanistan-Pakistan Foreign Ministers' Dialogue", Chinese Ministry of Foreign Affairs, 26 December 2017, at https://www.fmprc.gov.cn/eng/gjhdq_665435/2675_665437/2676_663356/2678_663360/201712/t20171228_509669.html.

157 Ibid.

158 "China, Afghanistan and Pakistan Hold the 3rd Trilateral Practical Cooperation Dialogue", Chinese Ministry of Foreign Affairs, 28 May 2018, at https://www.fmprc.gov.cn/eng/gjhdq_665435/2675_665437/2757_663518/2759_663522/202406/t20240607_11411991.html.

159 "Foreign Minister Sergey Lavrov's Remarks at the International High-Level Conference on Afghanistan: 'Peace Process, Security Cooperation and Regional Connectivity', Tashkent, March 27, 2018", Russian Ministry of Foreign Affairs, 27 March 2018, at https://mid.ru/en/maps/af/1566946/.

160 Ibid.

161 "Xi Jinping Meets with President Mohammad Ashraf Ghani of Afghanistan", Chinese Ministry of Foreign Affairs, 10 June 2018, at https://www.fmprc.gov.cn/eng/gjhdq_665435/2675_665437/2676_663356/2678_663360/201806/t20180612_509709.html.

162 "China to Continue to Help Promote Afghan Reconciliation, Reconstruction: Premier", Chinese Ministry of Foreign Affairs, 13 October 2018, at https://www.fmprc.gov.cn/eng/gjhdq_665435/2675_665437/2676_663356/2678_663360/201810/t20181015_509715.html.

163 "Statement of the Ministry of Foreign Affairs of the Islamic Republic of Afghanistan on the Onset of the Moscow Meeting", Afghan Ministry of Foreign Affairs, 9 November 2018, at https://www.mfa.gov.af/press-releases/statement-of-the-ministry-of-foreign-affairs-of-the-islamic-republic-of-afghanistan-on-the-onset-of-the-moscow-meeting.html.

164 "Foreign Minister Sergey Lavrov's Remarks at the Second Meeting of the Moscow Format Consultations on Afghanistan, Moscow, November 9, 2018", Russian Ministry of Foreign Affairs, 9 November 2018, at https://mid.ru/en/maps/af/1577961/.

165 Bill Roggio, "At Moscow Conference, Taliban Refers to Itself as the 'Islamic Emirate' 61 Times", *Long War Journal*, 9 November 2018, at https://www.longwarjournal.org/archives/2018/11/at-moscow-conference-taliban-refers-to-itself-as-the-islamic-emirate-61-times.php.

166 "Remarks by Spokesman of Islamic Emirate regarding Moscow Conference", Al Emarah, 8 November 2018, at http://www.alemarah-english.org/?p=37276.

167 "Joint Statement of the 2nd Afghanistan-China-Pakistan Foreign Ministers' Dialogue", Chinese Ministry of Foreign Affairs, 17 December 2018, at https://www.fmprc.gov.cn/eng/wjdt_665385/2649_665393/201812/t20181217_679554.html.

168 Ibid.

169 "Foreign Ministers of China, Afghanistan and Pakistan Hold Second Dialogue", Chinese Ministry of Foreign Affairs, 15 December 2018, at https://www.fmprc.gov.cn/eng/gjhdq_665435/2675_665437/2757_663518/2759_663522/202406/t20240607_11412021.html.

170 "Wang Yi Talks About the Six Aspects of Consensus Reached at China-Afghanistan-Pakistan Foreign Ministers' Dialogue", Chinese Ministry of Foreign Affairs, 15 December 2018, at

https://www.fmprc.gov.cn/eng/gjhdq_665435/2675_665437/2676_663356/2678_663360/201812/t20181225_509726.html.

171 "Joint Statement of the 3rd China-Afghanistan-Pakistan Foreign Ministers' Dialogue", Pakistan Ministry of Foreign Affairs, 7 September 2019, at https://mofa.gov.pk/joint-statement-of-the-3rd-china-afghanistan-pakistan-foreign-ministers-dialogue/.

172 "Wang Yi on the Three Principles on the Political Arrangement for Afghanistan in the Future", Chinese Ministry of Foreign Affairs, 8 September 2019, at https://www.fmprc.gov.cn/eng/gjhdq_665435/2675_665437/2676_663356/2678_663360/201909/t20190910_509750.html.

173 Donald J. Trump, X Post (formerly Twitter), 8 September 2019, 4:21 AM, at https://twitter.com/realDonaldTrump/status/1170469618177236992.

174 Shamil Shams, "Afghan Taliban Meet with Chinese Officials After Talks with US Collapse", *Deutsche Welle* (DW), 22 September 2019, at https://www.dw.com/en/afghan-taliban-meet-with-chinese-officials-after-talks-with-us-collapse/a-50540037; Abdul Qadir Sediqi and Rupam Jain, "Afghanistan's Taliban meets Chinese government in Beijing", *Reuters*, 22 September 2019, at https://www.reuters.com/article/us-afghanistan-taliban-china-idUSKBN1W70I3.

175 "Taliban Delegation Holds Talks in China as Part of Peace Push", *Reuters*, 20 June 2019, at https://www.reuters.com/article/us-china-afghanistan-idUSKCN1TL0V9.

176 "Wang Yi Meets with Former President Hamid Karzai of Afghanistan", Chinese Ministry of Foreign Affairs, 3 December 2019, at https://www.fmprc.gov.cn/eng/gjhdq_665435/2675_665437/2676_663356/2678_663360/201912/t20191205_509776.html.

177 "State Councilor and Foreign Minister Wang Yi Talked about Afghanistan at the Press Conference of the third Session of the 13th National people's Congress", Chinese Embassy in the Islamic Republic of Afghanistan, 25 May 2020, at http://af.china-embassy.gov.cn/eng/sgxw/202005/t20200525_1180576.htm.

178 "Joint Press Release of the 3rd Round China -Afghanistan-Pakistan Trilateral Vice Foreign Ministers' Strategic Dialogue", Chinese Embassy in the Islamic Republic of Afghanistan, 7 July 2020, at http://af.china-embassy.gov.cn/eng/sgxw/202007/t20200708_1180602.htm.

179 "Wang Yi Attends the First Video Opening Ceremony of Intra-Afghan Negotiations", Chinese Ministry of Foreign Affairs, 13 September 2020, at https://www.fmprc.gov.cn/eng/gjhdq_665435/2675_665437/2676_663356/2678_663360/202009/t20200915_509807.html.

180 "Remarks by State Councilor and Foreign Minister Wang Yi at the Ninth Ministerial Conference of The Heart of Asia-Istanbul Process", Chinese Ministry of Foreign Affairs, 30 March 2021, at https://www.fmprc.gov.cn/eng/gjhdq_665435/2675_665437/2676_663356/2678_663360/202103/t20210330_9168620.html.

181 "Wang Yi Elaborates China's Position on Current Situation in Afghanistan", Chinese Ministry of Foreign Affairs, 11 May 2021, at https://www.fmprc.gov.cn/eng/gjhdq_665435/2675_665437/2676_663356/2678_663360/202105/t20210512_9168626.html.

182 "Wang Yi Elaborates China's Position on Current Situation in Afghanistan", Chinese Ministry of Foreign Affairs, 11 May 2021, at https://www.fmprc.gov.cn/eng/gjhdq_665435/2675_665437/2676_663356/2678_663360/202105/t20210512_9168626.html.

183 "Joint Statement of the Fourth China-Afghanistan-Pakistan Trilateral Foreign Ministers' Dialogue—On Afghanistan's Peace and Reconciliation Process", Chinese Ministry of Foreign Affairs, 3 June 2021, at https://www.fmprc.gov.cn/eng/gjhdq_665435/2675_665437/2676_663356/2678_663360/202106/t20210604_9168629.html.

184 Ibid.

185 "Wang Yi Talks about the Five Propositions for Advancing Peace and Reconciliation in Afghanistan", Chinese Ministry of Foreign Affairs, 4 June 2023, at https://www.fmprc.gov.cn/eng/gjhdq_665435/2675_665437/2676_663356/2678_663360/202106/t20210604_9168632.html.

186 "Wang Yi Meets with Afghan Foreign Minister Mohammed Haneef Atmar", Chinese Ministry of Foreign Affairs, 15 July 2021, at https://www.fmprc.gov.cn/eng/gjhdq_665435/2675_665437/2676_663356/2678_663360/202107/t20210715_9168636.html.

187 "Xi Jinping Speaks with Afghan President Mohammad Ashraf Ghani on the Phone", Chinese Ministry of Foreign Affairs, 16 July 2021, at https://www.fmprc.gov.cn/eng/gjhdq_665435/2675_665437/2676_663356/2678_663360/202107/t20210717_9168637.html.

188 "External Security Commissioner of the Foreign Ministry Cheng Guoping Meets with Afghan Ambassador to China Javid Ahmad Qaem", Chinese Ministry of Foreign Affairs, 6 August 2021, at https://www.fmprc.gov.cn/eng/gjhdq_665435/2675_665437/2676_663356/2678_663360/202108/t20210807_9168639.html.

189 "Wang Yi Meets with Head of the Afghan Taliban Political Commission Mullah Abdul Ghani Baradar", Chinese Ministry of Foreign Affairs, 28 July 2021, at https://www.fmprc.gov.cn/eng/gjhdq_665435/2675_665437/2676_663356/2678_663360/202107/t20210729_9168638.html.

190 Ibid.

191 Ibid.

192 Ibid.

"*China is our most important partner and represents a fundamental and extraordinary opportunity for us, because it is ready to invest and rebuild our country...In addition, China is our pass to markets all over the world.*" *

—Taliban Spokesperson Zabihullah Mujahid to *la Repubblica*
1 September 2021.

* "Afghanistan: Taliban to Rely on Chinese Funds, Spokesperson Says", *Al Jazeera*, 2 September 2021, at https://www.aljazeera.com/news/2021/9/2/afghanistan-taliban-to-rely-on-chinese-money-spokesperson-says.

3

China and the Second Taliban 'Emirate'
Proactive Diplomatic Engagement

China was among the few countries—besides Russia, Iran and Pakistan—that kept its diplomatic mission open even as the Haqqani–Taliban fighters entered Kabul in mid-August 2021. It has since gone into a diplomatic overdrive to project itself as the 'most reliable friend' and a 'strategic partner' of the Afghan people. It has cast a web of diplomatic initiatives with its old trilateral mechanism with Pakistan and Afghanistan at the core of it. Beijing has added more and more layers to its diplomatic forays on the Afghan issue, drawing in Central Asian countries in the process. While Moscow has been engaged in a wider confrontation with the West in Ukraine over the past three years now, Beijing has been working overtime to expand and consolidate its diplomatic spheres to both north and south of Amu Darya. While much of what Beijing claims to be doing in the Taliban-led Afghanistan appears as high on optics and hope as before, nevertheless, given the changed ground situation in Afghanistan, it is worth examining the kind of diplomatic and economic initiatives it has (re)launched as the 'Islamic Emirate' continues to unfold.

China at G20 Foreign Ministers' Conference on Afghanistan

On 23 September 2021, Chinese Foreign Minister Wang Yi while speaking at the Group of 20 (G20) Foreign Ministers' Video Conference on Afghanistan stated that "the changes in the situation in Afghanistan have aroused widespread concern in the international community, and how it will evolve subsequently will have greater implications for international and regional peace and stability." He further remarked that "the destiny of Afghanistan is once again in the hands of the Afghan people, yet there is still uncertainty in its future development." He put forth five points as way forward on Afghanistan:

> First, humanitarian assistance is a task which brooks no delay. We should redouble efforts on and speed up the provision of assistance to Afghanistan, and in particular lend the Afghan people a helping hand in time to address their most urgent needs. China has decided to provide 200 million yuan worth of related materials to Afghanistan, including the donation of the first three million doses of COVID-19 vaccine.
>
> Second, economic sanctions must be stopped. All kinds of unilateral sanctions or restrictions on Afghanistan should be lifted. Afghanistan's foreign exchange reserves are its national assets, and should be owned by and used for the people, rather than being used as a bargaining chip to exert political pressure on Afghanistan.
>
> Third, interactions and contacts should be inclusive. On the premise of respecting the sovereignty, independence and territorial integrity of Afghanistan, we should support the Afghan people in independently choosing a development path suited to its national conditions and eventually building a broad and inclusive political structure which respects the basic rights of minority groups, women and children, and pursues a foreign policy of peace advocating good neighborliness with all countries, especially with neighboring countries.
>
> Fourth, counter-terrorism cooperation needs to be deepened. Afghanistan must earnestly honor its commitments by making a clean break with and resolutely fighting all kinds of international terrorist forces.
>
> Fifth, both the symptoms and root causes of the refugee issue must be addressed. The United States and the North Atlantic Treaty Organization (NATO) countries should take the primary responsibility for solving the issue of Afghan refugees and migrants. The economic reconstruction of Afghanistan is the fundamental solution to the issue of refugees and migrants.
>
> Sixth, mechanisms of all sorts should coordinate for higher synergistic effects. China supports the United Nations (UN) in acting as the main channel for maintaining peace and stability in Afghanistan and offering humanitarian assistance, and urges the UN Assistance Mission in

> Afghanistan (UNAMA) and other UN agencies to effectively carry out their responsibilities. China welcomes multilateral mechanisms on Afghanistan to give play to their respective advantages and pool efforts to assist Afghanistan.[1]

China at G20 Extraordinary Leaders' Meeting on Afghanistan

On 12 October 2021, President Xi Jinping's Special Representative, State Councilor and Foreign Minister Wang Yi attended the G20 Extraordinary Leaders' Meeting on Afghanistan held in Beijing via video link.

According to the Chinese foreign ministry press release, Wang Yi said that "Afghanistan today has come to a crossroads which may head to stability and prosperity or chaos and fall...Experience and lessons from Afghanistan over the past two decades have demonstrated again that the right way to get along between countries is the respect for independent choices of development paths, and mutual inclusiveness and mutual learning among different civilizations." He cautioned that "imposing one's own ideology on others, arbitrarily interfering in the internal affairs of other countries, or even resorting to military intervention will only bring about continuous turmoil and poverty, and cause serious humanitarian disasters." Wang Yi put forward four suggestions:

> First, put people's well-being first to help Afghanistan cope with the humanitarian crisis. China is accelerating the provision of emergency assistance to Afghanistan worth 200 million yuan in food, winter materials, vaccines and medicines.
>
> Second, pursue both current and long-term interests to drive Afghanistan onto an open and inclusive development path. The international community should proceed with dialogue and contact with all parties in Afghanistan from a rational and pragmatic perspective, support the Afghan people in independently choosing a development path suited to their national conditions, encourage and guide Afghanistan to eventually build a broad and inclusive political structure which implements moderate and prudent domestic and foreign policies.
>
> Third, adopt a zero-tolerance approach to ensure that Afghanistan keeps itself far away from terrorism.
>
> Fourth, build broad consensus to promote the formation of synergy among various mechanisms on Afghanistan. The G20 should uphold the role of

> the UN as the main channel for promoting peace and stability, as well as humanitarian assistance in Afghanistan, and push various multilateral mechanisms on Afghanistan to supplement one another and form synergy.[2]

Wang Yi–Mullah Baradar Meeting in Doha

On 25 October 2021, Foreign Minister Wang met with Acting Taliban Deputy Prime Minister Mullah Baradar in Doha during his visit to Qatar. He also met Acting Taliban Foreign Minister Amir Khan Muttaqi.

According to the Chinese foreign ministry press release, Wang Yi in his interaction with Mullah Baradar stated that Afghanistan is "standing at a critical stage of transforming from chaos to governance" and is "currently facing a historic opportunity to truly master its own destiny, achieve inclusiveness and reconciliation, and advance national reconstruction." He was of the view that "Afghanistan is facing quadruple challenges, namely the humanitarian crisis, economic chaos, terrorist threats and governance difficulties. Overcoming these challenges requires more understanding and support from the international community." He added that "China hopes that the Afghan Taliban can further demonstrate openness and inclusiveness, unite all ethnic groups and factions in Afghanistan to work together for peaceful reconstruction," and which "should effectively protect the rights and interests of women and children, adopt a friendly policy toward its neighboring countries, and build a modern country that conforms to the wishes of the people and the trend of the times."[3]

Wang was said to have further stated that China has "never interfered in the internal affairs of Afghanistan and never sought selfish gains or a sphere of influence, and it firmly pursues a friendly policy toward all the people of Afghanistan"; "China urges the Western countries led by the United States as a whole to lift sanctions, and calls on all parties to engage with the Afghan Taliban in a rational and pragmatic manner"; "China is willing to continue to provide humanitarian material assistance to Afghanistan within its capacity and work with the international community." He also emphasised that the ETIM is "an international terrorist organization designated by the UN Security Council" and it "not only poses a real threat to China's national security and territorial integrity, but also jeopardizes the domestic stability and long-term stability and security in Afghanistan." He added that China hopes and believes that "the Afghan Taliban will make a clean break with the ETIM and other terrorist organizations, and take effective measures to resolutely crack down on them."[4]

Baradar briefed Wang Yi on the current situation in Afghanistan and claimed that "the overall situation in Afghanistan is under control and improving, with the governments at all levels being gradually established and government decrees being carried out effectively," and that his government is "working hard to meet the needs of the people." He was said to have assured the Chinese foreign minister that his government "has taken and will continue to take inclusive measures to expand the representation of the regime" and "strengthen the efforts to protect the rights and interests of women and children" and "not deprive them of the rights to education and work". He added that "women in medical institutions, airports and other places have resumed their work, and girls in primary and secondary schools in many provinces have returned to school". He hoped that "China and the international community will increase assistance to Afghanistan to help it overcome the humanitarian crisis and return to the right track of development."[5]

The Chinese press release stated that Baradar emphasised that "China is an important neighbor of Afghanistan…and pursuing a friendly policy toward China is the firm choice by the Afghan Taliban, and Afghan [istan] hopes to strengthen cooperation with China in various fields." He was said to have further stated that his government "attaches great importance to China's security concerns" and "will resolutely honor its promise and never allow anyone or any force to use the Afghan territory to harm China."[6]

Later, addressing the media before leaving Qatar, Wang said that China has put forward four expectations for the future of Afghanistan, including:

> first, build a more open and inclusive political structure in which all ethnic groups and factions should participate and play a role; second, implement moderate and prudent domestic and foreign policies, including the protection of the legitimate rights and interests of women and children; third, make a clear break with all terrorist forces including the Islamic State and the East Turkestan Islamic Movement and take measures to resolutely combat them; fourth, pursue a peaceful foreign policy and live in harmony with other countries, especially its neighbors.[7]

Chinese foreign minister claimed that "the expectations put forward by China have become the consensus of the international community. The key is how to achieve them." He added that China does not "approve of indiscriminately exerting pressure" and is "even more opposed to threats with sanctions." He further stated that "As long as we remain patient, proceed step by step, and actively interact with the Afghan interim government and other parties and ethnic groups, I believe the Afghan Taliban will be able to understand more clearly what actions are more in line with the fundamental and long-term interests of the Afghan people, as well as the expectations of all parties, in order to be more smoothly integrated into the international community."[8]

Second Foreign Ministers' Meeting of Afghanistan's Neighbours

Chinese Foreign Minister Wang Yi speaking via video from Europe at the Second Foreign Ministers' Meeting of Afghanistan's Neighbours hosted by Iran on 27 October 2021, proposed cooperation on the following four issues:

> First, making active engagement and *showing guidance*. We should attach importance to the opportunity that the *Afghan interim government is adaptable and shapable*, and get in touch and talk with it in a rational and pragmatic way to increase mutual trust and exert positive influence..
>
> Second, expanding multilateral coordination. We need to increase mutual reinforcement and build synergy between the various mechanisms on Afghanistan, and support the United Nations as a key coordinator in such fields as maintaining stability, preventing chaos, and providing emergency assistance. We should *urge the United States and other Western countries to take up their primary responsibility in helping Afghanistan emerge from hardship to vitality.*
>
> Third, strengthening counter-terrorism cooperation. Not only do we need to encourage the new Afghan authority to make a clean break with terrorist forces, we also need to support it in independently, resolutely and effectively combating all extremist and terrorist organizations including ISIL and the ETIM..
>
> Fourth, promoting peace and reconstruction. Afghanistan is in need of revival on all fronts, and development is the top priority. Only by finding a development path suited to its national conditions at an early date and integrating itself into the regional development architecture, can there be a basis to address the various challenges facing Afghanistan.[9]

Wang Yi also proposed two meeting mechanisms: (i) the special envoys/ representatives for the Afghan issue, and (ii) representatives of embassies in Kabul to follow through on the consensus of the meeting and push forward specific work through consultation.[10]

First Meeting of Bialteral Liaison Mechanism

On 30 December 2021, Director-General of the Department of Asian Affairs of the Chinese Foreign Ministry Liu Jinsong (earlier served as ambassador to Afghanistan from December 2017 to July 2019; Afghanistan was Liu's first ambassadorial assignment) and Director-General of the Third Political Department of the Afghan Ministry of Foreign Affairs co-chaired the first meeting of the China–Afghanistan liaison mechanisms at the working levels for humanitarian assistance and economic reconstruction via video link. The participants included officials from the Taliban-led Afghan ministries of finance, commerce, mines and petroleum, public health, and the Afghan Red Crescent Society, as well as from China's National Development and Reform Commission and from the Ministry of Commerce, China International Development Cooperation Agency, Ministry of Natural Resources, General Administration of Customs, Red Cross Society of China and other relevant departments attended the meeting.

Liu Jinsong in his remarks described China and Afghanistan as "good neighbors, good friends, good partners and good brothers." He pointed out that the meeting of the liaison mechanism is to jointly implement the consensus reached at the China-Afghanistan high-level meeting in Doha, comprehensively review the progress of bilateral cooperation in relevant fields, jointly solve the problems encountered in the process of cooperation, discuss the direction of cooperation for the next step and jointly embark on the road to common prosperity.

Liu said, "China is ready to share development experience with Afghanistan, help Afghanistan formulate long-term development plans and support Afghanistan in exploring a development path suited to its national conditions. China welcomes the export of Afghanistan's agricultural specialties such as pine nuts, saffron and pomegranate to China, and supports Afghanistan in turning its rich mineral resources into a driving force for future development.

China hopes that Afghanistan will provide a safe business, working and living environment for Chinese enterprises and citizens, protect their legitimate interests and send a signal to the international community that investment in Afghanistan is safe and secure." He added that China hopes that Afghanistan will "capitalize on its geographical strength as the 'Heart of Asia', seek synergy with the Belt and Road Initiative and the Global Development Initiative, and strengthen its capacity for self-driven development."[11]

Wang Yi's First Visit to Taliban-controlled Kabul

On 22 March 2022, Chinese foreign minister visited Kabul and met Acting Taliban Deputy Prime Minister Mullah Baradar and Acting Taliban Foreign Minister Muttaqi. In Kabul, Wang Yi introduced China's "Three Respects" and "Three Nevers" on the Afghan issue.

Wang Yi stated that "China and Afghanistan are friendly neighbors linked by mountains and rivers, with exchanges between the two countries dating back to more than a thousand years ago." Elaborating on "Three Respects," he stated that "China respects the independence, sovereignty and territorial integrity of Afghanistan, respects the independent choices made by the Afghan people, and respects the religious beliefs and national customs of Afghanistan." As for the "Three Nevers," he stated that "China never interfered in Afghanistan's internal affairs, never seeks self-interests or the so-called spheres of influence in Afghanistan." Wang pointed out that "China is the only major country that has never hurt Afghanistan. We are proud of this and are ready to carry forward the traditional friendship between the two peoples, develop normal and friendly neighboring relations with Afghanistan on the basis of the Five Principles of Peaceful Coexistence, and help Afghanistan achieve true independence and self-generated development, thus taking the future of Afghanistan into its own hands."[12]

In his meeting with Mullah Baradar, Chinese foreign minister emphasised China's abovementioned policy of "Three Respects" and "Three Nevers" towards Afghanistan and noted that "the Afghan Interim Government is committed to peaceful reconstruction and has taken a series of positive measures to respond to the concerns of the international community. China expects the Afghan side to continue to build an inclusive government, exercise prudent governance, and better safeguard the rights and interests of women and children, so as to demonstrate the tolerance and friendliness of Muslims." He assured the Taliban side that China "is ready to carry out mutually beneficial cooperation with Afghanistan in an orderly manner, so as to *help Afghanistan turn its resource advantage into a development advantage*. The cooperation will be based on the principles of giving priority to improving people's wellbeing, enhancing Afghanistan's capacity for self-generated development, and laying stress on substantial results rather than paying lip service." He further stated that China welcomes Afghanistan's active participation in the BRI and "is ready to make efforts to extend the China-Pakistan Economic Corridor to Afghanistan, so as to replicate more successful experiences and make Afghanistan, which is located in the 'Heart of Asia,' a bridge for regional interconnectivity." Chinese foreign minister appreciated Taliban's "clear declaration and solemn commitment" to "not allow any external forces to use the Afghan territory to take actions against neighboring countries or harm the security of other countries" and hoped that the Taliban "will firmly and resolutely fulfill this commitment, which is necessary for Afghanistan to establish a positive image in the international arena and carry out normal international exchanges."[13]

In his meeting with Muttaqi, Wang Yi highlighted China's aid and assistance to Afghanistan since the Taliban came to power. He stated that "China has provided multiple batches of emergency humanitarian assistance to the Afghan side at the earliest time possible to help the Afghan people get through the winter in safety, and arranged 36 chartered flights to import Afghan pine nuts to help Afghanistan alleviate difficulties and improve people's livelihood, writing a new chapter of friendship between the Chinese and Afghan people. China is ready to continue to provide assistance within its capacity for Afghanistan's development and revitalization, actively carry out cooperation in such fields as medical care, poverty alleviation, agriculture, disaster prevention and mitigation, and welcomes Afghanistan's participation in Belt and Road cooperation. China will cooperate with international multilateral institutions to provide Afghanistan with food assistance, and is willing to offer COVID-19 vaccines to Afghanistan based on its needs."[14]

The visiting Chinese foreign minister also hoped that the Taliban side "will earnestly fulfill its commitment and take effective measures to resolutely crack down on all terrorist forces, including the ETIM." Muttaqi was quoted as having said that his government "is highly vigilant against the resurgence of terrorism and will take resolute and effective measures to eliminate terrorist forces in Afghanistan" and that the Afghan Taliban "fully understands China's concerns and will never allow any force to use the Afghan territory to engage in acts detrimental to Chinese friends."[15]

First China-led Informal Trilateral Meeting

On 30 March 2022, China hosted the Trilateral Foreign Ministers' meeting, first since the Taliban takeover but an informal one, in Tunxi, Anhui Province. The meeting was chaired by Chinese Foreign Minister Wang Yi and attended by Pakistan Pakistan Foreign Minister Shah Mahmood Qureshi and Acting Taliban Foreign Minister Amir Khan Muttaqi.

Wang Yi said, "China, Afghanistan and Pakistan, as traditional friendly neighbors linked by mountains and rivers and enjoying cultural affinity, jointly created the ancient Silk Road civilization and made important contributions to the East-West integration and mutual learning." Similar to what Chinese leaders and officials used to say in the 1950s and the 60s about their ties with Afghanistan, Chinese foreign minister said that "We share similar historical experience and have always supported each other in our struggle for national liberation and independence." He went on to add that "since the situation in Afghanistan has undergone fundamental changes, China and Pakistan have immediately engaged in dialogue and exchanges with the Afghan Interim Government in an equal and respectful manner, immediately provided emergency humanitarian assistance for Afghanistan despite difficulties, and immediately promoted the establishment of the foreign-minister-level mechanism of Afghanistan's neighboring countries." He further stated that "the two sides also encouraged and supported Afghanistan's inclusive government and prudent governance, urged the United States to lift its unilateral sanctions against Afghanistan, and built the international community's consensus on helping and supporting Afghanistan's peaceful reconstruction."[16]

Wang Yi suggested that the three countries "should restart the trilateral cooperation mechanism and advance cooperation in the three areas of politics, development and security based on the principles of mutual respect, equal-footed consultation and mutual benefit." Elaborating on the points, he said: "First, we should build political mutual trust among our three parties under the principle of good-neighborliness and friendship. We should uphold friendship and partnership with our neighbors, support each other's core concerns and safeguard our common interests. Second, we should promote trilateral practical cooperation to benefit the people. We should jointly advance Belt and Road cooperation and extend the China-Pakistan Economic Corridor to Afghanistan, and help Afghanistan participate in regional connectivity. Third, we should strengthen counter-terrorism and security cooperation under the guidance of the new vision of common, comprehensive, cooperative and sustainable security. We should adopt a comprehensive approach to address both the symptoms and root causes, and eliminate the breeding ground of terrorism, so as to achieve lasting peace and stability in the region." The three sides also agreed to hold a formal trilateral dialogue at an appropriate time.[17]

The Tunxi Initiative

The very next day, on 31 March 2022, China hosted the Third Foreign Ministers' Meeting on the Afghan Issue Among the Neighboring Countries of Afghanistan in Tunxi, Anhui Province. Chaired by Chinese Foreign Minister Wang Yi, the meeting saw the participation of Turkmen Deputy Prime Minister and Foreign Minister Rashid Meredov, Uzbek Deputy Prime Minister and Minister of Investments and Foreign Trade Umurzakov Sardor Uktamovich, Russian Foreign Minister Sergey Lavrov, Pakistan Foreign Minister Shah Mahmood Qureshi, Iranian Foreign Minister Hossein Amir-Abdollahian and Tajik Justice Minister Muzaffar Ashurion. UN Secretary-General António Guterres had delivered a video speech on the occasion. Chinese foreign minister summarised the "eight-pronged consensus" reached at the meeting.

> First, we stress our respect for the independence, sovereignty and territorial integrity of Afghanistan and our support for the Afghan people to independently determine their country's future and explore a development path that is in line with not only their own national conditions but also the development trend of the times.

> Second, we, on the whole, recognize the governance efforts of the Afghan Interim Government for more than half a year, and call on Afghanistan to achieve national reconciliation and domestic solidarity through dialogue and consultation, build a broad-based and inclusive government, exercise moderate and prudent governance, and adhere to good-neighborliness and friendship.
>
> Third, we express our common concern about the activities of terrorist forces in Afghanistan and urge Afghanistan to make a clean break with and firmly dismantle various terrorist organizations such as the Islamic State and the East Turkestan Islamic Movement, and ultimately eliminate them.
>
> Fourth, we are concerned about the severe humanitarian difficulties facing Afghanistan and decide to continue to provide humanitarian assistance for the Afghan people, support Afghanistan's economic reconstruction and self-reliant development, and strengthen regional connectivity.
>
> Fifth, we call on all parties to engage Afghanistan and conduct dialogue with it, support its economic and social development, oppose sanctions and pressure, and oppose the politicization of humanitarian assistance.
>
> Sixth, we urge the Western countries led by the United States to earnestly fulfill their primary responsibility for the reconstruction and development of Afghanistan, return the property of the Afghan people as soon as possible, and oppose attempts to create chaos in Afghanistan and bring disaster to the region.
>
> Seventh, we support the United Nations in playing its due role in promoting peace and stability and coordinating assistance in Afghanistan, and call on international financial institutions to actively inject liquidity into Afghanistan and help Afghanistan embark on a path of sound development.
>
> Eighth, we will continue to play a unique role in the mechanism of coordination and cooperation among Afghanistan's neighboring countries.[18]

During the meeting, each of the seven participating countries made various commitments aimed at facilitating Afghanistan's economic sustenance and development under six heads: (i) humanitarian assistance (ii) connectivity (iii) economy and trade (iv) agriculture (v) energy, and (vi) capacity building. Under the head 'Humanitarian Assistance', China announced that it will speed up the delivery of emergency humanitarian assistance such as food, winter supplies,

COVID-19 vaccines and medical equipment. On 'Connectivity', China stated that it supports the extension of CPEC and China–Central Asia–West Asia Economic Corridor to Afghanistan, synergy between the BRI and the development strategies of Afghanistan, and the smooth operation of China–Afghanistan freight train services.[19]

On economy and trade, China stated that it "supports its enterprises in investing and starting businesses in Afghanistan *when the security situation permits*, and in resuming projects such as the Aynak Copper Mine and the Amu Darya Oilfield in due course. China supports its enterprises to help Afghanistan improve its mobile network, and explore and develop mineral resources."[20]

On agriculture, China stated that it "supports Afghanistan in cultivating cotton, pepper, sunflower seeds and other agricultural products and exporting them to China, and will continue to facilitate the export of Afghan specialty agricultural products including pine nut, saffron, almond and pomegranate to China." China further stated that it "stands ready to, as needed by Afghanistan, provide seeds, fertilizers and agricultural materials and machinery to Afghanistan, and support the development of high-value-added agricultural industries such as greenhouse planting to help Afghan farmers raise income." It also "supports Afghanistan in strengthening agricultural infrastructure."[21]

On energy, China stated that it is "ready to continue discussions with Afghanistan on solar power station and other projects based on Afghanistan's needs and security condition, etc."[22]

On capacity building, China pledged to further strengthen human resource development cooperation with Afghanistan in key areas such as governance, health, poverty reduction and alleviation, disaster prevention and mitigation and trade and investment. In addition, China also expressed its willingness "to work with other neighbors of Afghanistan to provide joint training programs for Afghanistan."[23]

First Meeting of Foreign Ministers' of Neighbouring Countries

On 31 March 2022, China also hosted the First Meeting of "Neighboring Countries of Afghanistan Plus Afghanistan" Foreign Ministers' Dialogue. This event too was held in Tunxi, Anhui Province. According to the Chinese foreign ministry press release, foreign ministers and representatives of member states of the mechanism of coordination and cooperation among Afghanistan's neighboring countries (China, Iran, Pakistan, Russia, Tajikistan, Turkmenistan, Uzbekistan), as well as Acting Taliban Foreign Minister Muttaqi attended the meeting. Qatari Deputy Prime Minister and Foreign Minister Sheikh Mohammed bin Abdulrahman Al Thani and Indonesian Foreign Minister Retno Marsudi attended the meeting as guests.[24]

Extended Troika Meeting on Afghanistan

On the same day, 31 March 2022, China also hosted the Extended Troika Meeting on Afghanistan in Tunxi. Chaired by Foreign Minister Wang Yi, the meeting was attended by Chinese Special Envoy for Afghan Affairs of the Ministry of Foreign Affairs of China Yue Xiaoyong, Russian Special Presidential Representative for Afghanistan Zamir Kabulov, US State Department's Special Representative for Afghanistan Thomas West and Pakistan Prime Minister's Special Representative on Afghanistan Affairs Mohammad Sadiq. The visiting representatives of all four countries also met Acting Taliban Minister of Mines and Petroleum Shahabuddin Delawar.

According to the Chinese foreign ministry press release, the representatives of all four countries agreed that "a peaceful and stable Afghanistan is in the common interests of the international community"; "Afghanistan should not become a place for geopolitical rivalry, but a platform for international cooperation"; reiterated their "firm support for the Afghan people and stressed that more humanitarian assistance will be provided to Afghanistan"; called on "all parties in Afghanistan…to realize national reconciliation through substantive dialogue and negotiation, and work for a broader, more inclusive and united political architecture in Afghanistan"; stressed that "various terrorist forces entrenched in Afghanistan remain a threat to the security of the region, and called on relevant Afghan parties to take more visible measures to fulfill their counter-terrorism commitment and dismantle and eliminate all types of terrorist groups"; and finally "All sides are encouraged to work together with Afghanistan through commercial and market-oriented means such as economic and trade investment, connectivity and infrastructure construction to improve the level of practical cooperation and help Afghanistan improve its capacity for self-reliant development and achieve economic independence."[25]

Wang Yi Summarises the Outcomes

At the end of all three events held during 30–31 March 2022 in Tunxi, Chinese Foreign Minister Wang Yi summarised the important consensus and achievements of the meetings during a press conference.

According to the Chinese foreign ministry press release, Wang Yi informed that the outcomes of the meetings were mainly reflected in two documents, namely the Joint Statement of the Third Foreign Ministers' Meeting on the Afghan Issue Among the Neighboring Countries of Afghanistan, and the Tunxi Initiative of Afghanistan's Neighboring Countries on Supporting Afghanistan's Economic Reconstruction and Practical Cooperation. He stated that "these two documents reflect the common political position of neighboring countries" who have decided "to provide material support for Afghanistan in key areas such as humanitarian assistance, interconnectivity, economy and trade, agricultural development, energy and power, and capacity building." On the Tunxi Initiative, he stated that the initiative "embodies five features: First, not playing geopolitical games, but focusing on practical cooperation. Second, not imposing one's will on others, but advocating equality and voluntariness. Third, not making high-profile empty promises, but pursuing tangible results. Fourth, not acting without coordination, but striving for regional connectivity. Fifth, not seeking isolation and antagonism, but advocating openness and inclusiveness."[26]

Chinese Special Envoy Yue Xiaoyong's Brief

Chinese Special Envoy Yue Xiaoyong briefed several country representatives and senior officials on the outcomes of the series of meetings held on 30–31 March 2022. He is said to have briefed the Special Representative of the Federal Government of Germany for Afghanistan and Pakistan Jasper Wieck, EU Special Envoy for Afghanistan Tomas Niklasson, Director of the International Security Cooperation Department of the UAE Ministry of Foreign Affairs and International Cooperation Salem Mohammed Al Zaabi, Director-General of the Department of South Asia of Turkish Ministry of Foreign Affairs Hakan Tekin, UK Prime Minister's Special Representative for Afghanistan and Pakistan

Nigel Casey on the outcomes of the Third Foreign Ministers' Meeting Among the Neighboring Countries of Afghanistan. He also briefed the Deputy Foreign Minister of Turkmenistan Vepa Hajiyev, Special Representative of the Uzbek President for Afghanistan Ismatulla Irgashev, Special Envoy of Qatar's Minister of Foreign Affairs for Counterterrorism and Mediation in Conflict Resolution Mutlaq Qahtani, Head of Department of Strategic Studies of Tajikistan Vafo Niyatbekzoda on the Extended Troika Meeting on Afghanistan.[27]

Later, on 25 April 2022, according to the Chinese foreign ministry press release, Yue briefed foreign embassies on Foreign Minister Wang Yi's visit to Afghanistan and the series of meetings held on the Afghan issue. Representatives from more than 20 embassies, including those of Russia, Pakistan, Tajikistan, Uzbekistan, Turkmenistan, Turkey, ROK, Singapore, EU, Germany, Norway, Ireland, US, UK, Canada were said to have attended the session online. Yue introduced the abovementioned diplomatic events hosted by China using four key phrases, namely "Carrying forward the Traditional Friendship," "Strengthening Friendship and Mutual Assistance," "Building on the Consensus of All Parties" and "Persevering in Diplomatic Efforts."[28]

Second Meeting of Bilateral Liaison Mechanism

The second meeting of the liaison mechanism at the working level for economic construction, which was set up in December 2021, was held via video link on 28 June 2022, following the earthquake in eastern Afghanistan. It was co-chaired by Director-General of the Department of Asian Affairs of the Chinese Foreign Ministry Liu Jinsong and Director-General of the Third Political Department of the Taliban-led Afghan Foreign Ministry Zakir Jalaly. Jinsong stated that to help Afghanistan tide over the economic crisis, China imported Afghan agricultural products such as pine nuts, saffron, dried apricots, figs and raisins. In the first five months of the year 2022, China imported 200 tonnes of pine nuts from Afghanistan, which generated US$ 2.8 million for the Afghan people. He added that 81 Afghan pine nut enterprises had been registered in China until then. He further stated that China is ready to "speed up the return of the Afghan students to China for their studies, the resumption of direct flights and the visa application of Afghan businessmen to China and other issues of concern to Afghanistan, and support cooperation between sister provinces and regions at the sub-national level."

As was customary of Chinese official statements at the time, Jinsong criticised US for its hasty and irresponsible withdrawal and blamed it for the economic mess in Afghanistan. He also stated that relevant Chinese ministries have suggested the holding of a meeting of the China–Afghanistan Joint Economic and Trade Committee to discuss the prospect of providing technical support to help develop Afghanistan's agricultural sector and expand the export of Afghan agricultural products to China. The Taliban official Jalaly was stated to have expressed his government's desire to deepen practical cooperation with China in various sectors, including agriculture, economy and trade, energy, mining, health, finance, culture and people-to-people exchanges, and capacity building. He was also said to have assured the Chinese side of the safety of Chinese projects and personnel in Afghanistan.[29]

Wang–Muttaqi Meeting in Tashkent

On 28 July 2022, Chinese Foreign Minister Wang Yi met with Acting Taliban Foreign Minister Muttaqi on the sidelines of the SCO Foreign Ministers' meeting. Wang Yi appreciated "the Afghan Interim Government's unremitting efforts in overcoming the four challenges posed by the winter, earthquake, flood and sanctions" and hoped "to push the alignment of the Belt and Road Initiative with the development strategies of Afghanistan, support the extension of the China-Pakistan Economic Corridor to Afghanistan, and share China's development opportunities." He announced that China "will grant zero tariff treatment to 98 percent of the tariff lines of the Afghan products exported to China, and is willing to import more quality specialty products from Afghanistan." He added that China "appreciates Afghanistan's firm attitude to the counter-narcotics issue, and is willing to assist Afghanistan in planting alternative crops" and emphasised that China "will continue to urge the United States and other Western countries to remove unreasonable sanctions on Afghanistan, and earnestly fulfill its primary responsibility for the economic reconstruction of Afghanistan." He also pointed out that China hopes that Afghanistan "can build a broad-based and inclusive government and exercise moderate and prudent governance, maintain domestic stability and realize national harmony, take resolute measures to crack down on all terrorist forces, including the East Turkestan Islamic Movement, and actively respond to the concerns of the international community and gain more understanding and recognition."[30]

According to the articles posted on Chinese embassy website in November 2022, based on principles enunciated by Chinese President Xi in his report to the 20th National Congress of the CPC held in October, that China and Afghanistan "should seek common ground while reserving differences and coexist peacefully" and "strengthen exchanges in governance, deepen cooperation in economy and trade, agriculture, energy, minerals, health-care, education, finance, connectivity and capacity building." It further stated that China "will continue to provide development assistance and emergent humanitarian assistance such as food, winter supplies, COVID-19 vaccines and medical equipment"; "support enterprises in investing and starting businesses in Afghanistan on the basis of mutual benefit"; and "provide new humanitarian aids and economic reconstruction cooperation through bilateral and multilateral channels". It also stated that China is "ready to promote synergy" between the BRI and Afghanistan and is "willing to support the extension of the China-Pakistan Economic Corridor and the China-Central Asia-West Asia Economic Corridor to Afghanistan" to "support the smooth operation of the China-Afghanistan freight train services", and to "help Afghanistan better integrate into the regional economic integration process."[31] Again, in another article posted in December 2022, it stated that China and Afghanistan should follow "a path of peaceful development," "openness and inclusiveness," and "a path of solidarity".[32]

China's Position Paper on Afghanistan

On 12 April 2023, the Chinese foreign ministry published a position paper on the Afghan issue. It was a rehash of what Chinese Foreign Minister Wang Yi stated during his visit to Kabul and subsequently in various meetings held at Tunxi in March 2022. It listed out 11 elements, with some of them being repetitive, to the Chinese approach on the Afghan issue: (1) Adhering to the 'Three Respects' and 'Three Nevers' (2) Supporting moderate and prudent governance in Afghanistan (3) Supporting peace and reconstruction of Afghanistan (4) Supporting Afghanistan in countering terrorism resolutely and forcefully (5) Calling for greater bilateral and multilateral counter-terrorism cooperation (6) Working together to fight terrorism, separatism and extremism in Afghanistan (7) Urging the US to live up to its commitments and responsibilities to Afghanistan (8) Opposing external interference and infiltration in Afghanistan (9) Strengthening international and regional coordination on the Afghan issue (10) Facilitating solution to Afghanistan's humanitarian and refugee issues, and (11) Supporting Afghanistan's fight against narcotics (for details, see Appendix IV).[33]

Second Informal Foreign Ministers' Meeting

On 12 April 2023, the Second Informal Foreign Ministers' Meeting on Afghanistan was held in Samarkand, Uzbekistan. It brought together the foreign ministers of China, Russia, Pakistan and Iran. The meeting was chaired by the newly-appointed Chinese foreign minister, Qin Gang. Russian Foreign Minister Sergei Lavrov, Iranian Foreign Minister Hossein Amir-Abdollahian and Pakistani Minister of State for Foreign Affairs Hina Rabbani Khar attended the meeting.

According to Chinese foreign ministry spokesperson, Foreign Minister Qin referring to China, Russia, Pakistan and Iran as "the core force for regional coordination on Afghanistan issue" stated that "Under the new circumstances, the Cold War mentality and bloc confrontation must be abandoned for the political settlement of the Afghan issue". He suggested that "All countries concerned need to adhere to the principle of indivisible security, address both the symptoms and root causes, and guide the Afghan Taliban to exercise governance in a moderate and prudent way". Qin further stated that all the four countries "should work together to make the international community pay more attention to terrorism-related security issues in Afghanistan to help the country effectively address terrorist threats and make a clean break with all terrorist forces". He also stated that the four countries "will encourage and support the Afghan Taliban in pursuing a modernization path suited for its national conditions" and "help Afghanistan enhance self-driven development capacity and integrate itself into the regional economy".[34]

The outcomes of the meeting were as follows:

> First, the Ministers reiterated respect for the sovereignty, independence and territorial integrity of Afghanistan, and support for the "Afghan-led, Afghan-owned" principle to determine the country's political future and development path.

Second, the Ministers emphasized their deep concerns regarding the terrorism-related security situation in Afghanistan, and urged the Afghan Interim Government to take more visible measures in upholding its stated commitments on counter-terrorism, dismantling and eliminating all sorts of terrorist groups, with a view to preventing the soil of Afghanistan from being used by any terrorist group. The Afghan authority should take effective measures to protect the safety, security and legitimate rights of foreign institutions and citizens.

Third, the Ministers called on the Afghan authority to build an inclusive government and protect the basic rights and interests of all Afghans, including women, children and ethnic minority groups.

Fourth, the Ministers pointed out that the US and its allies, who bear historic responsibility for the predicament in Afghanistan, should instantly lift unilateral sanctions against Afghanistan and return its overseas assets, for the benefits of Afghan people. They firmly opposed the reestablishment of military bases in and around Afghanistan.

Fifth, the Ministers called on the international community to continue providing humanitarian assistance to Afghanistan, help Afghanistan effectively fight narcotics and develop alternative crops cultivation, and help the country strengthen capacity for self-driven and sustainable development.

Sixth, the Ministers supported all diplomatic efforts conducive to facilitating the political settlement of the Afghan issue, and support the international community, in particular the United Nations, the Shanghai Cooperation Organization, the Foreign Ministers' Meeting among Neighboring Countries of Afghanistan and Moscow Format Consultations, in playing a substantive role in this regard.[35]

Fourth China-led Trilateral Foreign Ministers' Dialogue

On 13 April 2023, following the Informal Foreign Ministers' Meeting on Afghanistan held on 12 April, the fourth Foreign Ministers' Meeting among the Neighboring Countries of Afghanistan was held in Samarkand. The meeting was chaired by the Acting Foreign Minister of Uzbekistan, Bakhtiyor Saidov. It brought together Russian Foreign Minister Lavrov, Iranian Foreign Minister Abdollahian, Foreign Minister of Tajikistan Sirojiddin Muhriddin, First Deputy Foreign Minister of Turkmenistan Vepa Hajiyev and Pakistani Minister of State for Foreign Affairs Khar.

According to the declaration issued by the six countries, which came to be known as the Samarkand Declaration, the participating countries stated:

> The Parties noted the importance of building *an inclusive and broad-based governance system in Afghanistan* that reflects the interests of all segments of Afghan society.
>
> The Parties noted that the terrorism-related security situation in Afghanistan was still severe and reaffirmed their commitment to enhance cooperation on counter-terrorism and security among neighboring countries and to develop a united front against terrorism.
>
> The Parties pointed out that all terrorist groups, namely the Islamic State of Iraq and the Levant (ISIL), Al-Qaeda, the Eastern Turkistan Islamic Movement (ETIM), the Tehreek-e-Taliban Pakistan (TTP), the Balochistan Liberation Army (BLA), Jundallah, Jaish al-Adl, Jamaat Ansarullah, the Islamic Movement of Uzbekistan (IMU), and other terrorist organizations based in Afghanistan continue to pose a serious threat to regional and global security.
>
> The Parties stressed the importance of combating the drug threat and called for support for the development of drug crop substitution programs, as well as for combating drug production and trafficking.
>
> The parties noted the relevance of coordinating regional and international efforts to ensure security and stability in the region, emphasizing the positive contribution of existing regional forums, including the Tashkent International Conference "Afghanistan: Security and Economic Development" and the Moscow Format Consultations on Afghanistan.
>
> The Parties reaffirmed the importance of countering attempts to politicize the provision of humanitarian assistance needed by the people of Afghanistan and stressed that the distribution and use of humanitarian assistance should serve for the benefit of the ordinary Afghan people.
>
> The Parties noted the fundamental significance of major international energy, transport, communication, infrastructure and other projects implemented by neighboring countries for socio-economic development of Afghanistan and its active integration into the world economy.
>
> The Parties took note of the initiative of Uzbekistan to create an International Negotiation Group under the auspices of the UN and Tajikistan's initiative on creating a "security belt" around Afghanistan, and look forward to receiving comprehensive concept notes from the initiators.

> The parties reaffirmed the launch of three working group meetings namely political and diplomatic, economic and humanitarian, security and stability at an early date.[36]

Fifth China–Afghanistan–Pakistan Foreign Ministers' Dialogue

On 6 May 2023, Chinese Foreign Minister Qin attended the fifth Foreign Ministers' Dialogue held in Islamabad. Chaired by Pakistani Foreign Minister Bilawal Bhutto Zardari, the dialogue was attended by Acting Taliban Foreign Minister Amir Khan Muttaqi.

Qin in his remarks stated that the hosting of the foreign ministers' dialogue marks the "restart of the China–Afghanistan–Pakistan cooperation mechanism." He added that China "stands ready to join hands with Afghanistan and Pakistan through bilateral and trilateral cooperation mechanisms to implement the Global Development Initiative, the Global Security Initiative and the Global Civilization Initiative, share development opportunities, meet security challenges together, jointly advance the progress of civilizations, set an example of cooperation among neighbors, through mini-multilateralism and on hotspot issues, and defend and promote regional stability and prosperity" and emphasized that the three countries "should strengthen cooperation on counter-terrorism and security affairs under regional multilateral frameworks including the mechanism of coordination and cooperation among Afghanistan's neighboring countries." Qin hoped that "Afghanistan and Pakistan will further strengthen safety and security measures for Chinese nationals, institutions and projects."[37]

The three countries also agreed "to restart the dialogue mechanism under the framework of the foreign ministers' dialogue, and strengthen exchanges and cooperation in such fields as economy, trade, agriculture, poverty reduction, and cultural and people-to-people exchanges, advance the Belt and Road cooperation, support the extension of the China-Pakistan Economic Corridor to Afghanistan, promote connectivity among the three countries and the region, and improve the cross-border trade system, with a view to enhancing economic integration among the three countries and achieving sustainable development."[38]

According to the joint statement issued, the three sides also stressed the importance of existing projects including CASA–1000, TAPI, Trans-Afghan Railways, etc. to fully harness Afghanistan's potential as a transit hub, emphasised the need to "push forward the 'hard connectivity' in infrastructure and 'soft connectivity' in norms and standards," and agreed to enhance transit trade through Gwadar Port.[39]

A few weeks later, on 29 May, China stated that its Global Security Initiative, proposed by Xi at Boao Forum for Asia held in April 2022, "provided further direction for addressing global governance challenges, including the issue of Afghanistan, and building a community with a shared future for mankind."[40]

Appointment of New Chinese Ambassador

In September 2023, China became the first country to send a new ambassador to Afghanistan since the Taliban takeover in August 2021.[41] The new Chinese ambassador, Zhao Xing, arrived in Kabul on 8 September. He succeeded Wang Yu, who was appointed in November 2019. On 13 September, Zhao also became the first foreign ambassador to present his credentials to Acting Taliban Prime Minister Mohammad Hassan Akhund. He also presented a copy of the credentials to Acting Taliban Foreign Minister Muttaqi on the same day.[42] While the Chinese embassy website barely provided any biographical information about the new ambassador,[43] media sources suggested that he had long served with the Chinese Foreign Ministry's Department of International Organisations and Conferences.[44]

Muttaqi–Baradar Meeting

In early October 2023, Acting Taliban Foreign Minister Muttaqi attended the third meeting of the Trans-Himalaya Forum for International Cooperation held in Tibet from 4 to 6 October. Wang Yi, who was then Director of the Office of the Central Commission for Foreign Affairs, met the visiting Taliban foreign minister on the sidelines of the forum. According to the Chinese foreign ministry press release, Wang Yi stated that both China and Afghanistan being in the trans-Himalaya region are "linked by mountains and rivers in geography" and have "mutual connectivity in history". He praised the participation of over 100 athletes from Afghanistan in the 19th Asian Games held in Hangzhou from 23 September to 8 October 2023.

Wang was said to have further stated that "China will, as always, support Afghanistan in building a broad-based and inclusive government, exercising moderate and prudent governance, adhering to good neighborliness and friendship, and cracking hard down on terrorism." He expressed hope that "Afghanistan will continue to take effective measures to crack hard down on terrorism, and thoroughly exterminate the terrorist forces of the East Turkestan Islamic Movement in Afghanistan."[45]

Interestingly, two Afghan contingents had participated in the Hangzhou Asian Games. One was the all-male contingent sent by the Taliban interim government, and the other was drawn from Afghan diaspora and it included 17 women players—a volley ball team trained in Iran, cyclists in Italy, and an athlete from Australia.[46]

Proactive Chinese Special Envoy

Acting Taliban Minister for Commerce and Industry Nooruddin Azizi visited Beijing to attend the Third Belt and Road Forum on International Cooperation held on 17–18 October 2023. On 19 October, Chinese Foreign Ministry's Special Envoy on Afghan Affairs Yue Xiaoyong met the visiting Taliban minister.[47] A month later, on 13 November, the Chinese Special Envoy addressed the opening ceremony of the China–Afghanistan–Pakistan Trilateral Workshop for Young Diplomats held at the China Diplomatic Academy.[48] Yue thereafter made several visits to Kabul as part of his tri-nation tours. From 11 to 19 December 2023, Yue visited the UAE, Tajikistan and Afghanistan. During his visit to Kabul, he met Taliban Foreign Minister Muttaqi.

Between 29 January and 3 February 2024, he visited Afghanistan, Iran and Pakistan. Yue visited Kabul on 29 January to participate in the Regional Cooperation Initiative, the first of its kind hosted by the Taliban interim government to project its "economic-centric" foreign policy. It is noteworthy that the Chinese foreign ministry press release stated that Yue "visited Afghanistan *collectively* with representatives of Russia, Iran and Pakistan on the Afghan issue" and together with them met with Taliban Foreign Minister Muttaqi. He immediately thereafter visited Iran and Pakistan.[49] Between 17 and 25 November 2024, Yue visited Pakistan, Turkmenistan and Afghanistan.

Yue had "in-depth exchanges" with senior Taliban officials on "practical cooperation in various fields" and met Taliban Deputy Prime Minister for Political Affairs Abdul Kabir.[50] Six months later, from 9 to 16 May 2025, Yue visited Afghanistan and Türkiye. During his visit to Kabul, Yue together with Pakistan Prime Minister's Special Representative on Afghan Affairs Mohammad Sadiq held a tripartite meeting with Acting Taliban Foreign Minister Muttaqi, Acting Taliban Industry and Commerce Minister Nooruddin Azizi, and Acting Taliban Interior Affairs Minister Sirajuddin Haqqani.[51]

China Accredits Taliban Ambassador

In late 2023, just over two years after the Taliban takeover, China became the first country to fully accredit a Taliban-appointment ambassador. According to the Afghan foreign ministry press release, the Taliban ambassador and special representative to China, Asadullah Bilal Karimi, who arrived in Beijing on 24 November 2023 and was received by Afghan embassy officials and Chinese Special Envoy on Afghan Affairs Yue Xiaoyong, handed over a copy of his credentials on 1 December to the protocol head of the Chinese foreign ministry. Finally, two months later, in early February 2024, Karimi presented his credentials, alongside ambassadors from 41 other countries, to Chinese President Xi Jinping in a ceremony organised in the Great Hall of the People in Beijing.[52]

Informal Trilateral Foreign Ministers' Meeting

On 21 May 2025, Chinese Foreign Minister Wang hosted an informal trilateral meeting with Pakistan Deputy Prime Minister and Foreign Minister Ishaq Dar and Taliban Foreign Minister Muttaqi in Beijing. The informal trilateral meeting took place in the backdrop of constant tension between Pakistan and Afghanistan, particularly in view of Pakistan's continued forced deportation of thousands of Afghan refugees and migrants. A key outcome of the informal meeting was that both Pakistan and Afghanistan agreed to elevate their diplomatic relations to the level of ambassadors. Wang, who chaired the meeting, later summarised the outcomes of the meeting and stated that the three countries have agreed to "enhance political mutual trust and uphold good-neighborliness"; "give play" to the role of the trilateral dialogue mechanism and strive to convene the sixth trilateral foreign ministers' dialogue in Kabul at an early date; Pakistan and Afghanistan "agreed in principle to exchange ambassadors"; deepen BRI cooperation and promote the extension of CPEC from Pakistan to Afghanistan; and security cooperation against terrorism.[53]

Here it is important to note that India considers so-called CPEC, which runs through Indian Territory that has been under Pakistan's forcible and illegal occupation since 1947, as *inherently illegal, illegitimate and unacceptable.* On 26 July 2022, the then official spokesperson of the Indian Ministry of External Affairs, Arindam Bagchi, stated the following in response to a media query regarding the participation of third countries in so-called CPEC projects:

> We have seen reports on encouraging a proposed participation of third countries in so-called CPEC projects.
>
> Any such actions by any party directly infringe on India's sovereignty and territorial integrity.
>
> India *firmly and consistently opposes* projects in the so-called CPEC, which are in Indian territory that has been *illegally occupied by Pakistan.*
>
> Such activities are *inherently illegal, illegitimate and unacceptable*, and will be treated accordingly by India (emphasis added).[54]

Humanitarian Aid and Bilateral Trade

According to the China–Afghanistan bilateral brief available on the Chinese foreign ministry website, as of June 2025, China has provided Afghanistan with humanitarian assistance worth more than 350 million RMB Yuan since the Taliban came to power in August 2021. It included cash, food, medicine, and wintering supplies.[55] In November 2024, Chinese Embassy donated 1,000 'care packages' to students at the Mashal Bayat School in Kabul. The donation was conducted through the Afghan Red Crescent Society and in the presence of its new Acting President Shahabuddin Dilawar. The care packages included school bags, thermos cups, pens, panda dolls, and other materials.[56]

The bilateral trade between China and Afghanistan stood at approx. 1.59 billion between January and December 2024, which was said to be a year-on-year increase of 19 per cent.[57] Here it is important to take note of the fact that the trade balance remains overwhelmingly in favour of China, as was the case before 2021, with rising Chinese exports and abysmally low imports from Afghanistan (see Table III).

Table III: China–Afghanistan Annual Trade: 2021 to June 2025 (In US$ Million)

YEAR (January to December)	*2021*	*2022*	*2023*	*2024*	*2025 (January to June)*
Exports to Afghanistan	472,113,930	549,712,624	1,268,793,829	1,543,937,090	916,228,632
Imports from Afghanistan	49,513,779	41,981,754	63,909,662	42,171,952	14,505,618
Total Trade	521,627,709	591,694,378	1,332,703,491	1,586,109,042	930,734,250

Source: Website of the General Administration of Customs, People's Republic of China.

It is noteworthy that in March 2025, Acting Taliban Minister of Industry and Commerce Nooruddin Azizi in his meeting with Chinese Ambassador Zhou Xing had "highlighted the critical importance of achieving a balanced trade relationship between their two countries". The key products identified to expand Afghanistan's exports to China included pine nuts, pomegranates, gemstones, and valuable minerals such as nephrite, onyx, lapis lazuli, and talc. The meeting was also said to have "addressed the necessity of streamlining the export process by reducing transit and transportation costs" to the benefit Afghan exporters.[58] The Taliban are also renegotiating huge investment projects contracted earlier to the Chinese state-owned corporations, leading to reported disagreements on both the Aynak copper mine and the Amu Darya energy projects.

Like the previous Afghan regime, the Taliban regime too has been pushing for a direct connectivity via the Wakhan Corridor and has been constructing the road leading to the border with China, but Beijing it appears has made it contingent upon the Taliban to first address its security concerns. Beijing instead continues to make efforts to integrate Afghanistan into the CPEC, hoping that it would help normalise ties between Pakistan and Afghanistan, expand regional connectivity, and with it its own influence in the region.

Summing Up

Over the past couple of years, Chinese diplomacy on Afghanistan has been proactive. Since the power transition in Kabul in August 2021, it has gone into an overdrive. Chinese ambassador is perhaps the most active of all foreign representatives based in Kabul. He is frequently in news visiting and meeting Taliban ministers and senior officials. Beijing has been articulating its position on the Afghan issue with clarity and is not inhibited in any manner in reaching out to the Taliban leaders, mostly the ones that have been diplomatically active, and also those whom it had known since the late 1990s. Successive Chinese ambassadors have also been regular contributing opinion pieces to the Afghan media to disseminate the Chinese narrative, presenting China as the harbinger of regional peace and development (see Appendix V).

Beijing's narrative on Afghanistan still revolves around the US role over the past two decades, and at times it comes out more prominently in its statements and articulations than that of the Taliban. Despite the Taliban's high hopes from Beijing, the latter has yet to effectively start implementing its economic commitments on the ground. Even as it eyes more infrastructure projects, key Chinese investment projects from before remain in limbo. Until then, if not anything else, the optics and the hope and hype that come with it would remain in the works.

NOTES

1 "Wang Yi Attends the G20 Foreign Ministers' Video Conference on Afghanistan", Chinese Ministry of Foreign Affairs, 23 September 2021, at https://www.fmprc.gov.cn/eng/gjhdq_665435/2675_665437/2676_663356/2678_663360/202109/t20210923_9580095.html.

2 "Wang Yi Attends the G20 Extraordinary Leaders' Meeting on Afghanistan", Chinese Ministry of Foreign Affairs, 12 October 2021, at https://www.fmprc.gov.cn/eng/gjhdq_665435/2675_665437/2676_663356/2678_663360/202110/t20211013_9550710.html.

3 "Wang Yi Meets with Acting Deputy Prime Minister of Afghan Taliban's Interim Government Mullah Abdul Ghani Baradar", Chinese Ministry of Foreign Affairs, 26 October 2021, at https://www.fmprc.gov.cn/eng/gjhdq_665435/2675_665437/2676_663356/2678_663360/202110/t20211026_10058258.html.

4 Ibid.

5 Ibid.

6 Ibid.

7 "Wang Yi Talks about China's Policy toward Afghanistan", Chinese Ministry of Foreign Affairs, 27 October 2021, at https://www.fmprc.gov.cn/eng/gjhdq_665435/2675_665437/2676_663356/2678_663360/202110/t20211027_10229574.html.

8 Ibid.

9 "Video Message by State Councilor and Foreign Minister Wang Yi to the Second Meeting of Foreign Ministers of The Neighboring Countries of Afghanistan", Chinese Ministry of Foreign Affairs, 28 October 2021, at https://www.fmprc.gov.cn/eng/gjhdq_665435/2675_665437/

2676_663356/2678_663360/202110/t20211030_10404010.html.

10 Ibid.

11 "China and Afghanistan Hold the First Meeting of the China-Afghanistan Liaison Mechanisms at the Working Levels for Humanitarian Assistance and Economic Reconstruction", Chinese Ministry of Foreign Affairs, 31 December 2021, at https://www.fmprc.gov.cn/eng/gjhdq_665435/2675_665437/2676_663356/2678_663360/202112/t20211231_10478089.html.

12 "Wang Yi Talks about China's 'Three Respects' and 'Three Nevers' on the Afghan Issue", Chinese Ministry of Foreign Affairs, 24 March 2022, at https://www.fmprc.gov.cn/eng/gjhdq_665435/2675_665437/2676_663356/2678_663360/202203/t20220325_10655537.html.

13 "Wang Yi Holds Talks with Acting Deputy Prime Minister of Afghan Interim Government Mullah Abdul Ghani Baradar", Chinese Ministry of Foreign Affairs, 24 March 2022, at https://www.fmprc.gov.cn/eng/gjhdq_665435/2675_665437/2676_663356/2678_663360/202203/t20220325_10655539.html.

14 "Wang Yi Holds Talks with Acting Foreign Minister of the Afghan Interim Government Amir Khan Muttaqi", Chinese Ministry of Foreign Affairs, 25 March 2022, at https://www.fmprc.gov.cn/eng/gjhdq_665435/2675_665437/2676_663356/2678_663360/202203/t20220325_10655541.html.

15 Ibid.

16 "Wang Yi Chairs the Foreign Ministers' Meeting among China, Afghanistan and Pakistan", Chinese Ministry of Foreign Affairs, 31 March 2022, at https://www.fmprc.gov.cn/eng/gjhdq_665435/2675_665437/2676_663356/2678_663360/202203/t20220331_10658064.html.

17 Ibid.

18 "Wang Yi Talks about Eight-pronged Consensus of the Third Foreign Ministers' Meeting on the Afghan Issue Among the Neighboring Countries of Afghanistan", Chinese Ministry of Foreign Affairs, 31 March 2022, at https://www.fmprc.gov.cn/eng/gjhdq_665435/2675_665437/2676_663356/2678_663360/202203/t20220331_10658195.html.

19 "The Tunxi Initiative of the Neighboring Countries of Afghanistanon Supporting Economic Reconstruction in and Practical Cooperation with Afghanistan", Chinese Ministry of Foreign Affairs, 1 April 2022, at https://www.mfa.gov.cn/eng/wjbzhd/202204/t20220401_10662024.html.

20 Ibid.

21 Ibid.

22 Ibid.

23 Ibid.

24 "Wang Yi Chairs the First 'Neighboring Countries of Afghanistan Plus Afghanistan' Foreign Ministers' Dialogue", Chinese Ministry of Foreign Affairs, 31 March 2022, at https://www.fmprc.gov.cn/eng/gjhdq_665435/2675_665437/2676_663356/2678_663360/202204/t20220401_10663013.html; "Chairman's Statement of the "Neighboring Countries of Afghanistan Plus Afghanistan" Foreign Ministers' Dialogue", Chinese Ministry of Foreign Affairs, 1 April 2022, at https://www.fmprc.gov.cn/eng/gjhdq_665435/2675_665437/2676_663356/2678_663360/202204/t20220412_10666956.html.

25 "China Chairs the Extended Troika Meeting on Afghan Issue", Chinese Ministry of Foreign Affairs, 1 April 2022, at https://www.fmprc.gov.cn/eng/wjbxw/202204/t20220401_10663273.html.

26 "Wang Yi Introduces the Important Consensus and Achievements of the Series of Meetings on the Afghan Issue", Chinese Ministry of Foreign Affairs, 1 April 2022, at https://www.fmprc.gov.cn/eng/gjhdq_665435/2675_665437/2676_663356/2678_663360/202204/t20220401_10663017.html.

27 "Special Envoy on Afghan Affairs of the Ministry of Foreign Affairs Yue Xiaoyong Briefed Relevant Parties on the Series of Meetings on the Afghan Issue", Chinese Ministry of Foreign Affairs, 20 April 2022, at https://www.fmprc.gov.cn/eng/gjhdq_665435/2675_665437/2676_663356/2678_663360/202204/t20220428_10675107.html.

28 "Special Envoy on Afghan Affairs of the Ministry of Foreign Affairs Yue Xiaoyong Briefed Embassies (Mission) in China on State Councillor and Foreign Minister Wang Yi's Visit to Afghanistan and the Series of Meetings on the Afghan Issue", Chinese Ministry of Foreign Affairs, 25 April 2022, at https://www.fmprc.gov.cn/eng/gjhdq_665435/2675_665437/2676_663356/2678_663360/202204/t20220428_10675113.html.

29 "Neighbors Need to Reach out to Each Other and Work Together for Development", Chinese Ministry of Foreign Affairs, 29 June 2022, at https://www.fmprc.gov.cn/eng/gjhdq_665435/2675_665437/2676_663356/2678_663360/202207/t20220707_10716967.html.

30 "Wang Yi Meets with Acting Foreign Minister of the Afghan Interim Government Amir Khan Muttaqi", Chinese Ministry of Foreign Affairs, 29 July 2022, at https://www.fmprc.gov.cn/eng/gjhdq_665435/2675_665437/2676_663356/2678_663360/202207/t20220729_10730548.html.

31 "Working Together to Meet the Challenges of World Recovery and Build a Better Future for China and Afghanistan", Chinese Embassy in the Islamic Republic of Afghanistan, 20 November 2022, at http://af.china-embassy.gov.cn/eng/sgxw/202211/t20221120_10978326.htm.

32 "Standing at the Crossroads of the New Era, Looking for the Vision of China-Afghanistan Friendship", Chinese Embassy in the Islamic Republic of Afghanistan, 4 December 2022, at http://af.china-embassy.gov.cn/eng/sgxw/202212/t20221204_10985078.htm.

33 "China's Position on the Afghan Issue", Chinese Ministry of Foreign Affairs, 12 April 2023, at https://www.fmprc.gov.cn/eng/gjhdq_665435/2675_665437/2676_663356/2677_663358/202304/t20230412_11057785.html.

34 "Foreign Ministry Spokesperson Wang Wenbin's Regular Press Conference on April 14, 2023", Chinese Ministry of Foreign Affairs, 14 April 2023, at https://www.fmprc.gov.cn/eng/xw/fyrbt/lxjzh/202405/t20240530_11347504.html.

35 "Foreign Ministry Spokesperson Wang Wenbin's Regular Press Conference on April 14, 2023", Chinese Ministry of Foreign Affairs, 14 April 2023, at https://www.fmprc.gov.cn/eng/xw/fyrbt/lxjzh/202405/t20240530_11347504.html; "Joint Statement of the Second Informal Meeting on Afghanistan Between Foreign Ministers of China, Russia, Pakistan and Iran", Chinese Ministry of Foreign Affairs, 14 April 2023, at https://www.fmprc.gov.cn/eng/zy/gb/202405/t20240531_11367493.html.

36 "Samarkand Declaration of the Fourth Meeting of Foreign Ministers of Afghanistan's Neighboring States", Chinese Ministry of Foreign Affairs, 14 April 2023, at https://www.fmprc.gov.cn/eng/zy/gb/202405/t20240531_11367494.html.

37 "Qin Gang Attends the Fifth China-Afghanistan-Pakistan Foreign Ministers' Dialogue," Chinese

Ministry of Foreign Affairs, 7 May 2023, at https://www.fmprc.gov.cn/eng/gjhdq_665435/2675_665437/2676_663356/2678_663360/202305/t20230508_11073154.html.

38 Ibid.

39 "Joint Statement of the 5th China-Afghanistan-Pakistan Foreign Ministers' Dialogue", Chinese Ministry of Foreign Affairs, 9 May 2023, at https://www.fmprc.gov.cn/eng/gjhdq_665435/2675_665437/2676_663356/2678_663360/202305/t20230509_11073522.html.

40 "The Global Security Initiative Provides a Chinese Solution for Promoting Peace and Development in Afghanistan", Chinese Embassy in the Islamic Republic of Afghanistan, 29 May 2023, at http://af.china-embassy.gov.cn/eng/sgxw/202305/t20230529_11085470.htm.

41 "President Xi Jinping Appoints New Ambassadors", Chinese Ministry of Foreign Affairs, 8 October 2023, at https://www.fmprc.gov.cn/eng/gjhdq_665435/2675_665437/2676_663356/2678_663360/202310/t20231009_11158080.html.

42 "The Newly-appointed Chinese Ambassador to Afghanistan Zhao Xing Presents the Credentials to Mohammad Hassan Akhund, Acting Prime Minister of the Afghan Interim Government", Chinese Embassy in the Islamic Republic of Afghanistan, 15 September 2023, at http://af.china-embassy.gov.cn/eng/sgxw/202309/t20230915_11143508.htm.

43 "Curriculum Vitae of H.E. Zhao Xing, Ambassador of the People's Republic of China to Afghanistan", Chinese Embassy in the Islamic Republic of Afghanistan, 15 September 2023, at http://af.china-embassy.gov.cn/eng/dsxx/dsjl/#:~:text=Ambassador%20Extraordinary%20and%20Plenipotentiary%20to,the%20 Communist%20Party%20of%20China.

44 "Report: Zhao Xing and China's Diplomatic Priorities in Afghanistan", *China Diplomatic Digest*, 18 September 2023, at https://www.chinadiplomaticdigest.com/p/report-zhao-xing-and-afghanistan.

45 "Wang Yi Meets with Acting Foreign Minister of the Afghan Interim Government Mawlawi Amir Khan Muttaqi", Chinese Ministry of Foreign Affairs, 5 October 2023, at https://www.fmprc.gov.cn/eng/gjhdq_665435/2675_665437/2676_663356/2678_663360/202310/t20231012_11159970.html.

46 David Rising, "Taliban Send All-male Team to Asian Games But Afghan Women Come from Outside", *Associated Press*, 22 September 2023, at https://apnews.com/article/asian-games-taliban-afghanistan-teams-women-e8de2badcc8fa82953a09d757511c648; Ian Ransom, "Displaced Afghan Women Athletes Defy Taliban at Asian Games", *Reuters*, 27 September 2023, at https://www.reuters.com/sports/displaced-afghan-women-athletes-defy-taliban-asian-games-2023-09-27/; "Afghanistan's 'Flying Angels' Will Inspire Women Around the World at Hangzhou Asian Games", Olympic Council of Asia, 6 September 2023, at https://oca.asia/news/4252-afghanistans-flying-angels-will-inspire-women-around-the-world-at-hangzhou-asian-games.html.

47 "Special Envoy on Afghan Affairs of the Ministry of Foreign Affairs Yue Xiaoyong Meets with Acting Minister of Commerce and Industry of the Afghan Interim Government", Chinese Ministry of Foreign Affairs, 23 October 2023, at https://www.fmprc.gov.cn/eng/gjhdq_665435/2675_665437/2676_663356/2678_663360/202310/t20231023_11165911.html.

48 "Special Envoy on Afghan Affairs of the Ministry of Foreign Affairs Yue Xiaoyong Attends the China-Afghanistan-Pakistan Trilateral Workshop for Young Diplomats", Chinese Ministry of Foreign Affairs, 14 November 2023, at https://www.fmprc.gov.cn/eng/gjhdq_665435/2675_665437/2676_663356/2678_663360/202311/t20231114_11179938.html.

49 "Special Envoy on Afghan Affairs of the Ministry of Foreign Affairs Yue Xiaoyong Visits

Afghanistan, Iran and Pakistan", Chinese Ministry of Foreign Affairs, 5 February 2024, at https://www.fmprc.gov.cn/eng/gjhdq_665435/2675_665437/2676_663356/2678_663360/202402/t20240206_11241381.html.

50 "Special Envoy on Afghan Affairs of the Ministry of Foreign Affairs Yue Xiaoyong Visits Pakistan, Turkmenistan and Afghanistan", Chinese Ministry of Foreign Affairs, 28 November 2024, at https://www.fmprc.gov.cn/eng/gjhdq_665435/2675_665437/2676_663356/2678_663360/202412/t20241218_11498319.html.

51 "Special Envoy on Afghan Affairs of the Ministry of Foreign Affairs Yue Xiaoyong Visits Afghanistan and Türkiye", Chinese Ministry of Foreign Affairs, 19 May 2025, at https://www.fmprc.gov.cn/eng/gjhdq_665435/2675_665437/2676_663356/2678_663360/202505/t20250521_11629984.html.

52 "The President of the People's Republic of China H.E. Xi Jinping, accepted the letter of credence of Mawlawi Asadullah (Bilal Karimi) as the Ambassador Extraordinaire and Plenipotentiary of the Islamic Emirate of Afghanistan to China," Ministry of Foreign Affairs, Afghanistan, 4 February 2024, at https://mfa.gov.af/en/16271.

53 "Wang Yi on the Outcomes of the Trilateral Meeting of Foreign Ministers of China, Afghanistan and Pakistan", Chinese Ministry of Foreign Affairs, 21 May 2025, at https://www.fmprc.gov.cn/eng/gjhdq_665435/2675_665437/2676_663356/2678_663360/202505/t20250521_11629994.html.

54 "Official Spokesperson's Response to Media Queries Regarding Participation of Third Countries in CPEC Projects", Ministry of External Affairs, Government of India, 26 July 2022, at https://www.mea.gov.in/response-to-queries.htm?dtl/35542/official+spokespersons+response+to+media+queries+regarding+participation+of+third+countries+in+cpec+projects.

55 "China and Afghanistan", Chinese Ministry of Foreign Affairs, at https://www.fmprc.gov.cn/eng/gjhdq_665435/2675_665437/2676_663356/.

56 "Embassy of China in Afghanistan Donates 'Care Packages' to Afghan Children", Chinese Embassy in the Islamic Republic of Afghanistan, 13 November 2024, at http://af.china-embassy.gov.cn/eng/sgxw/202411/t20241113_11525505.htm.

57 "China and Afghanistan", Chinese Ministry of Foreign Affairs, at https://www.fmprc.gov.cn/eng/gjhdq_665435/2675_665437/2676_663356/.

58 "Trade Ties Strengthened Between Afghanistan and China", *Bakhtar News Agency*, 26 March 2025, at https://www.bakhtarnews.af/en/trade-ties-strengthened-between-afghanistan-and-china/.

Observations

China's Afghan policy has largely been governed by its wider geo-strategic and security calculus than by cultural or historical ties. Chinese interest and involvement in the Afghan affairs have surged in the past in times of external interventions or internationalisation of the Afghan conflict, i.e., in the years following the Soviet intervention in 1979; and, in more recent times, since the US-led 'war on terror' in Afghanistan in late 2001; and following the US withdrawal in August 2021. Broadly, with the exception of the Soviet-backed regimes in Kabul in the 1980s, China has felt comfortable dealing with whosoever came to power in Kabul, including the Taliban in the late 1990s.

Since 2013–14, there has been a relatively greater clarity in the Chinese articulation on the evolving scenario in Afghanistan. As a Chinese scholar argued back then, China maintains an 'independent' but 'low key' policy vis-à-vis Afghanistan which reflects "the peculiarities of its interests, concerns and priorities," however, "domestic concerns about the security and stability of the largely Muslim region of Xinjiang, overwhelm all others"[1] and China views Afghanistan as "an inseparable part of building Xinjiang's security."[2]

Chinese Foreign Minister Wang Yi during his visit to Kabul in February 2014, as noted before in the book, had drawn a direct linkage between security in Xinjiang and the Afghan instability. Prior to it, in its position paper presented at the UN General Assembly in September 2012, without directly establishing the linkage between terrorism and insurgency in Xinjiang and the situation in Afghanistan, China in the section on "counter terrorism" had stated that despite the efforts of the international community "the breeding ground of terrorism has not been removed," and China has been a victim of terrorist plots instigated by "Eastern Turkestan" terrorist forces, to fight against whom "is an important part of the international anti-terrorism campaign." It then went on to state that the "situation in Afghanistan concerns peace and stability in the region and the world at large and affects the progress of the international counter-terrorism effort."[3] Despite diplomatic efforts at mediation between Pakistan and Afghanistan since 2014–15, Chinese security concerns and perceptions have remained the same to this day.

However, China at the same time had taken care not to mention the Taliban as a source of concern. It was, therefore, no surprise that China had not issued any official reaction on the issue of Taliban resurgence and violence, despite having "friendly" relations with the governments in Kabul. Perhaps, that was to be expressed through a multilateral forum like the SCO. China has used the SCO to further reinforce the fundamental aspects of its approach on the Afghan issue.

As early as 2013, there were reports suggesting that China had established indirect contacts with the Quetta *Shura* of the Taliban through Pakistan.[4] Moreover, given China's long-standing strategic relationship with Islamabad and latter's influence over sections of the Taliban regime, China was pushing for an inclusive dispensation in Kabul. Driven by its wider economic interests in the south-central Asia region, including attempts at making investments in the Afghan resources, China was not averse to the idea of the Taliban being part of a broad coalition in Kabul, as the Taliban had re-emerged as a force to reckon with. Until 2021, the fundamental question remained: whether the Quetta *Shura* and its various allies were at all willing for a negotiated political settlement of conflict with the 'Islamic Republic' of Afghanistan, and, more importantly, whether the Taliban were willing to accept the social and political diversity of the country which remains at the heart of the long-standing conflict within the country?

Though it was more than two decades ago when Beijing established its first contacts with the Taliban in 1998–99, and had since consciously avoided directly criticising the Haqqani–Taliban network or the Pakistani military-intelligence apparatus for sustaining them, the Uighur militants continued to find support among various groups/networks active in the tribal areas of Pakistan, as well as parts of northern and eastern Afghanistan.

Rise in religious extremism and sectarian violence within Pakistan, particularly the rapid proliferation of various militant Islamist networks/groups in the Pakistani polity, has been of concern to Beijing. Until the emergence of the Taliban regime in the mid-1990s, China probably never felt threatened by the spectre of religious extremism and violence spilling over into its predominantly Muslim Xinjiang region, but that perhaps is not the only concern any longer.

While the post-2001 Kabul, under both Hamid Karzai and Ashraf Ghani, tried hard to leverage its engagement with Beijing, hoping that the latter would prevail upon its 'all weather friend' Pakistan and help facilitate reconciliation with the Taliban, but as expected, Beijing went along with the Taliban and Pakistan. Post-August 2021, China proactively engaged the Taliban, and held out several proposals to invest in Afghanistan. Chinese ambassadors have in recent years been the most active foreign diplomats in Kabul. They have been in the news for frequently meeting various Taliban ministers to explore prospects of investment, particularly in mineral and energy sectors. Their opinion articles have been frequently published or republished in leading Afghan news dailies (see Appendix V).

While Beijing realises the menace of terrorism and at every forum reiterates and reaffirms its commitment towards jointly addressing the issue of religious extremism and terrorism, its approach towards state-sponsored cross-border terrorism has remained as discriminatory and selective as that of its 'all weather friend' Pakistan. It was no surprise that al Qaeda chief Osama bin Laden was found hiding deep inside Pakistan, for well over a decade, and diverse militant groups of several nationalities, including the Uygur militants from China, have had safe havens along the tribal frontiers of Pakistan and Afghanistan.

Beijing has long advocated the policy of non-interference in the internal affairs of the other countries, and had opposed the Soviet invasion of Afghanistan in the 1980s and latter the US military role and presence in the country after 2001, it has not extended such criticism to the direct role of Pakistan in the overthrow and installation of regimes in Kabul.

China is more likely to continue to work closely with the Taliban regime in Kabul and with the Pakistani military establishment in the hope that both would rein in the Uygur militants and ensure a stable regional environment.

Now with the Taliban at the helm in Kabul, and still awaiting recognition from the international community, it is not understood as to how threat from Uygur militants to China or from other foreign militant groups to the region could be eliminated. All such groups continue to sustain and motivate each other. The evolving security situation in Afghanistan and the unprecedented levels of violence and sectarian divide inside Pakistan has only brought out the futility of a narrow and selective approach towards fighting forces of militant extremism and terrorism that continue to proliferate in the region.

Beijing remains wary of the Taliban regime's linkages with the ETIM and also that of the IS-K as it retains its appeal among sections of the ETIM. The attack on a hotel in Kabul in December 2022 in which five Chinese nationals were injured was claimed by the IS-K. Chinese nationals have since been targeted inside Afghanistan and are likely to face increased threat as intra-Islamist competition gathers pace.

As of now, there are no discernible trends indicating any strategic shift in China's thinking as far as its relationship with Pakistan or its response to the Afghan uncertainty is concerned. However, the prospect of China re-strategising or re-aligning its policy in the long-term cannot be ruled out.

Where would Afghanistan figure in China's long-term regional and overall security calculus, and whether Pakistan would continue to be an asset or prove to be a growing liability in China's own re-balancing of priorities, is difficult to envision. Nevertheless, the rising threat of religious extremism and narcotics from Afghanistan and Pakistan and frequent attacks on Chinese personnel in Pakistan will, in all likelihood, necessitate a greater Chinese security interest in developments close to its western frontiers.

Beijing's current approach does not seem to be entirely driven by the projected security threats from the ETIM. In view of its burgeoning regional and extra-regional economic stakes manifest in its Belt and Road Initiative and increased investments in the Central Asian energy resources. Xi Jinping's Beijing appears far more concerned about the safety and security of the flagship CPEC project.

It is believed that Beijing cannot be supporting Kabul at the expense of its strong strategic ties with Pakistan. However, given its rising economic ambitions and with it the quest for a stable neighbourhood, Beijing could gradually be looking for ways to widen the space needed to diplomatically manoeuvre or politically manipulate even its strategically significant partnership with the Pakistani military establishment, which has thus far failed to ensure the security of Chinese personnel engaged in several projects in Pakistan. Even in such a scenario, Kabul is unlikely to emerge as the first rank economic or political partner of Beijing. The hope and hype around Beijing's proactive diplomatic engagement with Kabul is intended at presenting the former as a benign and sole harbinger of peace and development in the region, and not as the saviour of Afghanistan.

China hopes to contain the negative influence of possible Afghan instability by engaging the Taliban regime in Kabul, and also by continuing to work closely with the Pakistani security establishment. Though China has had cordial relations with Kabul and more than cordial ties with Islamabad, it is not clear to what extent Beijing's mediation would temper and transform the historically complex relationship Kabul and Kandahar have had with Pakistan. So far it has not led to any notable change in the Pakistani behaviour either. Beijing has also cautiously avoided giving Kabul any impression of a Sino-Pakistan axis seeking to influence the politics of Afghanistan.

As stated earlier, Kabul remains keen on Beijing playing an active role in facilitating the economic development of Afghanistan. In the post-2021scenario, the Taliban regime is unlikely to seek direct Chinese diplomatic intervention in resolving tensions along the Durand Line with Pakistan. China's investments in BRI–CPEC and the management of the Gwadar Port in Pakistan are, however, only likely to reinforce China's strategic stakes in the region.

In case of any threat from Afghanistan, China is unlikely to assume any direct military role inside Afghanistan in the foreseeable future. Instead, China may assert its position through increased cooperation and consultations with Afghanistan and Pakistan and declarations and joint statements in trilateral and multilateral forums like the SCO. It seems to prefer a broader security approach towards Afghanistan. In the long run, much would depend on China's own threat perceptions, evolving security situation within both Afghanistan and Pakistan, the nature of future US engagement again with both Afghanistan and Pakistan, the overall trajectory of the US–China relations, and changes in the wider regional geopolitics.

NOTES

1 Zhao Huasheng, "China and Afghanistan: China's Interests, Stances and Perspectives", A Report of the CSIS Russia and Eurasia Programme, Centre for Strategic and International Studies, Washington, D.C., March 2012, p. 1.

2 Ibid., p. 5.

3 "Position Paper of the People's Republic of China at the 67th Session of the United Nations General Assembly", Chinese Embassy in the Republic of Indonesia, Posted 20 September 2012, at http://id.china-embassy.gov.cn/eng/sgdt/201209/t20120920_2048361.htm.

4 Andrew Small, "China's Afghan Moment", *Foreign Policy*, 3 October 2012, at https://foreignpolicy.com/2012/10/03/chinas-afghan-moment/. Also see, Andrew Small, "Why is China Talking to the Taliban?", *Foreign Policy*, 21 June 2013, at https://foreignpolicy.com/2013/06/21/why-is-china-talking-to-the-taliban/.

APPENDICES

APPENDIX I

Boundary Agreement between the Royal Afghan Government and the People's Republic of China Signed on 22 November 1963 in Peking

(Official Gazette of Afghanistan, No. 4, 7 May 1966.)

The full text of the treaty is as follows:

The Chairman of the CPR [Chinese People's Republic] and His Majesty the King of Afghanistan;

With a view of insuring [*sic*] the further development of the friendly and good neighborly relations which happily exist between the two independent and sovereign states, China and Afghanistan;

Resolving to delimit and demarcate formally the boundary existing between China and Afghanistan in the Pamirs in accordance with the principles of respect for each other's sovereignty and territorial integrity and mutual nonaggression and the Ten Principles of the Bandung Conference, and in the spirit of friendship, cooperation, and mutual understanding;

Firmly believing that the formal delimitation and demarcation of the boundary between the two countries will further strengthen the peace and security of this region;

Have decided for this purpose to conclude the present treaty, and appointed as their respective plenipotentiaries;

For the Chairman of the CPR: Chen I [Chen Yi], Minister of Foreign Affairs;

For His Majesty the King of Afghanistan: Al-Qayyum [A. Qayyum], Minister of the Interior;

Who, having examined each other's full powers and found them to be in good and due form, have agreed upon the following:

Article 1. The contracting parties agree that starting from a peak with a height of 5,630 meters—the reference coordinates of which are approximately 37 degrees 03 minutes north, 74 degrees 36 minutes east—in the southern extremity, the boundary line between the two countries runs along the Mustagh Range water divide between the Karachukur Su River, a tributary of Tashkurghan River, on the one hand, and the sources of the Aksu River and the Wakhjir River, the upper reaches of the Wakhan River, on the other hand, passing through South Wakhjir Daban (called Wakhjir Pass on the Afghan map) at the elevation of 4,923 meters, North Wakhjir Daban (named on the Chinese map only), West Koktorok Daban (named on the Chinese map only), East Koktorok Daban (called Kara Jilga Pass on the Afghan map), Tok Man Su Daban called Mihman Yoli Pass on the Afghan map), Sirik Tash Daban (named on the Chinese map only), Kokrash Kol Daban (called Tigarman Su Pass on the Afghan map) and reaches Peak Kokrash Kol (called Peak Povalo Shveikovski on the Afghan map) with a height of 5,698 meters.

The entire boundary line as described in the present article is shown on the 1:200,000 scale map of the Chinese side in Chinese and the 1:253,440 scale map of the Afghan side in Persian, which are attached to the present treaty. Both of the above-mentioned maps have English words as an auxiliary.

Article 2. The contracting parties agree that wherever the boundary between the two countries follows a water divide, the ridge thereof shall be the boundary line, and wherever it passes through a daban—pass—the water-parting line thereof shall be the boundary line.

Article 3. The contracting parties agree that:

1—As soon as the present treaty comes into force a Chinese–Afghan joint boundary demarcation commission composed of an equal number of representatives and several advisers from each side shall be set up to carry out on location concrete surveys of the boundary between the two countries and to erect boundary markers in accordance with the provisions of Article 1 of the present treaty and then draft a protocol relating to the boundary between the two countries and prepare boundary maps setting forth in detail the alignment of the boundary line and the location of the boundary markers on the ground.

2—The protocol and the boundary maps mentioned in paragraph one of the present article, upon coming into force after being signed by the representatives of the two governments, shall become annexes to the present treaty, and the boundary maps prepared by the joint boundary demarcation commission shall replace the maps attached to the present treaty.

3—Upon the signing of the above-mentioned protocol and boundary maps, the tasks of the Chinese–Afghan joint boundary demarcation commission shall be terminated.

Article 4. The contracting parties agree that any dispute concerning the boundary which may arise after the formal delimitation of the boundary between the two countries shall be settled by the two parties through friendly consultation.

Article 5. The present treaty shall come into force on the day of its signature.

Done in duplicate in Peking on 22 November 1963, in the Chinese, Persian, and English languages, all three texts being equally authentic.

(Signed) Chen I [Chen Yi], plenipotentiary of the CPR.

(Signed) Al-Qayyum [A. Qayyum], plenipotentiary of the Kingdom of Afghanistan

---

Source: "International Boundary Study: Afghanistan–China Boundary", The Geographer, Office of Strategic and Functional Research, Bureau of Intelligence and Research, US Department of State, No. 89, 1 May 1969.

APPENDIX II

Joint Statement between the People's Republic of China and the Islamic Republic of Afghanistan

20 June 2006

I. At the invitation of President Hu Jintao of the People's Republic of China, Hamid Karzai, President of the Islamic Republic of Afghanistan, paid a state visit to the People's Republic of China from 18 to 21 June 2006.

II. President Hu Jintao held official talks with President Karzai. Mr. Wu Bangguo, Chairman of the Standing Committee of the National People's Congress and Mr. Jia Qinglin, Chairman of the National Committee of the Chinese People's Political Consultative Conference, met with President Karzai respectively. In a cordial and friendly atmosphere, the leaders of the two countries had in-depth exchange of views and reached broad agreement on expanding and deepening China-Afghanistan relationship of good-neighborliness, friendship and cooperation, on international and regional issues of mutual interest.

During his visit, President Karzai gave two speeches to representatives of the Chinese academic and intellectual communities at the China Institute of Contemporary International Relations and Beijing University. He met with business leaders of the two countries to brief them on trade and investment opportunities in Afghanistan and had numerous interviews with the Chinese media.

III. The leaders of the two countries spoke highly of the growth of bilateral relations since the establishment of diplomatic ties in 1955 and expressed satisfaction with the rapid resumption and fast growth of bilateral relations after the formation of the Interim Administration of Afghanistan. Both sides held that enhancing China-Afghanistan good-neighborly relationship and mutually beneficial cooperation serves the fundamental interests of the two countries and their peoples, and contributes to peace, stability and development of the region and the world at large. The two sides agreed to establish China-Afghanistan Comprehensive and Cooperative Partnership in order to consolidate their traditional friendship and broaden cooperation in all fields.

IV. The two sides reaffirmed the guiding role of the Treaty of Friendship and Non-Aggression Between the People's Republic of China and the Kingdom of Afghanistan signed in 1960 in deepening the bilateral relationship and agreed to sign, on that basis, the Treaty of Good-Neighborliness and Friendly Cooperation Between the People's Republic of China and the Islamic Republic of Afghanistan. The two sides agreed to abide by the principles of the Treaty and continue to enrich the partnership of all-round cooperation for the benefit of the two countries and their peoples and in the interest of peace, stability and development in the region.

V. The Chinese side spoke highly of the achievements made by the Afghan Government and people in the peace process and economic reconstruction over the past four years since the beginning of the Bonn Process. The Chinese side expressed the hope and belief that with the concerted efforts of the Afghan Government and people, Afghanistan will realize enduring peace and prosperity in the nearest future. The Chinese side reiterated that it will continue to support and take an active part in Afghanistan's economic reconstruction. China will provide Afghanistan with another 80 million RMB gratis this year. On behalf of the Afghan Government and people, President Karzai extended sincere thanks to the Chinese Government and people for their long time and selfless help to Afghanistan's peaceful reconstruction.

VI. The two sides held that trade and economic relations are an important part of China-Afghanistan good-neighborliness and friendly cooperation. To strengthen their trade and economic ties, the two sides decided to sign the Agreement on Trade and Economic Cooperation Between the Government of the People's Republic of China and the Government of the Islamic Republic of Afghanistan, establish the China-Afghanistan Joint Economic and Trade Committee. Both parties agree to intensify cooperation in infrastructural areas such as natural resources development, power generation and road construction. To help increase Afghanistan's export to China, the Chinese side announced that it would grant zero-tariff treatment to 278 items of Afghan exports to China as of 1 July 2006. The two sides will continue to explore new channels and ways to expand and deepen trade and economic cooperation.

VII. The two sides agreed to expand cooperation in agriculture, culture, education, transportation, energy and investment on the basis of equality and mutual benefit. To support Afghanistan's national reconstruction, the Chinese side will train 200 Afghan professionals in the coming two years and will offer 30 government scholarships to Afghanistan annually starting from 2007.

VIII. The two sides emphasized that strengthening cooperation in national defense, security and police affairs is an important part of their bilateral relationship. They will actively enhance cooperation in pragmatic terms in the aforementioned fields.

IX. The Afghan side reaffirmed that there is only one China in the world that the Government of the People's Republic of China is the sole legal Government representing the whole of China and that Taiwan is an inalienable part of the Chinese territory. The Afghan side expressed support to China's efforts in safeguarding sovereignty and territorial integrity and its opposition to any attempt of the Taiwan authorities to create "two Chinas", "one China, one Taiwan" or "Taiwan independence", including "de jure Taiwan independence". The Chinese side reiterated that it respects the independence, sovereignty and territorial integrity of Afghanistan, supports its efforts to safeguard its independence, sovereignty, territorial integrity and internal security, and opposes any attempt that will jeopardize Afghanistan's stability.

X. Both sides agreed that terrorism constitutes an international menace, as it poses a grave threat to world peace and security. China and Afghanistan are both victims of terrorism and they both firmly oppose terrorism of any form. The Chinese side supported Afghanistan's efforts in combating terrorism and safeguarding national stability and is ready to work with the Afghan side to fight terrorism, separatism, extremism, organized crime as will [*sic*] as illegal immigration, drug trafficking and illegal arms trade. The Afghan side reaffirmed its strong support to the Chinese side in combating the three forces.

XI. The Chinese side appreciated the efforts of the Afghan side in promoting regional cooperation and welcomed Afghanistan's relationship with the Shanghai Cooperation Organization within the context of "Contact Group Protocol". The Chinese side expressed readiness to enter into cooperation in pragmatic terms with the Afghan side within the framework of regional cooperation. The Afghan side welcomed China becoming an observer of the South Asian Association for Regional Cooperation (SAARC) and supported China in carrying out mutually beneficial cooperation with SAARC.

XII. During the visit, the two sides signed: Treaty of Good-Neighborly Friendship and Cooperation between the People's Republic of China and the Islamic Republic of Afghanistan, Agreement on Cooperation between the Government of the People's Republic of China and the Government of the Islamic Republic of Afghanistan in Combating Transnational Crime, Agreement on Trade and Economic Cooperation between the Government of the People's Republic of China and the Government of the Islamic Republic of Afghanistan, Agreement on Economic and Technical Cooperation between the Government of the People's Republic of China and the Government of the Islamic Republic of Afghanistan, Exchange Letter for China Granting Zero Tariff Treatment to Certain Goods Originated in Afghanistan, Air Service Agreement between the Government of the People's Republic of China and the Government of the Islamic Republic of Afghanistan, Protocol on Institutionalizing Consultations between Officials of the Ministry of Foreign Affairs of the People's Republic of China and the Ministry of Foreign Affairs of the Islamic Republic of Afghanistan, Memorandum of Understanding on Agricultural Cooperation between the Ministry of Agriculture of the People's Republic of China and the Ministry of Agriculture, Animal Husbandry and Food of the Islamic Republic of Afghanistan, Memorandum of Understanding between the State Administration of Cultural Heritage of the People's Republic of China and the Ministry of Information, Culture, Tourism and Youths of the Islamic Republic of Afghanistan on Cooperation in the Maintenance and Preservation of Cultural Heritage, Memorandum of Agreement between the Afghanistan Chamber of Commerce and Industry and the China Council for the Promotion of International Trade, Memorandum of Agreement between the Afghanistan Investment Support Agency and the China Council for the Promotion of International Trade.

XIII. President Karzai invited President Hu Jintao to pay a state visit to Afghanistan at a time convenient to him. President Hu expressed his thanks for the invitation.

Source: Consulate-General of the People's Republic of China in San Francisco, 20 June 2006, at http://sanfrancisco.china-consulate.gov.cn/eng/xw/200606/t20060620_4376026.htm.

APPENDIX III

Joint Declaration between the People's Republic of China and the Islamic Republic of Afghanistan on Establishing Strategic and Cooperative Partnership

8 June 2012

At the invitation of President Hu Jintao of the People's Republic of China, President Hamid Karzai of the Islamic Republic of Afghanistan participated in the 12th Meeting of the Council of State Heads of Shanghai Cooperation Organization Member Countries and visited China on 5-8 June 2012, and had a bilateral meeting with President Hu Jintao on 8 June. In a candid and friendly atmosphere, the two leaders had in-depth exchange of views on bilateral relations, regional and international issues of common interest and reached broad consensus.

The two leaders reviewed the history of China-Afghanistan relations in an all-round way, and agreed that, since the establishment of diplomatic ties on 20 January 1955, the two countries have abided by the Five Principles of Peaceful Co-existence and treated each other with mutual respect, trust and support, deepening the traditional friendship. In 2002, Afghanistan launched its peace and reconstruction process, and a new chapter of China-Afghanistan relations has been opened since. With increasing mutual political trust and expanding cooperation, our Comprehensive and Cooperative Partnership featuring good-neighbourliness and friendship has enjoyed smooth development.

The two leaders agreed that the regional and international situation is undergoing profound and complex changes. In order to jointly tackle challenges and uphold regional peace, stability and development, the two countries should view and develop the bilateral relations from a strategic and long-term perspective. For this purpose, the two countries decided to establish the China-Afghanistan Strategic and Cooperative Partnership, and assigned their respective Ministry of

Foreign Affairs to take lead in formulating an action plan for implementing the China-Afghanistan Strategic and Cooperative Partnership.

As for the content and basic principles of this Strategic and Cooperative Partnership, the People's Republic of China and the Islamic Republic of Afghanistan (hereinafter referred to as the "two sides") hereby state as follows:

1. The two sides would like to establish China-Afghanistan Strategic and Cooperative Partnership on the basis of the Five Principles of Peaceful Co-existence, in line with the purposes and principles of the Charter of the United Nations and widely recognized norms of international laws, as well as the basic principles for bilateral relations enshrined in the Treaty of Good-neighbourliness and Friendly Cooperation Between the People's Republic of China and the Islamic Republic of Afghanistan signed in 2006 and other bilateral documents.
   The two sides agreed that the Strategic and Cooperative Partnership will be an enduring and comprehensive relationship between the two nations which will serve the fundamental interests of two countries and peoples, facilitate the efforts to consolidate the traditional friendship of the two countries, expand cooperation in various fields, including political, economic, cultural and security. The China-Afghanistan Strategic and Cooperative Partnership will also contribute to the peace, stability and development in the region and beyond.
2. The two sides agreed that their cooperation in the political, economic, cultural and security fields, as well as on regional and international affairs, are the five pillars that will underpin the China-Afghanistan Strategic and Cooperative Partnership.
3. The two sides believed that high-level exchanges are of special significance to the growth of the bilateral relations and political mutual trust is the foundation of the China-Afghanistan relations. The two sides will actively promote the exchanges between their leaders, including arranging meetings between the leaders on the sidelines of international and multilateral occasions, where they will be able to exchange views on the bilateral relations and major international and regional issues and enhance strategic communications. The two sides will further promote the exchanges and cooperation between the two governments, legislatures and political parties, with a view to increasing mutual understanding and trust.

The two sides have undertaken to firmly support each other on issues concerning national sovereignty, unity and territorial integrity, and not allow their respective territory to be used for any activities targeted against the other side. The Afghan side reaffirmed that it is committed to the one-China policy, and that the government of the People's Republic of China is the sole legal government representing the whole China. It expressed its firm support for China's positions on the Taiwan, Tibet-related, Xinjiang-related and other major issues concerning China's core interests. The Chinese side reaffirmed its commitment to respect Afghanistan's independence, sovereignty, territorial integrity and national unity, and reiterate its respect for Afghan people's choice of development path suited to their national conditions, and its support for the national reconciliation process in Afghanistan. The Chinese side believes that, with the determination of the Afghan people,as well as support and cooperation from its regional and international partners, Afghanistan will achieve peace, stability and development at an early date.

4. The two sides agreed that, on the basis of the Agreement Between the Government of the People's Republic of China and the Government of Islamic Republic of Afghanistan on Trade and Economic Cooperation signed in 2006, they will continue to explore new channels and methods to expand bilateral trade and investment and deepen economic cooperation. The two sides agreed to continually strengthen the pragmatic cooperation in such fields as resources and energy development, infrastructure development, engineering and agriculture. The Chinese side reaffirmed its support for the peaceful reconstruction process in Afghanistan. It will as always provide assistance to Afghanistan within the realm of its capabilities, and continue to encourage capable Chinese enterprises to participate in the construction and development of Afghanistan. The Chinese side announced that the Chinese government will provide 150 million RMB grant to the Afghan government during 2012. The Afghan side appreciated China's selfless assistance for Afghan peace and reconstruction over the years, and thanked the Chinese side for the new pledge of assistance.
5. The two sides pointed out that China and Afghanistan have a long history of friendly exchanges and traditional friendship. The people-to-people exchanges enjoy sound foundation and are of great significance. The two

sides will work vigorously to promote exchanges and cooperation in the cultural, educational, health, media and other fields, carry out people-to-people exchanges in various forms to further enhance understanding and friendship between the two peoples. The two sides will create favorable conditions for deepening and expanding the above-mentioned exchanges and cooperation. The Chinese side will continue to train the Afghan technical personnel, provide opportunities, including government-sponsored scholarships, to more Afghan youths to study in China, in an effort to support the development of Afghanistan.

6. The two sides expressed strong rejection of all forms of terrorism, extremism, separatism and organized crimes. The two sides agree to intensify exchanges and cooperation in security by way of jointly combating such transnational threats as terrorism, illegal immigration, illegal arms and drug trafficking, and enhancing intelligence exchanges and border management. The two sides will also strengthen cooperation in prevention of infectious diseases, disaster prevention and reduction, and other non-traditional security areas. The Chinese side firmly supports Afghanistan's efforts in combating terrorism and drug trafficking and safeguarding national stability, and calls on the international community to support this cause. The Afghan side reiterated its continued and firm support for China in combating the "three forces" of terrorism, extremism and separatism. It will take tangible measures to enhance the security of Chinese insitutions [*sic*] and people in Afghanistan.
7. The two sides pointed out that facing the profound and complex changes in regional and international situation, China and Afghanistan will enhance coordination and cooperation under the United Nations and other multilateral frameworks, stay in contacts and coordinate positions on major regional and international issues. The two sides will further the coordination and cooperation in SARRC. The Chinese side welcomes a bigger role played by Afghanistan in the SCO, including in its new role as an observer country, supports Afghanistan's efforts in improving and developing its relations with regional countries. The two sides also emphasise their commitment to countinue [*sic*] their cooperation within the Istanbul Process, which helps build confidence at the regional level in support of peace, stability and development in Afghanistan and the regional as a whole.

8. The establishment of China-Afghanistan Strategic and Cooperative Partnership is aimed to further deepen the traditional friendship and cooperation between the two countries. Both sides will fully respect and accommodate regional countries' reasonable concerns and interests, and work to promote regional peace, stability and development. This Partnership is not directed against any third party.
9. President Hamid Karzai expressed appreciation for President Hu Jintao's invitation for him to participate in the 12th Meeting of the Council of State Heads of SCO Member Countries and visit China and congratulated China on the success of the meeting.

Beijing, 8 June 2012

Source: "Joint Declaration between The People's Republic of China and The Islamic Republic of Afghanistan on Establishing Strategic and Cooperative Partnership", Chinese Ministry of Foreign Affairs, 8 June 2012, at https://www.fmprc.gov.cn/eng/zy/gb/202405/t20240531_11367266.html.

APPENDIX IV

China's Position on the Afghan Issue

12 April 2023

China and Afghanistan are close neighbors with longstanding friendship between the two peoples. Under the current situation, China's position on the Afghan issue is as follows:

1. Adhering to the "Three Respects" and "Three Nevers". China respects the independence, sovereignty and territorial integrity of Afghanistan, respects the independent choices made by the Afghan people, and respects the religious beliefs and national customs of Afghanistan. China never interferes in Afghanistan's internal affairs, never seeks selfish interests in Afghanistan, and never pursues so-called sphere of influence.
2. Supporting moderate and prudent governance in Afghanistan. China sincerely hopes that Afghanistan could build an open and inclusive political structure, adopt moderate and prudent domestic and foreign policies, and engage in friendly exchanges with all countries especially neighboring countries. We hope the Afghan Interim Government will protect the basic rights and interests of all Afghan people, including women, children and all ethnic groups, and continue working actively to meet Afghan people's interests and the international community's expectations.
3. Supporting peace and reconstruction of Afghanistan. China will continue to do its best to help Afghanistan with reconstruction and development, make plans with Afghanistan and fulfill its assistance pledges, promote steady progress in economic, trade and investment cooperation, and actively carry out cooperation in such fields as medical care, poverty alleviation, agriculture, and disaster prevention and mitigation, so as to help Afghanistan realize independent and sustainable development at an

early date. China welcomes Afghanistan's participation in Belt and Road cooperation and supports Afghanistan's integration into regional economic cooperation and connectivity that will transform Afghanistan from a "land-locked country" to a "land-linked country".

4. Supporting Afghanistan in countering terrorism resolutely and forcefully. Security is the foundation and prerequisite of development. The East Turkestan Islamic Movement (ETIM) is a terrorist organization listed by the UN Security Council and designated by the Chinese government in accordance with law. The ETIM forces in Afghanistan pose a severe threat to the security of China, Afghanistan and the region. China hopes that Afghanistan will fulfill its commitment in earnest and take more effective measures to crack down on all terrorist forces including the ETIM with greater determination, and earnestly ensure the safety and security of citizens, institutions and projects of China and other countries in Afghanistan.
5. Calling for greater bilateral and multilateral counter-terrorism cooperation. As Afghanistan faces pronounced terrorism-related security issues, it is necessary for the international community to strengthen counter-terrorism security cooperation at both bilateral and multilateral levels and provide Afghanistan with much-needed supplies, equipment and technical assistance. Afghanistan should be supported in taking comprehensive measures to address both the symptoms and root causes of terrorism and prevent the country from again becoming a safe haven, breeding ground and source of terrorism.
6. Working together to fight terrorism, separatism and extremism in Afghanistan. Terrorism, separatism and extremism in Afghanistan remain a major security threat to the region and the world. China calls on the international community to firmly support Afghanistan's fight against terrorism, separatism and extremism and its active measures to cut off the channels of terrorist financing, to counter recruitment and cross-border movement of terrorists and the spread of violent terrorist audio and video materials, to contain extremism, youth radicalization and the spread of terrorist ideologies, and to eliminate sleeper cells and terrorist safe havens.
7. Urging the US to live up to its commitments and responsibilities to Afghanistan. It is a widely-held view in the international community that, by seizing Afghanistan's overseas assets and imposing unilateral

sanctions, the US, which created the Afghan issue in the first place, is the biggest external factor that hinders substantive improvement in the humanitarian situation in Afghanistan. The US should draw lessons from what happened in Afghanistan, face squarely the grave humanitarian, economic and security risks and challenges in Afghanistan, immediately lift its sanctions, return the Afghan overseas assets, and deliver its pledged humanitarian aid to meet the emergency needs of the Afghan people.

8. Opposing external interference and infiltration in Afghanistan. It is a shared view of regional countries that the military interference and "democratic transformation" by external forces in Afghanistan over the past 20-odd years have inflicted enormous losses and pain on Afghanistan. It will be difficult to eliminate the negative impacts for many years to come. To help Afghanistan achieve sustained peace and stability, relevant countries should not attempt to re-deploy military facilities in Afghanistan and its neighbourhood, practice double standards on counter-terrorism, or advance their geopolitical agenda by supporting or conniving at terrorism.
9. Strengthening international and regional coordination on the Afghan issue. Under the new circumstances, Afghanistan should be a platform for cooperation among various parties rather than geopolitical games. China supports all plans and measures that are conducive to political settlement of the Afghan issue, and will actively engage in multilateral coordination through such mechanisms and platforms as the Foreign Ministers' Meeting on the Afghan Issue among the Neighboring Countries of Afghanistan, the Shanghai Cooperation Organization (SCO)–Afghanistan Contact Group, the Moscow Format Consultations on Afghanistan, the China-Afghanistan-Pakistan Trilateral Foreign Ministers' Dialogue, the Informal Meeting of China-Russia-Pakistan-Iran Foreign Ministers on Afghanistan, the Troika Plus Meeting and the United Nations, in an effort to build consensus and synergy for stability in and assistance to Afghanistan at regional and international levels.
10. Facilitating solution to Afghanistan's humanitarian and refugee issues. China is concerned about the situation of Afghan refugees and will continue to provide assistance through bilateral and multilateral channels. China supports relevant UN agencies in playing a positive role in this regard, applauds the efforts by regional countries, and calls on the international community to provide continuous humanitarian and

development assistance to jointly help Afghanistan rebuild its economy and create favorable conditions for the final settlement of the refugee issue.

11. Supporting Afghanistan's fight against narcotics. China looks forward to and supports more concrete actions by Afghanistan to counter narcotics cultivation, production and illicit trafficking, and will work with the international community to help Afghanistan with alternative development and crackdown on cross-border drug-related crimes, so as to eliminate the source of narcotics in the region.

Source: "China's Position on the Afghan Issue", Chinese Ministry of Foreign Affairs, 12 April 2023, at https://www.fmprc.gov.cn/mfa_eng/gjhdq_665435/2675_665437/2676_663356/2677_663358/202304/t20230412_11057785.html.

APPENDIX V

Opinion Pieces by Chinese Ambassadors and Embassy Officials Published/Republished in Afghan Media

(Articles were translated into Dari and English)

"Carry Forward the Five Principles of Peaceful Coexistence, Open New Pages for Friendly Cooperation between China and Afghanistan"
By Chen Shijie, Chinese chargé d'affaires ad interim in Afghans
Daily Outlook Afghanistan, 3 July 2014.

"Commemorate the Chinese People's War of Resistance against Japanese Aggression to Jointly Safeguard World Peace"
By Deng Xijun, Chinese Ambassador to Afghanistan
Daily Outlook Afghanistan, 6 September 2014.

"A Unique and Fruitful State Visit"
By Deng Xijun, Chinese Ambassador to Afghanistan
Daily Outlook Afghanistan, 7 November 2014 and *Afghanistan Times*, 8 November 2014.

"Accelerating Building of the Belt and Road, Forging China-Afghanistan Community of Common Destiny"
By Deng Xijun, Chinese Ambassador to Afghanistan
Daily Outlook Afghanistan, 15 April 2015.

"China's Foreign Aid: Mutual Benefits and Win-Win"
By Deng Xijun, Chinese Ambassador to Afghanistan
Daily Outlook Afghanistan, 12 May 2015.

"History Must be Remembered to Cherish Peace"
By Deng Xijun, Chinese Ambassador to Afghanistan
Daily Outlook Afghanistan, 29 August 2015.

"The Belt and Road Upgrades China-Afghanistan Relations"
By Yao Jing, Chinese Ambassador to Afghanistan
Kabul Times, 22 March 2016.

"BRF Promotes Win-Win Cooperation for China and Afghanistan"
By Yao Jing, Chinese Ambassador to Afghanistan
Daily Outlook Afghanistan, 13 May 2017.

"Open a New Chapter for China-Afghanistan-Pakistan Trilateral Cooperation"
By Zhang Zhixin, Chargé D'Affaires of Chinese Embassy in Afghanistan
Daily Outlook Afghanistan, 30 December 2017.

"If there is Any Person to Suffer, It's Not Child"
By Liu Jinsong, Chinese Ambassador to Afghanistan
Daily Outlook Afghanistan, 30 January 2018.

"What is the Chinese Path?"
By Liu Jinsong, Chinese Ambassador to Afghanistan
Daily Outlook Afghanistan, 21 February 2018.

"What is the Chinese Path? (Part 2)"
By Liu Jinsong, Chinese Ambassador to Afghanistan
Daily Outlook Afghanistan, 22 February 2018.

"Women Hold Up Half of the Sky both in China and Afghanistan"
By Liu Jinsong, Chinese Ambassador to Afghanistan
Daily Outlook Afghanistan, 8 March 2018.

"Forging Peace Together: At the 64th Anniversary of Establishment of Diplomatic Ties between China and Afghanistan"
By Liu Jinsong, Chinese Ambassador to Afghanistan
Daily Outlook Afghanistan, 20 January 2019.

"The Truth about the Issues of Human Rights in Xinjiang"
By Wang Yu, Chinese Ambassador to Afghanistan
Afghanistan Times, 9 July 2020.

"Economic Recovery in China Brings Hope for World Economy to Move out of Darkest Hour"
By Wang Yu, Chinese Ambassador to Afghanistan
Afghanistan Times, 25 July 2020.

"Xi's Thought on Diplomacy Guides China and Afghanistan towards a Deeper and Richer Relationship"
By Wang Yu, Chinese Ambassador to Afghanistan
Afghanistan Times, 5 August 2020.

"China's New Development Pattern: Opportunities for Afghanistan, Source of Confidence for Whole World"
By Wang Yu, Chinese Ambassador to Afghanistan
Afghanistan Times, 10 September 2020.

"All Under Heaven are of One Family: Let's Jointly Build a Community of Shared Future for China and Afghanistan"
By Wang Yu, Chinese Ambassador to Afghanistan
Afghanistan Times, October 2020.

"Fostering China-Afghanistan Common Understanding, Maintaining Existing International Order and Promoting Peaceful Development Together"
By Wang Yu, Chinese Ambassador to Afghanistan
Afghanistan Times, 16 October 2020.

"China and Afghanistan: Together for a Community of Shared Future Featuring Peace, Development and Prosperity"
By Wang Yu, Chinese Ambassador to Afghanistan
Afghanistan Times, 28 October 2020.

"Entering a New Development Phase, China Voices a Fortissimo for Peaceful Development and Win-Win Cooperation"
By Wang Yu, Chinese Ambassador to Afghanistan
Afghanistan Times, 15 November 2020.

"Shanghai Cooperation Organization Summit Draws a New Blueprint for China-Afghanistan Relations"
By Wang Yu, Chinese Ambassador to Afghanistan
Afghanistan Times, 18 November 2020.

"Countless Stories of Happiness in Xinjiang"
By Wang Yu, Chinese Ambassador to Afghanistan
Afghanistan Times, 23 November 2020.

"Let's Build a Community of Shared Future for Mankind and a Better World Together"
By Wang Yu, Chinese Ambassador to Afghanistan
Afghanistan Times, 2 December 2020.

"China Plays an Active and Constructive Role in Afghan Peace and Reconciliation Process"
By Wang Yu, Chinese Ambassador to Afghanistan
Afghanistan Times, 29 January 2021.

"The Communist Party of China's View on Governance"
By Wang Yu, Chinese Ambassador to Afghanistan
Afghanistan Times, 31 January 2021.

"China Pursues an Independent Foreign Policy of Peace"
By Wang Yu, Chinese Ambassador to Afghanistan
Afghanistan Times, 5 February 2021.

"President Xi Jinping's holistic view of national security Guides China-Afghanistan Security Cooperation to a New High"
By Wang Yu, Chinese Ambassador to Afghanistan
Afghanistan Times, 8 February 2021.

"China Actively Upholds Multilateralism, Jointly Building a Community with a Shared Future for Mankind with Afghanistan"
By Wang Yu, Chinese Ambassador to Afghanistan
Afghanistan Times, 22 February 2021.

"China Willing to Share its Experience in Poverty Reduction with Afghanistan"
By Wang Yu, Chinese Ambassador to Afghanistan
Afghanistan Times, 17 March 2021.

"Friedrich Engels: The Afghans are Brave, Hardy, and Independent"
By Zhao Haihan, Chargé d'Affaires of the Chinese Embassy in Afghanistan
The Heart of Asia, 16 August 2023.

"The Belt and Road Initiative Belongs to the World, Including Afghanistan!"
By Zhao Haihan, Chargé d'Affaires of the Chinese Embassy in Afghanistan
Bakhtar News Agency, 2 September 2023.

"China Provides Certainty to The Uncertain World"
By Zhao Xing, Chinese Ambassador to Afghanistan
Tolo News, 23 March 2025.

Source: Official Website of the Chinese Embassy in the Islamic Republic of Afghanistan and Afghan Newspapers and Web Sources.

Index